Invisible in Austin

Invisible in Austin

Life and Labor in an American City

EDITED BY JAVIER AUYERO
WITH AN AFTERWORD BY LOÏC WACQUANT

University of Texas Press ◆ *Austin*

Requests for permission to reproduce material from this work should be sent to:
    Permissions
    University of Texas Press
    P.O. Box 7819
    Austin, TX 78713-7819
    utpress.utexas.edu/rp-form

♾ The paper used in this book meets the minimum requirements of ANSI/NISO
Z39.48-1992 (R1997) (Permanence of Paper).

Library of Congress Cataloging-in-Publication Data
Invisible in Austin : life and labor in an American city / edited by Javier Auyero ;
with an afterword by Loïc Wacquant. — First edition.
    pages   cm
    Includes bibliographical references.
    ISBN 978-1-4773-0364-1 (cloth : alk. paper) — ISBN 978-1-4773-0365-8
(pbk. : alk. paper) — ISBN 978-1-4773-0366-5 (library e-book) —
ISBN 978-1-4773-0367-2 (non-library e-book)
    1. Marginality, Social—Texas—Austin.   2. Austin (Tex.)—Social
conditions.   3. Austin (Tex.)—Economic conditions.   4. Poor—Texas—
Austin.   5. Minorities—Texas—Austin.   I. Auyero, Javier, editor.
    F394.A99I58   2015
    976.4'31—dc23   2014046938

doi:10.7560/303641

Contents

Acknowledgments

This book would not have been possible without the cooperation and generosity of the people whose lives we portray in the pages that follow. They opened their homes and their hearts to us, and we are immensely grateful for the opportunity they gave us to learn from them. We hope we did justice to their stories.

Three years ago, after a particularly intense graduate seminar, a few of us decided to embark on this collective project. From the very beginning, we were blessed with the unwavering support of the chair of the Sociology Department at the University of Texas at Austin, Christine Williams. It was Christine who first conceived the Urban Ethnography Lab—the intellectual home of this project—as an institutional space to support ethnographic work in sociology. She not only read and commented on several chapters of this book but also provided the intellectual leadership for our scholarly effort to germinate and blossom. Thank you, Christine. And thanks to Dean Randy Diehl at the College of Liberal Arts and to Mark Hayward, director of the Population Research Center at UT, for supporting the work we do in the lab. We are all extremely grateful to Philippe Bourgois, Robert Gay, and Loïc Wacquant for their detailed comments and criticisms on earlier drafts of this manuscript.

For the past two years the Urban Ethnography Lab was for us a place of fruitful intellectual exchange and scholarly production. It was also a space where we were able to share and debate the emotional ups and downs involved in ethnographic fieldwork. Various events at the lab such as brown bags, updates from the field, lectures, and workshops fed and nurtured our sociological imagination. From its inception this book has been a collective endeavor made possible, to a great extent, by this wonderful intellectual and affective atmosphere.

As the writing drew to a close photographer Julia Robinson joined the group and produced the wonderful images that illustrate each chapter. Thank you, Julia, and thank you, Eva Hershaw, journalist and photographer, for the beautiful portraits of Santos. More pictures, along with updates on the lives of some of the subjects of this book, can be found at www.othersidesofaustin.com.

Proceeds from this book will go to the Workers Defense Project in Austin, Texas.

INTRODUCTION

Know Them Well

JAVIER AUYERO

A tiny symbol, if one were needed, of all the million circumstances of the other fellow's life, of that blizzard of details that constitute the confusion of a human biography—a tiny symbol to remind me why our understanding of people must always be at best slightly wrong.
PHILIP ROTH, *THE HUMAN STAIN*

No social study that does not come back to the problem of biography, of history and of their intersections within a society has completed its intellectual journey.
C. WRIGHT MILLS, *THE SOCIOLOGICAL IMAGINATION*

It all began with a nagging discomfort that slowly metamorphosed into an incredible, expansive collective energy. It was the spring semester of 2012, and I was teaching a graduate seminar on poverty and marginality in the Americas in the Sociology Department at the University of Texas at Austin, my academic home since 2008. On a weekly basis I subjected my students, a heterogeneous group from my own discipline as well as from anthropology and social work, to the typical graduate seminar drill—three hundred pages or more of reading, electronic notes, and long hours of intense discussions devoted to reviewing past and present analyses of the nature and experiences of poverty and marginality in Latin America and in the United States, examining the most controversial issues and debates and exploring research topics emerging north and south of the border. The discomfort did not take long to emerge: although they were in agreement with diagnoses about the economic and political sources of dispossession, students were uncomfortable—distrustful and on more than one occasion angry—with the ways in which many a text represented the lives of those living at the bottom of the socio-symbolic ladder, including their daily predicaments, their beliefs, and their hopes. Oftentimes entire, and quite diverse, categories (the urban poor, young poor men, poor women) were reduced to one or two salient portrayals (single mother, welfare recipient, sex worker, drug dealer, gang member); other times the complex and changing character of their lives was truncated in order to make (more or less sophisticated) social scientific arguments. Doubts about how well researchers knew the people they were representing, and how well they were representing these people, lingered.

Readings from Pierre Bourdieu's now classic *The Weight of the World* changed the terms of our conversation and first planted the seed for this book. *The Weight of the World* was the product of many years of collaborative work under the direction of Bourdieu, France's best known sociologist. A group of twenty or so researchers examined the social, political, and economic forces producing novel forms of suffering, mostly in contemporary France (with two chapters devoted to the United States), and the many ways in which individuals—a teacher, a social worker, a factory worker, a migrant, an artisan, and others—deal and cope with the external forces that deprive them not only of their means of economic subsistence but also, and just as importantly, of the recognition and respect they once enjoyed. The book's publication was a major event in France, and it became an instant bestseller because, among other things, it depicts the suffering caused by a shrinking labor market and a retrenching welfare state through a series of lively, eye-opening (and oftentimes heartbreaking) one-on-one interviews with ordinary folks. Usually silenced in public debates, these people and the stories they told speak to larger pressing problems. They talked in highly personal terms about the social, economic, and political sources of their troubles—and about their unceasing struggles to regain control over their lives and maintain a sense of dignity in their existence.

Rereading chapters of that book, and with the students' shared discomfort in mind, it occurred to me that we could try something along similar lines in the city we call our home—an exploration of current forms of social suffering in Austin, Texas, a thriving, rapidly growing, highly unequal, and segregated technopolis. It was not, at the beginning, a well-conceived plan. There was no grant money to support the fieldwork it would require, and there were neither material nor symbolic rewards in sight for those willing to be part of it. I would be lying if I said that I have a clear idea about why students jumped at the opportunity—after all, the cutthroat competition that defines the field of academic production typically militates against collaborations of this kind.

The work that went into making this book was not part of a research project with a clearly defined objective, design, or timetable. Yet we were clear—adamant, in fact—about one thing. It was going to be a collective enterprise: students were not working as "research assistants" for a "principal investigator"; they were the protagonists of an intellectual adventure. Together we defined the end (and aim) of the journey in ambitious yet vague terms: we would write a book that people outside the restricted and restricting confines of academia would enjoy reading and that would make them think and reflect about the place where they live and the people whom they live alongside. It would be a book that would not be circumscribed to Austinites but could speak to the manifold ways in which inequality and social exclusion are lived and experienced in the United States. By attempting to gently and persuasively force readers to acknowledge the suffering they normally do not see, we thought of our group as engaging in a collective effort in public social science.

We first set up a Google Group (named OSA, for "the other side of Austin") where we circulated readings about a variety of topics: from Austin's socioeconomic indicators to the rapid urban transformation currently taking place in other similar American cities. We then began to meet, every month at first but eventually every week, in after-work sessions that were at first chaotic and later a bit more systematic but always long and vibrant. ("These nights," one of the collaborators reflected, "are what make me happy to be in graduate school.") Over potluck dinners at various group members' homes, we first talked in general terms about what our individual and collective efforts would entail, and we then began to carefully choose the subjects to be included in the book and, simultaneously, the criteria for including some and excluding others (more on this below). As students got to know their subjects, we discussed (and read about) best practices in in-depth interviewing and life history construction. As the project moved on, a parallel conversation emerged regarding writing. How could we best represent the lives of others in ways that made for engaging, readable stories? As this conversation progressed, the subjects of the students' interviews became the characters readers are now about to meet.

The Other Side of Austin

Even in a surface reading of Austin's newspapers, online news sources, and monthly magazines one cannot fail to notice a set of parallel (though hardly contradictory) images and trends. Glowing descriptions of a fast-growing city, a city for the young and creative, a "cool" place to live and raise a family, and a city of internationally famous events like South by Southwest and Formula One compete with (more or less concerned, depending on political orientations) portrayals of increasing socio-economic inequality and residential class, racial, and ethnic segregation. As Maggie Tate lucidly describes in the first chapter of this book, and as seen in many other American cities and metropolitan areas, wealth and poverty, material abundance and penury, are booming right along-side one another in contemporary Austin. As elsewhere, the sharpening of social inequality magnifies the effects of social insecurity (from job instability and precarity to fears of downward social mobility) and re-configures the cityscape. Rich and poor residents are increasingly sep-arated from each other in high- and low-income neighborhoods, with little mobility in between. New exclusive areas of prosperity emerge, while deprivation forces others to the edges, the crevices, or, as we intu-itively put it early on in our meetings, "the other side" of town.

From the beginning of this project we knew that for all its intuitive appeal the notion of another "side" was somewhat misleading: although it accurately encapsulates the residential displacements that are cur-rently taking place, and the clustering of high rates of poverty in spe-cific geographic areas, it implicitly conveys the idea of a dual city inhab-ited by people who are disconnected from one another. The individuals who clean residential homes, care for children while parents go to work, fix office machines, drive the cabs we take, cook and wash dishes in the restaurants where we eat, dance in clubs (some) men visit, and fix roofs around town do not live in another world. They (most often) live at the margins of the city—margins defined by daily environmental risk and the poor quality of housing, public services, schools, et cetera—but they are, as many a social scientific study has repeatedly shown, a constitutive part of the daily life of all city residents.

Conceptual and empirical flaws aside, the image of a less glamorous "side" of this creative, fast-growing, and hip city has a double virtue. On the one hand, it calls attention to the kinds of class, ethnic, and racial inequalities that are now a defining aspect of cities like Austin. On the other hand, it forces us to think hard about the predicament of those at the losing end of the urban boom who are nowhere to be seen or heard in public accounts of the city's "creativity," "coolness," "weird-ness," or "hipness." This was the political impetus behind the making of this book.

The social sciences, and sociology in particular, are on relatively secure ground when it comes to describing and explaining objective inequalities of class, race, and gender and the mechanisms that generate them. We are on less certain terrain when it comes to understanding the many ways in which individuals, alone or in groups, make sense of and cope with these inequalities. These experiences matter because they oftentimes do the cultural work necessary to perpetuate the social order, but at other times they serve as the basis for challenging it. As a group, we wanted to explore this more subjective dimension of inequality.

At a very basic level, we wanted to know what was going on in the lives of those working at the invisible bottom of the socio-symbolic order. We wanted to first understand (and then to write about) these lives as complex products of individual and social forces, of what Philip Roth aptly calls "that blizzard of details" that form a person's biography and the social, economic, and political circumstances beyond the individual's control. In other words, we wanted to examine, up close, the intersection of biography and history (the task of what C. Wright Mills famously called "the sociological imagination") at a particular moment in time, focusing on a few poignant examples.

"If localized, microscopic studies were really dependent for their greater relevance upon [the] premise . . . that they capture the great world in the little," writes anthropologist Clifford Geertz, "they wouldn't have any relevance." What are the eleven characters portrayed in this book representatives of? What do their stories show that others do not? These were the critical questions that recurred in different ways as each contributor delved more deeply into the subjects' lives and wrote each chapter. Let me be clear: Clarissa, Raven, Santos, Kumar, Inés, Chip, Ella, Manuel, Keith, Xiomara, and Ethan do not "represent" city life; they are not Austin writ small. They do, however, stand for something. They incarnate the lived experiences of inequality and social marginalization, the ways in which inequality and exclusion are intertwined with individual lives and embedded in the intricate seams of biographical issues. The question of how many Clarissas, Ravens, Santoses, Kumars, Ineses, Chips, Ellas, Manuels, Keiths, Xiomaras, and Ethans are out there is thus replaced by a scrutinization of the complex ways in which life histories are linked with structural inequality.

In other words, we did not choose the subjects for this book because they represent the entirety of daily life at the margins. No subject can do that. We chose each subject because she or he sheds light on particularly relevant features of the daily life of the dispossessed in a growing, increasingly unequal city: the lack of affordable housing, the meager safety net, the disciplinary and punishing state, the poverty generated by a highly polarized labor market, et cetera. But each chapter seeks to illustrate not only the operation of larger forces behind the backs and above the minds of the destitute but also, and as importantly, the subjects' engagement with those forces and their more or less sustained resilience in the face of oftentimes overwhelming odds.

Stories and Characters

We all agreed that before the writing was to begin, it was imperative to get to know the subjects well, to spend time with them, to immerse ourselves, as much as we could, in their lives, to figure out—in Geertz's famous phrasing—what the devil they thought they were up to. Only then, after many hours of talking with them and following them around, would contributors begin to write up each story. And here, in the write-up, lies both the difference between this book and *The Weight of the World* and the most difficult aspect of our joint enterprise.

After transcribing their many one-on-one interviews, the authors began writing each chapter, an activity that involved a trying balancing act. In the book that served as our main inspiration, contributors had edited their interviews and written a brief opening narrative to situate the particular transcript. Encouraged by current nonfiction writing in Latin America, I persuaded my students to undertake a different task. Instead of simply transcribing and editing the most important, luminous parts of the many hours of interviews, they needed to construct a narrative out of the interview material. They needed to become the writers, the authors, of a story. When the graduate students accepted the challenge of writing (as different from, and more demanding than, the transcription and editing of interviews), their *subjects* became *characters* in a story whose reconstruction was the intellectual responsibility of each author (we decided, in most cases, to use pseudonyms to protect the characters' identities, and in some cases we altered identifying details of their stories). As the authors were conducting interviews and writing each story, the group discussed the material and suggested ways of sharpening the connections between biographical and social aspects and, just as important, of improving the narrative (more on this below). After that, each author shared a draft with the subject, who gave revisions and, eventually, the final approval for publication.

Thus, in our attempt to see the ways in which the social order imposes the material and symbolic circumstances under which men and women live their lives and make history, our intellectual effort was not different from the one undertaken by the contributors to *The Weight of the World*. The difference lies in the way in which the material produced jointly by researchers and subjects is presented here. The chapters to follow were, to reiterate, *fashioned* by the authors out of many hours of engaged conversation and active listening, and also out of the collective discussions we had as a group about what would be the most important set of social, economic, and political dimensions to highlight in each particular chapter. For all the attention given to individual details, the chapters emphasize the operation of the social order in the making of each character's biography.

The basic premise underlining the construction of each story and the portrayal of each character was deceptively simple: the authors should seek to understand their subjects (and to convey this understanding in their writing); they should try to imagine themselves in the characters' places, or, in other words, they should strive to take (to dare to take) the characters' points of view—which are nothing other than views of the social world from particular positions in the social structure.

The agreed-upon task, then, was to write a *story* that would delve into individual, idiosyncratic trajectories but would also illuminate the economic, social, and political forces that mold them. Some of these forces are particular to this city, while others are more general to the United States or operate in all contemporary capitalist societies. Out of Roth's "million circumstances" that shape each biography, the authors constructed a narrative that showed in clear relief the presence of one or more of those external forces and the work they did in shaping and constraining individual choices. The interpretive keys planted throughout each story—sometimes in the form of an absent welfare state or a present punitive one, other times in the form of a particularly exploitative job or a particularly harmful piece of legislation—push readers to realize that the chapter they are reading is, say, not only about an adolescent's daily efforts at improving himself and "making it" but also about a particularly vindictive migration policy; about a poor single mother's plight but also about a disciplinary state; about a woman's downward mobility and search for some sense of control but also about an almost nonexistent safety net for the most vulnerable; about a young woman's pernicious addiction but also about a malignant and violent patriarchal order; about the misfortunes of one particular manual laborer or housecleaner or musician but also about the bifurcated nature of a labor market with extremely low material and symbolic rewards and a high physical toll at its bottom; about ups and downs in the life of one woman in a poor neighborhood but also about the historic nature of residential segregation.

We are not animated by a voyeuristic desire to pry into the suffering of others. Our shared underlying assumption is that sight (what we see and we don't see about a city and its residents) has a politics (i.e., it is part of a power struggle), and our attempt here is to make a modest contribution to what is being said and seen (and what is being denied and hidden) in the city's public sphere. We want readers to start seeing the city we all love (or any other American city, for that matter) in a different light, so that the next time they encounter or read a story about a Xiomara cleaning homes with dangerous chemicals, a Clarissa losing her home, a Kumar being harassed in his cab, a Manuel being deported, an Ethan going to jail, a Santos fixing roofs and mowing lawns, a Chip working hard to keep a job he has trouble performing, a Keith struggling to pay the bills, a Raven overdosing or being raped, an Ella doing community work, or an Inés worrying about her daughter's school, they reflect back not only on the particularities of each story but on the contexts that have produced them.

A Work of Scholarly Love

Over the course of the more than two years that we worked on this project, I often wondered how I would be able to describe the *economy of efforts* and the *economy of feelings* that went into the making of this book. How could I convey in writing the exhilaration, the passion, the both intellectual and political commitment that we came to share over this time? Although I assumed the initial responsibility for the project—and took the initial leap of faith, betting not only on each contributor's energy and dedication but also on the eventual publication of a book with truly unusual features—it took less than two months for the graduate students to take ownership. A shared sense of collective purpose emerged and sustained us over time—but not without difficulties. As we moved forward, we jointly settled debates (heated at times) about the best way of writing about other people's lives, about the aspects to be emphasized ("the angle," as we called it) and the most adequate balance between authors' and subjects' voices, about the ethical obligations toward our subjects and their ultimate right to approve the story to be published, and about the intellectual and political reasons behind our joint enterprise.

Each contributor experienced the construction of each chapter in a different way—more than once our work sessions transformed into instances in which authors vented their frustrations with their subjects, expressed excitement about new developments, interrogated their own feelings about the stories they were creating, and speculated about alternative interpretations. From my own perspective, and whatever the specific merits of this book, the time spent in its making was a marvelous pedagogical experience. At its early stages, I did (I confess) doubt the overall feasibility of the project and the likelihood of its publication. As each contributor made progress with each chapter, I wondered if the aspects that authors chose to emphasize were the aspects I would have chosen (and said so out loud). But the pedagogical value of what we were doing was never in dispute. Whatever ultimately happened with the stories the authors constructed (whether they found their way into print or not), each contributor was learning to listen, to interpret, to put himself or herself in someone else's shoes, to write, to collaborate, to criticize and be criticized. I never abandoned this conviction, and although occasionally I could not tell whether the final product was going to be good or not, I was certain that as long as we continued to meet, struggling to find the next word in each other's chapters and fighting over possible interpretations, I was doing what I had to do, fulfilling my role as a teacher—encouraging and facilitating a cooperative way of learning from, and writing about, folks living under difficult, taxing circumstances.

Road Map

The book begins with a chapter by Maggie Tate that shows that the persistence of inequality in contemporary Austin has seeds in the city's earliest days. This chapter digs into Austin's history to unearth lesser-known roots of durable inequality and places the city's past and present in the context of broader understandings of American urbanism and industrial growth. The socially produced invisibility of narratives of inequality and oppression is highlighted against the backdrop of the hipness, creativity, and tolerance that have made Austin a city to be celebrated. This historical and social context provides the foundation from which the individual narratives in this book emerge.

In the second chapter, Jacinto Cuvi reconstructs Santos's life. A jack-of-all-trades, Santos walked to the United States all the way from a small village in Mexico's southwest. After years of wandering through many states, he settled in Austin, where he worked in crews that built bridges and hospitals, installed pipes, and set up telephone lines. Now old and ailing, dependent on his family for daily survival, he took the opportunity afforded by the many interviews with Cuvi not only to reflect on the ups and downs of a life defined by the double condition of being a poor migrant and an informal worker but also to express his dreams of financial relief. Taken out of context, Santos's illusions about "winning big" might seem unrealistic (and his desire to purchase a unicorn, pointless fantasy), but Cuvi's reconstruction helps readers to make sense of them—to see them as products of a difficult life and as attempts to fill what undoubtedly is one of the most hurting needs: the absence of clear future prospects.

Reading next about Clarissa in Kristine Kilanski's chapter, one cannot help but think, all at the same time, about the callousness with which the social world treats the most vulnerable, the role of chance in determining sudden downfalls, and the human perseverance that emerges in the face of terrible circumstances. The insistence with which Clarissa seeks to be treated as a "real person" and her endless search for respect and dignity (intricately associated with her ceaseless attempts to detach herself from negative stereotypes associated with homeless people like herself) illuminate society's rather skewed distribution of not only material but also symbolic opportunities and rewards and the strenuous efforts that individuals on the losing end have to make to live a life they consider decent.

Like Santos, Inés illegally crossed the border into the United States, traveling with her daughter Araceli "strapped" to her back. A thirty-eight-year-old woman and single mother of two, Inés works full-time busing tables and replenishing the all-you-can-eat salad bar at a deli that primarily serves local college students and professionals. Over the last three years Inés has lost many hours at work due to the demands of the local Disciplinary Alternative Education Program (DAEP) her daughter has been forced to attend. A cross between a penal and an educational institution, the DAEP attempts not only to discipline Araceli but also to control Inés's life. Jessica Dunning-Lozano's chapter takes readers into the unexplored, Kafkaesque universe of the DAEP (a direct product of Bush-era zero-tolerance policies in schools) and into the lives of a mother and a daughter trapped in its punitive dragnet.

In the next chapter, Eric Borja describes how Chip's many years of hard work have paid off—he was able to "put the kids through college." But, as is the case for many a manual laborer in contemporary America, his strenuous work and long hours of commuting did not secure a stable life for him and his wife. Now he resides at the edges of a city whose cost of living he can no longer afford. Chip's callous and increasingly unresponsive hands, his overused vehicle, his steadily deteriorating eyesight become, in Borja's reconstruction, the defining elements of a life that is hanging by a few precarious threads.

It would be easy to focus on the most extreme aspects of Raven's life (her recurrent addiction to pills, her stripping, her escorting) at the expense of her ordinary, but mostly fruitless, attempts to secure a stable job in the formal sector. Her "bad" choices, which make for an all too stereotypical "fast life," appear at first glance to be solely of her own manufacture. But upon closer look, Caitlyn Collins's reconstruction reveals a woman who, despite being marked by abuse, neglect, and sexual violence, is in a determined (though oftentimes risky) search for recognition—a recognition that, in Raven's eyes, can come mostly from men, be they more or less stable boyfriends or more or less good clients. Her unflagging optimism in the face of considerable heartache is a testament to the resilience and tenacity of the human spirit, particularly and especially for those occupying the bottom rungs of the socioeconomic ladder.

A political refugee from Nepal, Kumar works twelve hours a day, six days a week driving a cab around town. Katherine Jensen's chapter devotes equal attention to the particular set of circumstances that brought Kumar to Austin and to the trials and tribulations of driving a taxi on the night shift. Yet Kumar copes with the descent to nighttime cab driver from the lawyer and political science professor he was in Nepal by finding solace in his passion for writing poetry and love for his recently reunited family, and by morally differentiating himself from others near but just below him at the bottom of the socio-symbolic structure.

High-end service work might be one of the last places that comes to mind when thinking about social suffering, but at a luxury hotel catering to the young and successful, a hub for local celebrities and wannabes, Katherine Sobering encounters Ethan—the "$30,000 millionaire" living on the $30,000 salary of a hotel manager. That contrast, and his constant yearning to belong to a glittering crowd that only wants to be served, goes a long way to helping readers make sense of Ethan's rollercoaster life, his addiction to drugs and alcohol, and ultimately his legal distress.

No book about the landscape of labor and daily life in Austin, the "Live Music Capital of the World," could be complete without the story of a musician. Amias Maldonado illuminates singer Keith's struggles to keep doing what he loves—writing music, rehearsing, and performing—in a city that claims to share the same passions but seems to have less and less space for folks like him. As Keith points out, Austin may profess to be the capital of live music, yes, but "not here, not in this zip code."

The last three chapters direct readers' attention to collective forms of dealing with the risks and penury that define the lives of those struggling; and they provide a sliver of hope—a "collective light" at the end of a trying tunnel. Like many others currently living in Texas, Xiomara crossed the border into the United States on foot and has been struggling at the lower end of the labor market ever since. Jennifer Scott reconstructs the path that Xiomara, together with a few colleagues and the support of a local grassroots organization, took to successfully establish her own cooperative business in an effort to improve working conditions for herself and others. As with Ella and Manuel in the chapters that follow, Xiomara shows us that collective action can mean a real difference—in her case better and more stable wages—in the lives of those living at the economic, social, political, or legal margins.

The next chapter takes us to a historically black neighborhood on the East Side of Austin, where Ella grew up and now lives. Ella's responsibilities as a single mother and her work as a plumber, a nurse's aide, and a halfway house monitor did not prevent her from becoming an active participant in community affairs. Now retired after many years of hard work, Ella devotes most of her time to a group of black and Latino teenage boys in her neighborhood, whom she feels almost everyone else has already given up on. In Pamela Neumann's recounting, Ella displays a truly inspiring determination to make a difference in the lives of those who, like her, have experienced neglect and discrimination firsthand.

At the end of this volume, we meet Manuel, a high-achieving college student and community activist. His undocumented status acts as a sort of Damoclean sword looming not only over his future opportunities but also over his present daily life. Born in Mexico twenty years ago, he was brought to the United States by his parents when he was eight years old. He learned about his undocumented status after getting into a fight in middle school, when his parents told him he did not have a luxury that others at his age and school took for granted—the luxury of defending himself. He was admonished that if he stood up for himself, either with fists or with words, his entire family could be deported. In the hands of Marcos Pérez, the story of Manuel not only illuminates the at once insurmountable and unjustifiable obstacles imposed by the political system on adolescents, but also reveals the makings and meanings of a social movement that feeds and is fed by the resilience and optimism shown by folks who, like Manuel, live in highly vulnerable conditions.

Context(s)

As said above, the points of view expressed by our book's characters are taken from specific points in the social space—a social space characterized by objective forces and regularities beyond the individuals' control. The authors of each chapter constructed the interview questionnaire, asked follow-up questions, and interpreted interview transcripts and notes from field observations in light of their subjects' positions and trajectories in their social worlds. In other words, the lines of inquiry that each contributor developed in the making of each chapter (the specific questions they asked, the themes they focused on, and the themes they discarded) did not emerge out of thin air (or out of the particular idiosyncrasies of individuals' lives) but out of an attentive consideration of the objective parameters within which the characters live.

The crafting of this "angle" and the defining of these objective parameters were driven by each student's area of interest within the discipline of sociology. First, authors intentionally selected subjects whose social locations and fields of work complemented their own areas of research. For example, Katherine Jensen specializes in race, migration, and the asylum process, making her an apt writer of Kumar's story as an asylum seeker and cab driver. Caitlyn Collins studies gender inequality in the workplace, so her expertise made her a good match in comprehending Raven's labor market experiences in the licit and illicit service sector. Jessica Dunning-Lozano's work, which lies at the crossroads of education, inequality, and racial domination, served her well in her understanding of Araceli's and Inés's experiences with the school system and their entanglement with the punitive state. And the same could be said about Jacinto Cuvi's expertise on the informal economy, Kristine Kilanski's on poverty, gender, and work, Jennifer Scott's on poor people's survival strategies, and so forth. Second, student researchers spent

considerable time before, during, and after the interview process famil-
iarizing themselves with the scholarly literature relevant to their subjects' lives, and they continued this research while writing their chapters. Third, our awareness of the objective parameters shaping the
respondents' lives translated into very specific ways of conducting interviews and of understanding what subjects said. For example, one subject's trip to the emergency room and mounting unpaid bills acquires
particular analytic relevance in view of the state of poor people's health
care and the retrenchment of the (already paltry) welfare state. And so
does an accident at work in the context of the highly exploitative character of the construction industry; a seemingly anecdotal comment about
miles put on an already weary car in light of the polarizing dynamics
of real estate and the expansion of precarious work; a weekly count of
hours spent behind the wheel in the context of the highly exploitative
cab industry; a casual comment about types of clients in view of the
class-, race-, and ethnic-based differences in strip clubs; or an apparently banal description of the daily life of an undocumented youngster
in the midst of highly restrictive (and merciless, one could say) migration policies.

Another benefit to the sort of longitudinal interviewing approach
we employed—in which students met with their respondents over a period of many months, and up to two years—is that students could follow up on anecdotes heard months before, observe what happened as a
job change unfolded, or ask additional questions that arose while writing field notes after accompanying a subject on his or her work shift.
Holding regular group meetings over two years also lent us opportunities to collectively reflect on each author's subject in considerable detail—to delve into one person's interviews to date, to press another to
reconsider perspectives, question assumptions, and uncover new paths
of inquiry. We enjoyed mutual collaboration from the project's inception, from data collection and analysis to the initial drafts and the many,
many revisions of each chapter.

In these ways, the construction of the interviews and the interpretation of the subjects' viewpoints were conceived of as recursive processes, a back and forth between what the subjects were asked about,
what they said, and the objective forces at play—each process illuminating the other. Although very much present in the authors' minds and as
constant topics of debate during the lively group sessions that helped to
construct each chapter, for narrative reasons the structural factors shap-

ing the individuals' lives are not fully displayed in the written text. They merit a description, albeit brief, here.

"From the 1970s to today," writes Marianne Cooper, "income stagnation, growing inequality, increasing economic instability, soaring debt, and rising costs [in health care, housing, education, etc.] have steadily eroded the well-being of American families." At the root of what Cooper calls a "reversal of fortune"—the widespread insecurity that now afflicts a majority of Americans but affects with extreme intensity those living at the bottom—are the rise of the service economy, the decline of unions, the impact of globalization, and most importantly, the adoption of neoliberalism as an ideology and as a set of concrete state policies.

The study of social suffering takes on particular relevance (and urgency) in the context of neoliberal governance in the United States, under which most previous forms of protection are being swiftly dismantled (e.g., welfare benefits, employer-provided health care coverage, traditionally defined retirement pensions, etc.) and the penal state is expanding exponentially in order to manage the effects of growing inequality at the bottom of the social hierarchy. In this neoliberal era, socially produced forms of suffering take on particularly alarming features.

This larger neoliberal context should be kept in mind when reading about the plight of the characters of this book. All are living in times when assistance to the poor has shrunk dramatically, and all are experiencing the consequences of lack of living wages, stable employment, educational access, health insurance, welfare aid, housing and unemployment assistance, et cetera. But the particular political economic context of Texas (we could call it "neoliberalism on steroids") should also be highlighted in order to better understand the predicament of folks like Santos, Clarissa, Chip, Manuel, Xiomara, and the others. Three examples should suffice to illustrate this more local environment.

When a construction worker falls from a roof and is left to his own devices by the contractor, or when he is not paid overtime or cannot request a sick day, the largely unregulated character of the construction industry in Texas, and in Austin in particular, comes into focus. This industry, in more than one way, epitomizes the production of precarity affecting the lives of many who are living in the lower echelons of the social structure. It should not come as a surprise to anyone that, in one of the fastest-growing urban areas in the country, the construction industry plays a key role in the local economy by being one of the most important employers in the city. According to the report *Building Austin, Building Injustice*, construction work in the city, whether it be the building of new housing, commercial buildings, or city infrastructure, is predominately low-wage work and increasingly comprised of Latino workers born outside the United States. Long hours and dangerous working conditions characterize most of the jobs in the industry. Abuses and federal and state employment violations run rampant (due, to a large extent, to the weak state labor laws characteristic of the laissez-faire environment in which the industry operates). These abuses and violations (which we see determining the lives of some of the characters of this book, or their relatives) include poverty level wages, failure to be paid (known as "wage theft"), meager employment benefits (such as lack of health insurance, sick leave and vacation days, and pensions), high rates of dangerous and unsafe working conditions, and denied legal protections. To witness: as of 2008, Texas is the only state in the country that makes workers' compensation insurance coverage optional for any employer. "Austin's rapid expansion," concludes the report, "has come at the expense of construction workers' safety, health, wages, and quality of life." We ask readers to keep this in mind when immersing themselves in the lives of folks like Santos, Xiomara, and Manuel.

When an undocumented migrant walks four miles to work instead of driving her car, or avoids reporting an accident she was involved in even if it was not her fault, the operation of the Secure Communities program becomes poignantly evident. This program fosters cooperation between the local police and U.S. Immigration and Customs Enforcement (ICE). Any individual who comes in contact with the police (for example, by driving without a license, a document that is not available to immigrants in Texas without legal status) can be arrested and deported. As a result of this program and the compliance of Austin's local county jail with ICE detainers, over the last four years approximately 4,600 people were deported from Travis County.[1] It is little wonder that widespread fear pervades the lives of the undocumented.

A particularly revealing illustration of punitive neoliberalism in Texas is the mounting role of private prisons in housing the undocumented. The Lone Star State has more immigration detention beds than any other state and also has the largest number of beds operated by private prison companies.[2] The private prison industry, it should be noted, makes huge profits off of immigration detention—by, for example, using the detainees themselves to conduct much of the work within the facility (serving food in the cafeteria, performing janitorial work, etc.) at a pay rate of only one to two dollars a day.

When someone moves out of the city center because he cannot pay increasing rental prices or property taxes, or another individual dwells with her few belongings in a storage space or is pushed into homelessness, the increasingly exclusionary features of Austin's housing market are made patently visible. In different ways, the stories of Chip, Clarissa, and Ella demonstrate the interplay between a fast and furious process of gentrification and the cumulative scarcity of affordable housing. They illustrate the highly skewed character of the booming housing market in the city, where prices rise faster than incomes and fewer and fewer low-income residents can afford to live. As recently reported in the *Austin Chronicle*, in a story suggestively entitled "Exiled from Main Street," increasing numbers of low-income populations are now finding Austin unaffordable. As a result they are being forced to move to the city's outskirts—displaced to areas with worse educational, cultural, health, and transportation services and, thus, diminished economic opportunities. This exclusionary process is disproportionately affecting Latinos and African Americans.

The above examples—Austin's unregulated construction industry, the punitive Secure Communities program, and the increasingly segregated and polarized housing market—are only three of the social and political forces at play in the individual lives reconstructed by the contributors. Readers should keep in mind these influences, as well as others (harsher migration policies, exacerbation of punitive policies against the poor, increasing inequality in access to health services, etc.), in order to avoid leaving these pages with the mistaken impression that the misfortunes reconstructed here are simply the result of bad luck. True, being hit by car, as Clarissa was, could be viewed as one individual's unfortunate circumstances, but her lack of health insurance—in a state with the highest rate of uninsured individuals and families in the country—and the exorbitant hospital bills she could not afford to pay, and that resulted in her losing her housing, were not. The same social logic applies to "accidents" at work and other seemingly individual misfortunes endured by the characters of this book.

Many of the subjects of this book express aspirations and expectations that, in principle, seem implausible given the difficulties they experience daily—from the desire to become a teacher without a degree in hand coupled with the almost certain prospect of a felony conviction, to the wish of obtaining a well-paid job in the formal sector without the requisite educational credentials or work experience. Before assuming an all too common "blame-the-victim" mindset and passing judgment on these hopes, as well as the subjects who express them, readers should be reminded that one's dreams and expectations are intricately related to the degree of control—the power—one has in daily life. Given the bleakness and unpredictability characterizing the lives of many who populate these pages, having big dreams—albeit perhaps unrealistic—may be a basic means of survival. "The more power one has over the world," writes Pierre Bourdieu, "the more one has aspirations that are adjusted to their chances of realization. . . . [B]elow a certain level, on the other hand, aspirations burgeon, detached from reality and some-times a little crazy, as if, when nothing was possible, everything became possible, as if all discourses about the future . . . had no other purpose than to fill what is no doubt one of the most painful of wants: the lack of future." That, in a nutshell, is the reality that many of the subjects of the book are confronted with. Inhabitants of a "forward-looking," fast-growing city, they are—knowingly or unknowingly—stripped of prospects, and they express their predicament in these "little crazy" yearnings. A vision of an entirely different life may provide the buoy-ancy necessary to stay afloat amidst great turmoil—a life raft to cling to when a sense of powerlessness feels all too consuming.

The Clarissas, Ravens, Santoses, Kumars, Ineses, Chips, Ellas, Keiths, Manuels, Xiomaras, and Ethans of Austin and of many other cities in the United States are not simply playthings of political, social, economic, and legal misfortunes. Under circumstances not of their own choosing, they are active protagonists in the making of their own his-tory and in that of the city in which they live. We hope readers join us in seeing that while the daily aggravations they have to confront are in-deed to be lamented, their shows of strength against all odds, as well as their thirst—and endeavor—for recognition, are also to be acknowl-edged and respected.

Notes

I am extremely grateful to Philippe Bourgois, Robert Gay, Denise Gilman, and Loïc Wacquant for their comments and suggestions.

Excerpt from *The Sociological Imagination*, by C. Wright Mills, reprinted by permission of Oxford University Press, USA.

1. See Barbara Hines et al., letter to the Travis County Commissioners Court, "End Participation in Immigration and Customs Enforcement (ICE) Detainer Program under Secure Communities" (April 2014).

2. The Detention Watch Network report states, "In 2009, ICE had an adult average daily population (ADP) of 32,606 in a total of 178 facilities. Of these, 15,942 detainees—or 49%—were housed in 30 privately-operated detention centers. Of the private facilities, the states with the highest ADP were Texas (6,115), Georgia (1,804) and Arizona (1,779)." See http://www.detentionwatch network.org/privateprisons.

References

BBC Research and Consulting. 2014. *2014 Comprehensive Housing Market Analysis*. City of Austin. http://austintexas.gov/sites/default/files/files /Housing/Reports_and_Publications/Community_Reports/2014_Compre hensive_Housing_Market_Analysis_062414__reduced_.pdf.

Bourdieu, Pierre. 1990. *In Other Words: Essays Toward a Reflexive Sociology*. Stanford, CA: Stanford University Press.

———. 2000. *Pascalian Meditations*. Stanford, CA: Stanford University Press.

Bourdieu, Pierre, et al. 2000. *The Weight of the World: Social Suffering in Contemporary Society*. Stanford, CA: Stanford University Press.

Cooper, Marianne. 2014. *Cut Adrift: Families in Insecure Times*. Berkeley: University of California Press.

Geertz, Clifford. 1973. *The Interpretation of Cultures*. New York: Basic Books.

Mills, C. Wright. 1959. *The Sociological Imagination*. London: Oxford.

Pagano, Elizabeth. 2013. "Exiled from Main Street." *Austin Chronicle*, June 28.

Workers Defense Project. 2009. *Building Austin, Building Injustice: Working Conditions in Austin's Construction Industry*. A Report from Workers Defense Project in Collaboration with the Division of Diversity and Community Engagement at the University of Texas at Austin.

CHAPTER 1

Austin, Texas, in Sociohistorical Context

MAGGIE TATE

Flooding the Way for Progress

A crack rang out like a gunshot. The sound, it would soon become known, was caused by a sharp and sudden split down the middle of the massive red granite wall of the Austin dam. Built to hold back the flood-waters of the lower Colorado River, the dam was tested by the torrent of rain that descended on the Austin area on April 6, 1900. And the dam failed. Though it stood an impressive sixty feet high, the dam could no longer hold back the force of water rushing down the river. As the dam gave way on the morning of April 7, chunks of granite and limestone rubble were carried as far as sixty feet downstream. Lives and property were lost, as has been the case in the more than eighty recorded major floods in the lower Colorado basin since 1800. But this flood was dev-astating for more than this reason. With those broken pieces went the promise of Austin as the industrial center of the South, a vision toward which Austin residents had invested $1.4 million in bonds just nine years earlier. In today's dollars that amount would be roughly $35 million.

This chapter begins with the 1900 flood because had it not been for the destruction of the Austin dam, the course of Austin's economy would likely have taken a different trajectory. The failure of this monumental project, by disallowing Austin to develop into an early industrial center of the South, is one of the main events in local history that shaped the city into what it is today. This event explains in part why Austin's econ-omy remained relatively undeveloped for many decades. The economic dormancy that followed the destruction of the dam meant that entre-preneurs could later capitalize on developments in the technology industry. So, in a sense, the breaking of the Austin dam flooded the way for Austin's later success as the high-tech center dubbed "Silicon Hills."

The story of the failed dam also provides insight into the persistence of inequality in Austin. While quality of life has been a steady concern for urban entrepreneurs, only some Austin citizens have been able to experience high living standards. The debt that the city accrued during the building of the dam meant that very few resources were left to go toward other urban necessities, such as paved roads, adequate utilities, and public housing. This would not have been devastating had the dam actually produced the power and industry it promised, because Austin residents would have gotten a return on their investment. Given the dam's failure, they were left with nothing but debt. The city therefore selectively used what funds were still available to make Austin a residential draw for upper- and middle-class whites. Black, Mexican American, and poor white residents were left with dirt roads, backyard outhouses, and forced segregation.

The persistence of inequality despite the vast accumulation of wealth in the more recent history of Austin's success has seeds in these early days. The purpose of this chapter is to explore some of those early, lesser-known stories as a way of highlighting their continuing significance. This chapter situates the Austin dam and other lost opportunities in the context of a broader understanding of American urbanism and industrial growth. It emphasizes the existence of inequality and oppression against the backdrop of the hip, creative, tolerant city of popular lore that is characterized in the phrase "Keep Austin Weird." First coined by Red Wassenich while pledging money to an Austin public radio station in 2000, the phrase has since been adopted by many as a way of promoting local businesses and tourism. The social and historical context that follows implicitly questions what this phrase means and also provides the foundation for the individual narratives in this book.

Austin Exceptionalism

That Austin is exceptional has become commonplace in the public imagination over the past few decades. The city is set apart from the rest of the state of Texas through the popular saying "an island of blue in a sea of red." Descriptions of Austin's exceptionalism describe the enjoyable qualities of the natural landscape, the tolerant people, the creative energy, and the thriving economy that draw more and more people to settle in the Austin metropolitan area. The city is among the fastest growing in the nation, along with Raleigh, Las Vegas, Orlando, Charlotte, and others. As of 2012, the population was 842,592 within the Austin city limits and 1.8 million in the metro area. By the time this book reaches publication, these numbers will likely be much higher because, according to city demographer Ryan Robinson, the city nets 110 new residents each day. The *Austin American-Statesman* has run numerous stories about Austin growth, one of which informed readers that Austin is the fastest-growing metro area among those with populations of one million or more (Castillo 2013).

Aside from population growth, the stories of Austin's success also focus on growing economic possibilities and expanding wealth. However, the median household income of $50,520 reported in the 2010 U.S. Census seems quite modest compared to the city's supposed affluence. In fact, it varies little from the reported median income of both Texas and the nation as a whole. That Austin's median income is 2.2 percent higher than the state average and 3.5 percent lower than the national average appears unremarkable. But a look at the per capita income data tells a more interesting story. The income per capita in Austin is 32.1 percent greater than the Texas average and 17.4 percent greater than the national average. Because income per capita does not eliminate the mathematical influence of high salaries, this measure of wealth reveals an income gap that causes Austin to no longer hover around average.

Images of an affluent Austin today often clash with those of "old Austin," where, as the story goes, "we were dirt cheap; this is where slackers and creatives and musicians could crash" (Moreau quoted in Pagano 2013). Over the last decade, Austin has become more expensive to live in, and as a result higher-income groups have grown faster than the working class. At the neighborhood level, this trend has produced high levels of displacement, with working-class individuals and families no longer able to afford the cost of living in Austin neighborhoods. This trend has also put Austin's progressive reputation on the line, and the standard refrain of "Keep Austin Weird" can no longer universally stand for a culture of tolerance and inclusion.

Joshua Long's book *Weird City* attempts to describe exactly what it is that gives Austin a reputation of weirdness and tolerance. The book characterizes Austin as having "nonconforming quirkiness" and "cultural diversity" (Long 2010). Long interviewed residents of Austin to get a sense of what this means, through which he heard repeated stories of "eccentric people they regularly encounter, the oddly decorated yards in their neighborhood, or the strange protest signs they had recently read" (Long 2010, 19). He found that Austinites who embrace the city's weird identity often do so to distinguish Austin from the rest of Texas; for them, Austin history tells a narrative of political defiance against the conservative tendencies of the rest of the state.

Other work in the social sciences has also popularized the notion of Austin as an exceptional city. This is most evident in the work of Richard Florida, who uses Austin as one of the shining examples of creative cities that support the creative class. Other cities identified as creative are San Francisco, Seattle, Boston, and Portland. For Florida, the centrality of a creative class is a requirement for booming growth in the current knowledge economy. This is because, he claims, creativity has become the single driving force in the growth and development of particular places. His argument defines a trajectory in the history of the U.S. economy, as it has transformed from primarily agricultural, to industrial, to today's creative economy.

The parameters of this creative economy are unclear, particularly because Florida's definition of the creative class is broad: he includes science and engineering, research and development, technology-based industries, arts, music, culture, aesthetic and design work, as well as the knowledge-based professions of health care, finance, and law. Additionally, Florida's assertion that the creative economy causes economic growth lacks empirical evidence and mistakes correlation for causation (Peck 2005). Despite this, Florida's ideas have gained popularity amongst urban planners throughout the United States and globally. Planners who have incorporated the creative class thesis have focused on what Florida refers to as the three T's: technology, talent, and tolerance.

The ubiquity of the creative class thesis has provided a popular language through which to spin the growth of Austin's economy over the past few decades. According to one economist, Austin's creative industries were reportedly responsible for $4 billion in economic activity in 2010 (Kanin 2012). In 2002, then council member Will Wynn put support for the creative class into official city policy when he implemented the Keep Austin Weird Initiative as head of the Task Force on the Economy. The work he did as part of this initiative earned him the visibility that got him elected mayor in 2003, a position in which he served two terms.

Shaping a city toward the creative economy has its drawbacks. For one, many people in the creative class may not directly benefit. This is perhaps the flaw of Florida's vast grouping. Scientists, technology workers, and some types of designers are gaining financially from the Austin tech boom, but artists and musicians are experiencing a different fate. While Wynn has been credited with supporting the creative class by forming the Health Alliance for Austin Musicians (HAAM), one might also consider this a sign of the uneven nature of creative economic development. The reason that HAAM exists is because musicians are not making enough money to be able to afford health care within a privatized, insurance-based system.

Creative workers like artists and musicians often do not support themselves with their creative work and instead are employed in what one writer for the *Austin Chronicle* has called the "day-job infrastructure" (Erard 2003). With low pay and poor benefits, day jobs such as Whole Foods cashier or Caffe Medici barista are included in the low-skilled labor market and frequently get ignored in the discussion of Austin's high-skilled success. Because of their flexible hours, jobs in the service industry allow some artists or musicians to support themselves and still have time to produce their creative work. This source of income makes it possible for them to provide live music in bars inside and outside of the entertainment district, the prevalence of which has led to Austin being labeled the "Live Music Capital of the World."

A Residential Mecca

Inequality reveals itself in perhaps the most visible way in the area of housing. The history of Austin exposes deep disparities related to affordable housing and residential segregation that still shape the lives of current residents. Current growing pains regarding housing inequality are felt in both the buying and renting markets. Construction for new homes can barely keep ahead of demand. As this book goes to press, the average cost to buy a single family home in Austin is over $200,000 and on some months reaches as high as $300,000. Construction for apartment buildings is behind demand as rental rates continue to increase due to lack of vacancies. According to a 2010 study by Elizabeth Mueller of the School of Architecture at the University of Texas at Austin, apartment complexes built during the 1970s and 1980s serve as a primary source of housing for Austin's low-income renters. However, many of these complexes are falling into disrepair and being replaced by

Figure 1.1. "Pease Mansion 1903," detail, J. M. Kuehne. John Matthias Kuehne Collection, di_04417, the Dolph Briscoe Center for American History, the University of Texas at Austin.

mixed-use developments. This real estate upswing has made affordable housing scarce for Austin's current and potential residents.

Historically, there has been a consistent failure on the part of city actors to make affordable housing a necessary part of urban growth in Austin. During the nineteenth century, a building boom propelled the population from less than two hundred during the late 1840s to more than three thousand by the mid-1850s. During this time, Austin boasted high per capita wealth, as evidenced by the construction of many Greek revival mansions, several of which still stand as historic landmarks. The demand for building materials was high due to the building boom, and as a result the housing circumstances of the economically disadvantaged became ever more tenuous.

The building boom of the 1850s drove rapid growth, attracting newcomers whose skill sets changed the economic possibilities; these new arrivals included artisans such as bookbinders, photographers, and metalsmiths, as well as merchants and lawyers—workers whom Florida might call the creative class of the time. Even as growth continued and more Austinites profited from the new economy, "hundreds were impoverished and hundreds more enslaved" (Humphrey 1985, 43). Many who came to Austin with high hopes had those hopes dashed by the reality of life in the nascent state capital, a life that included droughts, freezes, floods, unpaved streets, little infrastructure, and limited trade.

During the early years of industrialism in the South, which occurred in the late nineteenth century following the Civil War, one of the dynamics limiting economic expansion in Austin was that vocal antigrowth Austinites expressed resistance to tenement housing. This type of low-cost, multioccupancy structure has historically served as an infrastructural backbone in urban areas by housing low-wage workers. Without places for workers to live in Austin, there could be few factories, because it was typically the availability of workers that kept the manufacturing economies in industrial cities functioning and prosperous.

Instead of building an industrial city, early developers of Austin focused instead on building a residential mecca as the primary strategy of economic development. Tenement housing and other forms of public housing were not the kinds of residences that these early visionaries imagined. One early industrialist claimed that local business owners who had power in the city during this time did not want the ugly tenement buildings to disturb the look of the developing city, nor did they want to have housing that would attract immigrant workers (Orum 1987).

Having been unable or unwilling to capitalize on modes of industrial growth during much of the nineteenth and early twentieth centuries, city leaders struggled to make Austin a distinctive place worthy of drawing in more settlers. Part and parcel of selling Austin as a pleasant place to live was the implementation of racial segregation both in jobs and in neighborhoods (Busch 2013). Segregation took overt form when a businessman named Monroe Shipe built a "whites only" community called Hyde Park in 1891.

Hyde Park was Austin's first suburb, and that it was a "whites only" community was one of the features highlighted by Shipe as he attempted to sell property there. The building of Hyde Park changed the story of residential living in Austin in other ways as well. Shipe built an electric streetcar that would travel from the city center to the suburb, making the latter highly accessible. The neighborhood had Austin's first lit moonlight tower, or "moontower," a form of lighting that is now used to represent the city's uniqueness, as in films such as *Dazed and Confused*.

Figure 1.2. "Congress Avenue Street Car—Austin (n.d.)," detail, J. M. Kuehne. John Matthias Kuehne Collection, di_09719, the Dolph Briscoe Center for American History, the University of Texas at Austin.

In addition, saloons were prevented from being built in this area. More "wholesome" pleasure took the form of concerts, plays, and other performance arts.

In the early part of the 1900s, Austin remained a viable city by serving as both the political and educational center of Texas. People moved to the city if they were somehow affiliated with either state politics or the University of Texas. Given that neither manufacturing nor trade had blossomed in Austin, prosperity was primarily achieved by attracting people to settle there and buy the goods and services that were available. But given that the population remained relatively constant during this time, urban entrepreneurs had to sell the city to potential residents in other ways. Thus urban entrepreneurs sought to make Austin distinctive through the city plan of 1928.

Much of the plan is strikingly similar to contemporary efforts aimed at making Austin a desirable place to live, including the beautification of streets and sidewalks to make public spaces more pleasant. What makes this plan notable is that it changed the shape of racial segregation in the city and has had a lasting effect on present forms of informal segregation. Prior to the passage of the 1928 plan, black residents were dispersed in different parts of the city, having settled there during the Reconstruction years following the Civil War. Freed slaves set up what would later become the historically black communities of Masontown, Pleasant Hill, Wheatsville, and Clarksville. However, the 1928 plan enforced residential segregation by locating facilities for blacks only east of East Avenue (today Interstate 35), resulting in the displacement of black residents in other parts of the city. The justification in the language of the city code was that it would eliminate the cost of duplicate buildings and facilities throughout the city for whites and blacks, as would have otherwise been mandated in order to comply with the Supreme Court's "separate but equal" interpretation of the Fourteenth Amendment.

As the 1900s progressed, so too did other segregating forces. In his 2012 report for the Institute for Urban Policy Research and Analysis at UT Austin, Eliot Tretter describes these forces as multifaceted, including public restrictions made by the local and federal government, such as those in the 1928 plan, as well as private land-use covenants that restricted the purchase or use of property to whites only. Tretter argues that these early policies of public and private zoning shaped segregation for the duration of the twentieth century, as similarly occurred in other cities throughout the United States. What makes Austin unique is that there has been a decline in Austin's black population since the early 1900s. At the end of the 1800s the black population of Austin had grown to 38 percent of the total population, as former slaves migrated to Austin from other areas of Texas and the South. However, by 1920 black residents had been reduced to 20 percent of the total population, and today that number has shrunk to a striking 8 percent. No other racial or ethnic group shares this pattern of decline in Austin. According to Eric Tang of the Institute for Urban Policy at UT, no other major city in the United States has experienced double-digit population growth while at the same time experiencing a decline in its black population (Tang 2014).

Private property rights, including the "right" to have racially discriminatory land-use covenants, were once common throughout the United States as a mechanism of residential segregation. This became a contested issue in Austin following the federal passage of the Fair Housing Act in 1968. The new act prompted the formation of the Austin Human Rights Commission, which would write local legislation in accordance with the federal law. The group drew up a document called the Austin Fair Housing Ordinance, which went to a vote at the city council shortly after its creation. The ordinance made it unlawful to discriminate against a potential renter, purchaser, or mortgage seeker based on race, religion, or national origin and was passed by the council without much debate. Immediately following its passage, however, stakeholders in the real estate business insisted that this type of decision should not be made by only a few government actors, and should instead be put to a city-wide vote so that Austin's residents could represent themselves on the matter.

Pitching it as freedom of private ownership, the Austin Board of Realtors' campaign to get the ordinance defeated was apparently persuasive. In 1968 the Austin Fair Housing Ordinance was overturned, making it virtually impossible for the federal Fair Housing Act to be enforced at the local level. Housing on the East Side, where Austin's non-white residents lived, was for the most part run-down and in disrepair. Additionally, the public services provided by the city, including things like libraries, parks, and utilities, were far inferior to those in west and north Austin. Therefore, even though the formal "separate but equal" segregation of the 1928 city plan was no longer in effect, private property owners were able to continue its work long after formal segregation was made unlawful.

Once legal segregation ended, many black residents with the means to do so left east Austin in pursuit of better economic opportunities. The out-migration of wealth from the neighborhood meant that the residents who remained were those without the means to leave or even to keep up the property they had. The disrepair progressed and became a significant concern for city leaders who wanted to foster the image of Austin as progressive and tolerant. As civil rights advancements were made in other parts of the country, the fact that blacks and Latinos were living in substandard housing became a potential blight on the wholesome image of Austin as a residential mecca.

What to do about East Side housing became a major concern for political leaders. The answer, it would seem, has turned out to be gentrification. Lower land values on the East Side meant that people who were getting priced out of other neighborhoods began investing in property there. The University of Texas even took part in this process during the 1980s by purchasing land for future development east of Interstate 35. In the current housing market, developers are buying blocks of land in east Austin and building large mixed-use developments that include luxury condominiums and boutique retail space.

These processes of gentrification have not been without pushback, however. In 1983 the Blackland Community Development Corporation

(CDC) was founded as a way to maintain some presence of affordable housing in east-central Austin. It was first founded by black middle-class residents as a way to purchase small plots of land that would interrupt the large blocks needed by the university to complete its eastward development plans. The university received negative press for appearing to bully the historically black community and eventually backed down during the 1990s. In the current housing market, the Blackland CDC owns forty-eight housing units, including duplexes, apartments, and houses. These are used to keep rent affordable for low-income residents and to offer transitional housing for people who have recently experienced homelessness.

As in many other urban areas in the United States, the Latino population has also experienced segregation. While Mexican Americans had previously developed a small area near Shoal Creek close to the city center, during the 1900s they began buying property on the East Side of the city where land was more affordable. It was during this time that east Austin's Mexican American community began to take shape. While the population was still relatively small, rising from three hundred residents in 1875 to over nine thousand by 1940, Mexican immigrants had a visible place in Austin's cultural landscape, largely through music and murals. These elements are still present, but often threatened, in contemporary Austin. While much of the city's Mexican American culture is commemorated and kept alive by its Mexican American Cultural Center, many a mural has long since been bulldozed or painted over by the changing forces of gentrification.

Preserving the Mexican American heritage of the East Cesar Chavez and Holly neighborhoods, which are in the southern section of the East Side, was the main concern of a 2012 report called *The Land of Broken Dreams and the Land of Opportunity*, authored jointly by the East Austin Conservancy and People Organized in Defense of Earth and Her Resources. The study looked at economic and housing trends at the neighborhood level and found that a primary threat for longtime residents in the area is the rising cost of property taxes. The report argues that rather than building affordable housing units, money would be stretched further by setting up an endowment that would serve as a homeowners' assistance program for low-income residents. This program currently exists under the name Eastside Guardians, but funding is so limited that in 2012 it was able to assist only twelve families, a number that is far lower than the hundreds whose homeownership is at risk due to the continuing rise in property taxes.

Building toward the Creative Class

Even though Austin did not develop into an industrial center, it has experienced its own forms of labor exploitation. This has occurred in a wide variety of fields, including construction, domestic labor, service industries, and the technology industry. Creative workers have been described as central to the making of contemporary Austin, but there are many other forms of labor that must take place in order for Austin to function. Some of those who do these types of labor are featured in the stories included in this book. Other stories reveal that exploited labor was paramount during Austin's formative years, as well as during later years of growth.

As with much economic growth in the United States, the story of labor exploitation in Austin has its own relationship to slavery. Documents from the early years of Austin's history show that slaves provided a major source of labor in building the original site from the ground up. The city officially took formation in 1839, when workers constructed temporary buildings modeled according to the directions of Edwin Waller, who was hired by then president Mirabeau Lamar to be the city's first urban planner. Waller's plan for the city was an organized grid of buildings located between Shoal Creek and Waller Creek (to the west and east, respectively) and between the Colorado River to the south and the capitol building to the north.

Waller's archival papers document that he paid for labor to build the early buildings and clear the land for the city grid. They also show that much of the money exchanged went to slave owners who hired out their slaves in order to profit from the building of the settlement. By 1860 Austin's population was about 3,500 people, 1,000 of whom were the enslaved blacks owned by more than one-third of Austin's white population. The percentage of the population that was enslaved was higher than in any other Texas municipality of the time. This fact stands in contradiction to the common narrative of Austin as unique in having relatively mild race-related conflict. The relatively high slave population created anxiety among white residents of Austin, who largely accepted slavery as legitimate and who feared a slave insurrection due to the sheer numbers of slaves. Hiring out slave labor was one key way that early Austinites made money during the building boom of the 1850s.

During the early decades of Austin's development, the number of Mexican American citizens was generally low. This was not by accident. Mexican immigrants troubled the black/white racial distinction that formed the logical justification for slavery. Because Mexican immigrants were free but were not white, it was believed that they instigated fantasies of freedom in the minds of the enslaved. In 1854 then mayor John Ford wrote an article for his paper, the *Texas State Times*, demanding the expulsion of any Mexican who was seen associating with a slave. He set up a "Vigilance Committee" for enforcement, and of course "associating with" was vague enough to allow for wide interpretation. The Mexican American population did not rebound until well into the 1900s. By 1930 Mexican Americans made up 10 percent of Austin's population. However, their position in the labor force was insecure. Business owners during the early twentieth century were particularly unfriendly toward Mexican Americans, viewing them as transient and hence unreliable labor.

Another important episode of labor exploitation occurred during the building of the new capitol, a site that today serves as both the center of political activity in Texas and an important tourist draw. After Texans finally resolved the conflict over where the capital would be located with a statewide vote in 1872, plans began to emerge to build an impressive new building that would reinforce the centrality of Austin in Texas politics. Difficult economic times prevented the plans from becoming a reality, however, until 1880, when city commissioners began taking bids. The project became more urgent in 1881, when the original capitol was destroyed in a fire.

The design, created by Elijah Myers of Detroit, laid the foundation for a massive building that was said to have surpassed all existing capitol buildings except the national Capitol in Washington, D.C. A railroad line was built specifically to bring materials to the new construction site. These materials included, according to the plans, several tons of limestone that had been quarried just nine miles west of Austin. The limestone proved to be of insufficient quality for the project, however. In order to keep the building materials of Texas origin, it was decided that the Capitol would instead be constructed from red granite, which required a new railroad line to the quarry roughly fifty miles from Austin. This change drastically extended both the time and costs of the project.

Not wanting to absorb the cost of this mishap, the contractors asked the state of Texas to provide both the granite and the labor for the project. The owners of Granite Mountain in Burnet County donated the granite. The governor agreed to supply the labor for quarrying and construction through "convict leasing," using prisoners from the Rusk Penitentiary. In response, the International Association of Granite Cut-

Figure 1.3. "Capitol from K. C. Miller House (New UT Press Bldg) (n.d.)," detail, J. M. Kuehne. John Matthias Kuehne Collection, di_09717, the Dolph Briscoe Center for American History, the University of Texas at Austin.

ters boycotted the construction project because the value of their labor was undercut by the utilization of the free labor of prisoners. In need of granite cutters but not wanting to give up the use of free labor, the contractors circumvented the union by hiring stonecutters from Scotland at a relatively low wage. Though the contractors were later found guilty of breaking the Alien Contract Labor Law, the fine was relatively low and the building construction was already well under way. The capitol officially opened on May 16, 1888.

The victory of the International Association of Granite Cutters over the contractors overseeing the building of the capitol represents a relatively rare occurrence in the history of union organization in Austin. Texas has historically had lower union participation than other U.S. states. Additionally, unions with high membership tended to be in areas where large industry had developed, which had not occurred in Austin. It was not until after World War II that union membership in Texas rose above 10 percent of the nonagricultural workforce. While other areas of Texas were becoming heavily industrialized during the mid- and late twentieth century, Austin was instead beginning to emerge as a technology center. This type of industry tended to have lower levels of union participation than did the heavier industry of manufacturing. The conservative leanings of Texas legislators, combined with the type of industry that was developing in Austin, meant that unions have had relatively little sway in the capital city.

The earlier moments in the history of Austin reveal that, as mentioned in the introduction of this volume, construction is an ongoing area of significant concern regarding labor, particularly during building booms. Given that population growth in Austin has also meant growth in the construction of both homes and office buildings, this pattern continues. In April of 2013 National Public Radio ran a story called "Construction Booming in Texas, But Many Workers Pay Dearly." The story unveiled the exploitation of construction workers in Texas. Of prominent concern, according to the Workers Defense Project (WDP), was wage theft. According to WDP, workers most often file complaints of partial payment and sometimes lack of payment. In addition, the story reported that construction companies rely on the labor of undocumented workers, who get paid in cash as independent contractors, allowing the companies to pay low wages and avoid the cost of federal income taxes.

In Austin, as in many other cities, construction workers are employed as independent contractors. This means that construction companies are not liable for workers' compensation when on-site accidents occur, as they frequently do. According to a report by the WDP in collaboration with the Division of Diversity and Community Engagement at UT Austin, more than one in five construction workers will require hospitalization for a work-related injury (Price, Timm, and Tzintzún 2013). Further, more construction deaths occur in Texas than in any other state. Recently, WDP has helped workers take legal action against one of the most prominent builders of luxury apartments in downtown Austin for wage theft and abusive working conditions.

Becoming Austin

The economic growth that had characterized Austin during its initial boom in the 1850s halted in 1861 as the Civil War got under way. Destitution was widespread during much of the 1860s as goods were in short supply and many soldiers died or were badly injured during the fighting. Disorder and unrest further ensued when the Union Army arrived in

Figure 1.4. "Bunch of cows, Capitol in distance, 1901," detail, J. M. Kuehne. John Matthias Kuehne Collection, di_09718, the Dolph Briscoe Center for American History, the University of Texas at Austin.

Galveston on June 19, 1865, and announced that all enslaved blacks were now freed. This was more than two years after the Emancipation Proclamation had ended slavery in the Confederate States. For fear of unrest, Union troops were sent into Austin, where they set up military occupation until 1870 to maintain order in the capital city. In addition to serving the needs and desires of these soldiers, economic activity during this time rested on the fact that Austin stood along a cattle drive trail, so it became a regular stop for cattlemen to purchase goods and services on their long journeys.

The emerging railroad system in the United States provided what appeared to be a new opportunity for economic growth. Work had begun on the first rail prior to the Civil War but ceased when the war got under way. Construction on a rail system did not resume until 1871, when the Houston and Texas Central line came to Austin and made it the westernmost railroad stop in Texas. At the time there were few rails in the area, so Austin initially became a trading center with a vibrant economy. Cotton farming, an important component of the economy in the American South, became a growing feature of Austin's economy because farmers could now export their crop yields relatively cheaply and much quicker. Trains allowed goods to be shipped to and from Houston, one of Texas's major port cities, in just a day rather than the two weeks it had previously taken to transport goods by wagon.

It appeared that Austin was becoming a city in its own right, as the population grew from 4,400 in 1870 to 10,400 by 1875. In 1872 Texans cast their final vote to make Austin the permanent capital of Texas. However, the economic activity that characterized the city during the 1870s was short lived. Because of competing railroad construction in other areas of Texas, Austin soon became a bypassed city. Trade and business growth came to a relative standstill, which was mirrored by a flattening in population growth between 1875 and 1880. With only modest growth in both manufacturing and the rail system, Austin stayed relevant largely through its role as the political center of Texas. To this end, the construction of the new capitol building was a focus of development during the 1880s.

It was during this time that the city also developed itself as an education center of the state. The first college to open was the Tillotson Collegiate and Normal Institute, which opened in January of 1881 and became a prominent historically black university. Tillotson Collegiate then merged with Samuel Huston College, which had opened in 1883 as Austin's second historically black university. The merger between the two in 1952 created Huston-Tillotson University. Although there were never any restrictions regarding race, it remained a primarily black university and is still in operation today.

Becoming home to the University of Texas was an important moment in Austin's claim as the education center of Texas. Though the university had existed in theory since 1839 in the form of a congressional land act, it was not operational until 1883. It was not even decided where the university would be located until 1881. During that year, Texas voters elected to have Austin serve as the main site for the university system, with Galveston becoming the site for the medical school. This vote followed a political contest between supporters of Austin and supporters of Waco that lasted for several months.

Given that the university would be a "whites only" institution for many years, it is ironic that a black reverend by the name of Jacob Fontaine was influential in the voting outcome (Goldstone 2006). Fontaine traveled throughout Texas making speeches and holding conventions to encourage black groups to vote for Austin to be the site of the university. Despite his efforts, the first black student was not admitted to the university until 1950, when Heman Sweatt was allowed to register in the School of Law. This followed a long and exhausting legal battle that had ended at the U.S. Supreme Court with a decision in Sweatt's favor. Despite efforts to increase diversity, the university is still a predominantly white institution, in particular among its faculty. As of 2010, 80 percent of faculty were white, 6.4 percent were Hispanic, and 3.5 percent were black. In comparison, of the students of the 2010 incoming freshman class, 48 percent were white, 23 percent were Hispanic, and 5 percent were black.

By the time of Sweatt's admission in the 1950s, the University of Texas had developed a promising reputation. However, its early years of operation were by contrast quite grim. For one thing, it took two years before the doors even opened to students, primarily due to lack of funding. Although the Board of Regents had acquired land in West Texas to develop a university endowment—a choice that would later have a great payoff in oil money—in these early years the university earned only a small income from land leases. While the university only attracted a modest number of students during its early years, averaging two hundred students in liberal arts and law, these students did generate some economic activity.

It was the discovery of oil in West Texas on land owned by the university that eventually led to the national prominence of the University of Texas. In 1923 the Santa Rita oil well became a profitable source of income for the university. While the university's lands in West Texas had previously garnered only around $40,000 per year, the Santa Rita oil well now accrued a profit of roughly $250,000 per month. This allowed for the construction of several new campus buildings and for the acquisition of land for further expansion.

Weathering the Depression

Surprisingly, the Depression era was a time of population growth for Austin, which saw an increase in population from fifty-three thousand to eighty-eight thousand by the end of the 1930s. Because it had failed to develop significantly in heavy industry or textile manufacturing, the city did not have a large industrial workforce to be suddenly out of work. However, black workers suffered the brunt of the economic consequences during this period, as they made up a large portion of the manual labor force. Those who could still find work were making only roughly half of what they had previously made. Austinites employed in government and education were hurt far less. These were by no means good economic years for the majority of Austin's residents, but in comparison to the rest of the nation, Austin's economy fared rather well due in large part to the New Deal.

Under the mayorship of Tom Miller, Austin sought New Deal assistance in the form of loans and grants through the Public Works Administration (PWA) of the federal government. New Deal money funded the building of badly needed roads, sewage facilities, utility infrastructure, and parks and allowed for the renovation of existing buildings. Miller started a "better streets" campaign that finally made paved streets the norm where dirt roads had previously remained. These projects laid the foundation for what is now considered Austin's high quality of life. In particular, the park system that was developed during the time has been integral to the selling of Austin as a residential city that has preserved the beauty of its green spaces. In addition, twenty new buildings were added to the University of Texas campus for a cost totaling $6 million, some of which were used for early research in the nascent days of Austin's technology industry.

The quality of life that was developed through PWA projects funded by the New Deal made Austin a place primed for growth as urban economies in the United States shifted from a manufacturing industrial base to a service industrial base. Military science in the 1950s "foreshadowed the shape of the Austin economy" when J. Neils Thompson and the University of Texas opened the Balcones Research Center, now the J. J. Pickle Research Campus (Orum 1987, 236). The building site had previously served as a magnesium plant for wartime manufacturing. After World War II, it became a university research facility that used the knowledge produced at the university and a large number of Department of Defense contracts to lay the groundwork for what would later become a tech boom.

The most well-known success in drawing business to Austin came in 1966, when IBM built a plant in the city and was shortly followed by Texas Instruments and Motorola. With the addition of these companies, the technology sector expanded beyond a focus on defense and became more multifaceted. By 1995 computer software and related work had become the largest employment sector of Austin's economy, with a base of 400 companies involved in the high-tech industry—a number that by 2012 had grown to 2,591. Austin continues to attract software, Internet, and technology companies, including large companies like Apple and Facebook, which recently opened offices in Austin.

Growth and Local Politics

The continuing story of the changing landscape of Austin reflects a tension between those who promote growth and those who wish to preserve an older Austin by fighting against the modernizing forces that are seen to threaten the city's weirdness. One such conflict that exemplifies this tension is the 2006 campaign called Responsible Growth for Northcross, which petitioned against the building of an enormous Wal-Mart near Burnet Road and Anderson Lane. As a result of this movement, the store that was built had a much smaller size and visible presence than either the developer or Wal-Mart had originally wanted.

Grassroots movements on the part of homeowners in Austin, such as Responsible Growth for Northcross, are often celebrated as a form of progressive politics. This can also be seen in the popularity and influence of the "buy local" movement, which has become another way of adhering to the slogan "Keep Austin Weird." The Austin Independent Business Alliance provides an online tool to help match consumers to local businesses based on their consumption needs. Yet many academic critics have pointed out that the consumer cost of buying local makes it a privilege not available to everyone. Anticorporate political action sometimes has the effect of making low-cost goods harder to find, contributing to the rising cost of living within the city. Further, buying local focuses on the celebration of consumption and does little to address worker rights abuses and labor inequality experienced by local people.

It could be argued that the kinds of grassroots politics that have taken shape in Austin's recent history have benefited the already privileged and contributed to the invisibility of other types of politics that could be or are taking place. The question of whether Austin can maintain its weirdness despite its rapid growth takes precedence in the public discourse about what change means in Austin. Therefore, it is rare for inequality to take center stage in the conversation about where the city stands on growth.

Because much of this chapter has focused on inequality furthered through policies that have deeply structured social relations in Austin, such as those relating to housing and employment, there has been much omitted on the movements and pressures to combat these structuring forces. In the book *Inequity in the Technopolis: Race, Class, Gender, and the Digital Divide in Austin* (Straubhaar et al. 2012), the authors look at the effect of what they refer to as top-down structuring policies as well as what they call bottom-up programs that seek to create digital inclusion, such as the Austin Free-Net program that began in 1995 to offer computer literacy training, technology support, computer donations, and free computer and Internet access. Despite these types of efforts, which apparently make Austin an exception among technopolitan and creative cities, the digital divide has become increasingly pronounced.

This chapter has emphasized the historical dimensions of inequality in order to make it more central to the understanding of how Austin came to be. Inequality has been systemic to the workings of the city, and making this visible is both an intellectual and political project. Our hope is that readers will begin to wonder what privileges, and what suffering, are produced from keeping Austin weird or from growing Austin into a hub of the technology industry. The stories in this book should not be seen as exceptional or extraordinary. They should be seen as everyday lives that make up this city and the joys and sorrows that such lives include. In this way, the myth of Austin exceptionalism will hopefully give way to an image of the city that sees beyond the trope of the weird and reveals the nuanced lives that are often made invisible in the process of narrating Austin's growth.

References

Busch, Andrew. 2013. "Building 'A City of Upper-Middle-Class Citizens': Labor Markets, Segregation, and Growth in Austin, Texas, 1950–1973." *Journal of Urban History* 20 (10): 1–22.

Castillo, Juan. 2013. "Old Story, New Chapter: Austin Leads U.S. in Growth among Biggest Metro Areas." *Austin American-Statesman*, March 15.

East Austin Conservancy and People Organized in Defense of Earth and Her Resources. 2012. *Land of Broken Dreams and Land of Opportunity*. Austin, Texas: Author.

Erard, Michael. 2003. "Creative Capital? In the City of Ideas, the People with Ideas Are the Ones with Day Jobs." *Austin Chronicle*, February 28.

Florida, Richard. 2005. *Cities and the Creative Class*. New York: Routledge.

Goldstone, Dwonna. 2006. *Integrating the 40 Acres: The Fifty-Year Struggle for Racial Equality at the University of Texas*. Athens: University of Georgia Press.

Goodwyn, Wade. 2013. "Construction Booming in Texas, But Many Workers Pay Dearly." *Morning Edition*. National Public Radio. April 10.

Humphrey, David C. 1985. *Austin: An Illustrated History*. Northridge, CA: Windsor Publications.

Kanin, Mike. 2012. "Hockenyos Gets Creative . . . Again: Austin should embrace its identity as a cultural mecca." *Austin Chronicle*, March 30.

Long, Joshua. 2010. *Weird City: Sense of Place and Creative Resistance in Austin, Texas*. Austin: University of Texas Press.

Mueller, Elizabeth. 2010. "Old Apartments and New Plans: Reconciling Planning and Housing Goals in Two Texas Cities." *Community Development* 41 (2): 121–140.

Orum, Anthony. 1987. *Power, Money and the People: The Making of Modern Austin*. Eugene, OR: Resource Publications.

Pagano, Elizabeth. 2013. "Exiled from Main Street: Can Austin's Stock of Affordable Housing Keep Pace with High-Speed Growth?" *Austin Chronicle*, June 28.

Peck, Jamie. 2005. "Struggling with the Creative Class." *International Journal of Urban and Regional Research* 29 (4): 740–770.

Price, Amy, Emily Timm, and Cristina Tzintzún. *Build a Better Texas: Construction Working Conditions in the Lone Star State*. Austin, Texas: Workers Defense Project.

Shank, Barry. 1994. *Dissonant Identities: The Rock'n'Roll Scene in Austin, Texas*. Middletown, CT: Wesleyan University Press.

Straubhaar, Joseph, Jeremiah Spence, Zeynep Tufekci, and Roberta G. Lentz. 2012. *Inequity in the Technopolis: Race, Class, Gender, and the Digital Divide in Austin*. Austin: University of Texas Press.

Swearingen, William Scott, Jr. 2010. *Environmental City: People, Place, Politics, and the Meaning of Modern Austin*. Austin: University of Texas Press.

Tang, Eric. 2014. "Outlier: The Case of Austin's Declining African-American Population." Institute for Urban Policy Research and Analysis.

Tretter, Eliot. 2012. "Austin Restricted: Progressivism, Zoning, Private Racial Covenants, and the Making of a Segregated City." Institute for Urban Policy Research and Analysis.

Waters, Andrew. 2003. *I Was Born in Slavery: Personal Accounts of Slavery in Texas*. Winston-Salem, NC: John F. Blair.

CHAPTER 2

Santos: The Gold Hunter

JACINTO CUVI

For a countryman like Santos who spent the first twenty years of his life harvesting maize and roping cattle, chipping cement under the eight-lane Mopac Bridge during its construction in the early 1970s hardly constituted an enjoyable task. But, then again, life for Santos was not about enjoyment.

In the half decade that followed, Santos toiled in more than a dozen industries. He washed dishes at La Cocina del Sur, a Mexican restaurant on Burnet Road, for about fifteen dollars a day; he cut wood boards at a factory on South Congress for $3.35 an hour; he cleared tables at Los Panchos, another Mexican restaurant; and a few years later he worked installing pipes that carried telecommunication cables alongside Oltorf Street. "I've had like ten thousand jobs," Santos told me with a smile. "And I never got in trouble. I never wasted my bosses' or supervisors' time." (Santos used the Spanish word "*mayordomos*" for the supervisors, an old-fashioned term meaning large estate stewards.) "But I always kept looking for new jobs. I wanted more, I was hungry."

Mexico

Santos's wandering life began sixty-five years ago on a farm near a remote, dirt-poor town in Mexico's western highlands. The town bears the peculiar name of Cutzamala de Pinzón and lies near the northwestern edge of the state of Guerrero. At the time that Santos was born, it had neither a church nor a school. These institutional voids conspired with the material needs of the household, as they so often do in rural Latin America, to deprive this modest farm boy of a single day of schooling. Santos was the third of three brothers whose dad died of an ordinary cold before Santos's second birthday. Thus, at the age of five, Santos was out in the fields, piling up corn stubble to be burned before the next sowing season. At seven, he was, in his own words, a "full-fledged peon" (*peón completo*), harvesting beans and clearing woods with his brothers and grandfather.

Looking back on his erratic career—if it can be called as much—Santos regrets that he never received any formal education. Even so, he traces what he sees as his stunted intellectual development to the shock he received from a lightning bolt that struck him, his brother, and two family friends as they walked home at the end of a long day of harvesting. Esteban, the middle child, took a full blow to the chest; he died in the field minutes later. Santos, who was nine at the time, survived the jolt without physical impairments. Yet he attributes his learning difficulties and short-term memory gaps to this childhood trauma.

In spite of the hardships he endured as a young boy, it was not poverty, or not poverty alone, that drove Santos from his godforsaken hometown to the United States. As they grew up, he and his older brother José learned to make the most of the two hundred hectares (roughly five hundred acres) that their dad had left them when he died. They built with their hands an adobe house that Santos describes as a mansion, a "casa de haciendado" (the house of a rich landowner of Spanish descent, normally pronounced "hacendado"), where the two brothers lived with their mother and José's wife.

Memories of this period of Santos's life are still colored by some moments of intense happiness. "Life was hard, but we had fun." Santos recalled for me the days following harvest, when he and other farmers would set up calf-roping contests—he boasted about the rowdiness of the young bulls they lassoed—or grill fresh corn on the range and devour as many as fifteen cobs apiece. "We were poor," Santos said, "but life was rich." What made Santos leave on his first northward journey, ignoring his mother's and his brother's pleas that he stay, was, in a way, curiosity.

Rumors of a foreign land where work was well paid had reached Santos's hometown through the stories of returning braceros, manual workers imported to the United States for temporary work stays, mostly in agriculture. Santos had heard you could make twenty-five cents for each box of strawberries you picked, and he figured he could fill one hundred boxes in a day. He had also heard on the radio news of the assassination of John F. Kennedy, and of a revolution on the remote island of Cuba.

By the time the bracero program ended in 1964, however, Santos was still under twenty-one, the minimum age for enrollment. To see that foreign land he would have to make the journey on his own.

"But didn't you think about finding a wife and settling down, like your brother had?" I asked him.

"Women, sure, I liked them, coveted them. But no, I was in love with El Norte."

"And what did you expect to find on your first trip?"

"I didn't know. I just wanted to see what it was like over there, how people lived, and then come back and tell my mother what I had seen. I wanted to tell her, 'Over there, people live in this way, and this way, and this way. . . .' That was my dream."

He left his rancho on foot on a blistering morning in March of 1968 with about thirty dollars in his pocket and a big, fuzzy, northward-pointing dream.

Santos now owns a house in a lower-middle-class, suburb-like neighborhood in south Austin. He lives with his wife, daughter, and two grandchildren. The house has a small backyard where Santos has carved a space for a vegetable garden. In it he grows corn, tomatoes, and red peppers, as well as other plants and spices from his homeland. He bought the house in the mid-1990s with a mortgage miraculously obtained by presenting a bank agent with pay stubs from his past jobs, at a time when the household was in deep financial straits.

Whatever prosperity Santos has achieved in this country, however, has come at the cost of a lifelong struggle.

In fact, his first sojourn in the United States lasted less than a week. In those days, nothing more than a barbed-wire fence divided the northern Mexican state of Sonora from Arizona, where Santos entered the United States for the first time. After spending a night at a hotel in San Luis, Sonora, the border town on the Mexican side, he jumped over the fence and found work picking oranges along the U.S.-Mexico border. But he was quickly rounded up by immigration officials, transferred to Yuma, Arizona, for a police check, and finally deported to Mexico by truck. Ten days later, having crossed into Arizona a second time to resume his orange picking job, he was back at Yuma's police station. The treatment he received this time around was far less courteous.

Santos was held for three days in solitary confinement in Yuma and then transferred to a prison in Chula Vista, California, where he spent three months. "I came out of there with white lice like dogs have." The night of his release, he was taken to the airport in Tijuana, handed a folding chair to sit on, and flown to León, Guanajuato, in a cargo plane along with other deportees. Those who had the money were asked to pay thirty-seven dollars for the trip.

His first entrance into Texas was scarcely more promising. To cross the U.S.-Mexico border, he walked alone in the desert for sixteen days, eating prickly pears and drinking water from the windmill-powered pumps that he came across every couple of days. On the morning that he first spotted a ranch on Texas soil, he had been without food or water for four days. He knocked on the farmhouse door and an old woman opened. He begged her for food and water. Using gestures, she told him that she had no food, signaled toward a spigot where he could refill his water bottle, and pointed in the direction of the road leading to the ranch. Santos understood that down this road he would find a place to eat. Instead, after walking a couple of miles, he ran into a police car. As it turned out, the woman had reported him.

In all, Santos was sent back to Mexico sixteen times. He made seventeen return trips to the United States.

"What were you looking for?" I asked him.

"Happiness," he replied. Upon reflection, he added, "But I didn't come to this country to stay. My plan was to go back to Mexico. I came here . . ." He paused. "I came here to 'harvest,' so to speak."

In the United States, he explained, life is only about work. In fact, even when he was young, he seldom attended dance parties organized by his fellow countrymen. "I didn't come here to drink, to burn rubber." In Mexico, though, things are different. "Life is good over there [allá se goza]."

As I came to realize through our talks and interviews, Mexico also occupies a special place in the imagination of this thwarted expatriate. It is an enchanted place, a wide world with room for heroic gestures and magical developments, events that would be unthinkable elsewhere. This mythical quality of his home country became apparent to me one day when we were riding in a truck he had bought to set up a moving business with his nephew—a short-lived enterprise, as it turned out, which ended when the nephew realized that he could make larger profits working on his own.

"I have a task for you," he told me. "I'll pay you."

"You don't need to pay me anything," I replied. "What can I do?"

"I need you to find out the market value of an olicorn."

"Do you mean a unicorn?"

"Yes, that's right, a unicorn."

"You mean those animals that look like horses with a horn in the middle of their foreheads?"

"Yes. I need you to find out how much I can buy one for, or, if I have one, for how much I can sell it."

I did not dare to ask on what side of the hypothetical transaction he stood, and I felt it would be discourteous to probe the concrete reasons behind his query at that point.

"I am not an expert in unicorns," I told him. "But most people I know doubt they ever existed."

"Well, I want you to research that too: where they existed, at what time, and whether they can still be found somewhere."

I had to wait until the following week to discover the motive behind his unusual request. By then, I had read on *Wikipedia* that unicorns were part of European mythology during the Middle Ages, that they could only be tamed by virgins, and that their horns held magical powers, including the ability to purify poisoned water and heal illnesses. It was a sunny Sunday afternoon, and we were sitting in Santos's backyard, chatting and drinking soda. He was showing me some treasures he had collected during his trips. Suddenly, he pulled out an ivory-colored object, two inches long and resembling an unearthed bone.

"This is what I was telling you about," he said. "This is from the unicorn."

He went on to explain that his grandmother had used powder that she ground from the horn to heal stomachaches and diarrhea. She had bestowed the object on Santos when he was a little boy.

Reflecting on this incident, I realized that the horn came from that same geographic and symbolic place where, Santos swears, he had once encountered the devil in the form of a red-eyed goat, the place where he had once escaped from a crowd of forty armed men, carrying his gun-wounded cousin on his shoulders in the middle of the night.

Whatever the reader may think about these wondrous anecdotes, they are an intrinsic part of how Santos sees the world. They coexist, moreover, alongside very detailed and realistic memories of his past travels and work experiences, which he recounts with surprising consistency across time and which he often buttresses with pictures and documents. Even his quixotic rescue of his cousin and their escape were related to me by him and his wife with such detail and in such a casual, candid way that I cannot help but think that most of it was real.

While Mexico captivates Santos's imagination, the nostalgia that he feels for his homeland stems from distinctively less miraculous experiences. "In Mexico," he once told me, "you can own a piece of land, and you can choose what to produce. Whether you farm maize, or beans, or raise pigs . . . it's your choice. And everything you produce on that land belongs to you. Here, in the United States, you work for others."

After a pause, and somewhat wistfully, he added, "My life has been working for others."

Working for Others

Santos's slim body bears witness to a life of hard labor. At 5′7″, he gives a peculiar and endearing impression, sitting in his Austin living room in a loose, oversized flannel shirt, sharp jeans, and polished cowboy boots. His skin is tanned and hardened, his gait not as light or brisk as it was in those early days. When he smiles or winces, crow's-feet frame his dark brown eyes. Santos seems accustomed to motion. He constantly sets forth to rein in a wayward grandson or lowers to retrieve a photo that will help him better tell his story. Yet his frame shows blatant signs of frailty brought on by years of lifting, pounding, and pushing, as well

as by a recent car accident, recounted below. When he speaks, however, he has an excitability, a stubborn sense of optimism that leaves its imprint on his audience.

Of all the jobs that Santos has held, the one he claims to have liked the most was at a chicken processing plant in San Antonio. He landed this job randomly (like most jobs he has had) after a conversation with a well-meaning Chicano at a cantina. Santos was stranded in San Antonio because he could not afford the final stretch of his trip back to the ranch of his *patrón*—an American rancher named Bill Pope who had taken Santos under his wing and who regularly rehired him when he returned from Mexico—a few miles west of Austin, near Oak Hill.

On the morning that Santos arrived at the processing plant for the first time, he was assigned ("with God's help") to the final stages of the work line. He remembers how his coworkers at the opposite end—where loads of live chickens were delivered by truck—would walk out covered in feathers and chicken excrement at the end of each day. Santos's task consisted of pulling defeathered carcasses out of a small washbasin and hanging them onto hooks attached to a conveyor belt. At first he shared the task with two other workers. In time, however, they were either dismissed or relocated, and Santos was left to process the full load on his own.

Santos speaks with pride about the thousands of carcasses he hung each day, his efficiency in adapting to new equipment, and the admiration that managers developed for his work. The job lasted until immigration officials raided the premises and Santos, who was deported to Matamoros, decided to stay his southward course and go visit his mother and check on the family land.

"But wasn't it boring to hang those chickens all day?" I asked him.

"That's the job I enjoyed the most [*el que más dominé*]."

This was neither the first nor the last time that being from another country would cost Santos his job. In fact, his immigrant status continued to undermine his prospects of stable employment even after he obtained a green card in the wake of the Immigration Reform and Control Act of 1986, as the following events illustrate.

In the early 1990s Santos had settled in on a ranch in central Mexico with his second wife and their three kids (his first wife died giving birth when Santos was twenty-four). He had bought the ranch with his savings and owned about sixty pigs, two horses, and a dozen dairy cows. "I was prosperous. I wanted to die on that rancho."

However, a series of misfortunes, including the near death of and expensive surgery for a son who was kicked in the face by an untamed mule, left the family in near financial ruin. To pay their debts and secure an income, they decided to move to Austin, Texas, where they hoped opportunities would be more numerous and generous. Following a month-long unsuccessful job search, during which the family ate on the floor and used Styrofoam containers for kitchenware, Santos and his wife found jobs with a local real estate developer. Santos painted walls while Sirila, his wife, worked as a cleaner at an apartment complex under construction near the corner of South Congress and Riverside—a few blocks from the heart of downtown Austin.

In a pattern that is sadly familiar among informal workers in Austin, twelve days later they were still waiting for their payment, which had been due at the end of the first week of employment. A series of tense encounters with their employer ensued, and Santos and his wife decided to stop working. "That amigo just used us," Santos concluded.

Santos made several attempts to recover his and his wife's unpaid wages. He once went to the house of his former boss, who had told him they could meet there and settle the dispute. Santos knocked on the door several times; no one answered. He then moved away from the door to peer into one of the nearby windows but suddenly got scared.

"What if the man called the police and told them I was a thief?" he told me, recounting the thoughts he had at the time. "What was I going to say?"

Santos left the house resigned and empty-handed.

Frustrated, Santos decided to seek redress through institutional channels. In this quest, he would experience once more the weight that a vertically structured social world exerts on the lowest rungs of the social ladder—where he consciously sits.

"What do you expect? To be treated like a little golden coin?" asked a man, whom Santos refers to as the consul of Mexico, on the other end of the phone.

The official was irritated by Santos's queries about measures taken by the consulate against the conning employer. Indeed, following the advice of a local nonprofit organization, Santos had reported the abuse to the Mexican consulate in Austin and was hoping that they would help him obtain some sort of reparation for the abuse he and his wife had suffered.

"I don't need you to remind me that I'm a fool!" Santos claimed he responded to the man. "I know that already. I'm asking for help defending my rights!"

Still shaken by the recollection of that incident, he told me, "The Mexican consul, he doesn't give a damn about people like me. I don't care how educated he is, I don't need him!"

Despite these moments of apparent helplessness, the notion that his checkered professional trajectory has been shaped by structural forces seems outlandish to Santos himself. When talking about a neighbor who stuck to his Wal-Mart job for more than twenty years and who, as a result, enjoys a small but secure pension, Santos pondered:

"I'm not like that. . . . And you know how much they pay you at those jobs? I have a cousin who's worked at the same company for eighteen years; he's lucky if he makes fifteen dollars [an hour]. It's not worth it. Besides, I had to go visit my mother. I never let a year go by without going to Mexico to check on her. To me, my mother was more important than any job."

As if his loyalty to his mother needed any justification, he added, poetically, "I didn't know how to write, you know. My visits back home . . . those were the letters I sent."

On a different occasion, he stressed his unsubmissive nature: "I never let anyone boss me around. As soon as they shouted at me, I took off.

That's why I've had so many jobs." He even went as far as to claim, on one afternoon when he felt tired and sick, that working "annoys" him (*me fastidia*).

There is, of course, more than a single cause or reason behind Santos's broken trajectory in the labor market. In fact, the reasons he invoked during our interviews speak as much to the motives behind past decisions as they do to his efforts to make sense of those decisions in the present. They also convey efforts to reclaim agency over events in which his personal wishes and attributes may have played only a marginal role—if any.

Where the actual line falls on the spectrum between structure and character is a matter of perspective. Conservative thinkers and politicians like to paint the successes and failures of individuals as a mechanical reflection of their personal choices. Sociologists, on the other hand, have warned against a blame-the-victim narrative that casts poverty, joblessness, and other social ills as the result of willful action taken by those who suffer the most from them (Bourgois 2003). Pervasive as it is in the media and public discourse, this blame-the-victim narrative can lead the "victims" to blame their own disgrace on themselves. Beyond anyone's ideological or methodological inclinations, however, the fact remains that Santos began working when he was five years old, and he has worked all his life, more and harder than many "successful professionals," at whatever job was available.

Santos worked all his life, that is, until an intoxicated driver going over the speed limit hit the side of his truck on March 29, 2012.

The accident took place at night, when Santos was driving home with his wife in his red Tacoma truck. As he came to a stop at the corner of Berkett Drive and Buffalo Pass in south Austin, he saw the headlights of a car coming from his left. The distance seemed to give him more than enough time to cross, and so he did.

The car slammed into the left side of his truck, just behind the driver's door. "Had it been on the door, I would be dead."

Santos got out of his truck, feeling dizzy. He stumbled and had to lean on the hood to keep his balance. His lower back ached. The other driver also got out of his car, visibly intoxicated. The man asked Santos not to call the police—or at least this is what Santos, who never learned English, understood. The man said that he would pay for the repairs. Santos, who had grabbed his cell phone, tried to explain to him through

gestures that he was calling a nephew who could come to the site and serve as an interpreter. Yet the man either misunderstood or did not believe Santos, and he reported the crash to the police himself.

When the police officer arrived, he offered to call an ambulance that would take Santos to the hospital. Santos, however, refused; he was worried about his truck. The car was to be picked up by a private towing company and delivered to his house. "I had to be there to make sure that they would bring my truck home," he told me. "I could not take that risk."

"That risk," one is left to infer, is the risk of there being another misunderstanding, of being cheated again, and of losing one of his few valuable assets.

Besides, Santos hoped that his pains would vanish on their own. The following morning, however, the pain in the nape of his neck and lower back was so acute that he had no choice but to go to the community clinic. He spent the whole day there, undergoing a range of medical exams, and walked out with a $2,000 bill—most of which was covered by Medicaid.

Since I met him three years ago, Santos has complained about a wide array of chronic ailments. Despite the pain, however, he has never stopped working. I was surprised to hear that during the winter of 2012, on days when the temperature dipped below freezing, he was still working at an open-air construction site at Lakeway Medical Center northwest of Austin, despite what sounded like whooping cough. Sweeping was the only task he felt strong enough to undertake, and his boss had agreed to keep him on the job.

Ever since the car crash, Santos has been unable to engage in any sustained physical activity. He still winces as he lifts himself off his sofa to grab a glass of Coke and hobbles when he crosses his garden to show me his corn plants. Yet his aspirations to reenter the job market one day have not dwindled. "I want to keep going," he said. "I have to. Before that amigo hit me, I felt like I was thirty."

Due to these setbacks and the resulting loss of income, Santos is now supported by his daughter, who waits tables, and his wife, who works for a costume-renting and party-organizing business. He cannot help but feel a certain shame about his situation of material dependency. To fill his time and make some money of his own, he has taken to collecting empty cans on the streets of his neighborhood, aided by a mechanical grabber that allows him to remain upright.

The gig is not new to this jack-of-all-trades. During the month-long period of unemployment that followed their return to Austin in the mid-1990s, Santos and his kids resorted to picking up cans to put food on the table—or, as was the case then, on the floor. "In a week," he once told a stranger sitting next to him at the community clinic, "I was able to gather about seventy dollars worth of cans. I took my wife and the kids to the supermarket and told them, 'Alright, we'll do this nice and cheap. Let's get some beans, some rice, a little bit of oil.' The whole family ate."

Nowadays, with the basic needs of the household covered by the salaries of his daughter and his wife, the money Santos makes through his can-picking efforts finances an old habit: buying lottery tickets. Two or three times a week Santos purchases scratch-off tickets. Since he does not know how to read, he usually takes the tickets home after scratching them and shows them to his daughter so she can decipher the results. Even though he seldom wins and has never made more than fifty dollars on a ticket, the hope of a drastic improvement in his living conditions has continued to fuel his lottery purchases for more than fifteen years.

In November of 2013 Santos bought a Weekly Grand lottery ticket at a convenience store not far from where he lives. He brought the ticket home and waited for his daughter to take a look at it, suspecting he had won some kind of prize. The daughter, however, came home late that night, and Santos did not get a chance to show her the ticket. Still, the next day, wanting to buy more tickets, he took the ticket with him to the gas station convenience store where he had purchased it.

"I never wanted to cash it!" he told me, visibly shaken. "I wanted my daughter to look at it first. If I had wanted to cash it, I would have said that to the cashier. I just wanted him to see the brand of tickets I wanted to buy. That's all I wanted!"

The problem, of course, was that Santos could not read (or even pronounce) the name of the brand of lottery ticket he intended to purchase. When he took the ticket out of his pocket and, holding it in the palm of his right hand, asked the cashier for another ticket from that same brand, the cashier looked intrigued. He asked to look at it more closely and, when Santos drew closer, he reportedly snatched the ticket from his hand. Santos was irate but could not utter a word. The cashier then swiped the ticket under the barcode reader and tossed four dollars on the counter. Recovering his breath, Santos shook his head, protested, and asked for his ticket back, but the cashier told him that it was too late; the ticket had already been entered in the system and Santos's prize had been redeemed.

Recounting these events as we sat in his truck, Santos recalled how his shaking hand tried to find its way into the pocket of his shirt to pay for his other purchases. "I even told [the cashier], 'Look! I can't even reach my wallet.'" Then, waving a threatening finger toward the dashboard of his truck, an infuriated Santos yelled, "I should have told him, 'Hum! You want it? You want a ticket? Well buy one!'"

"Why didn't you tell him that?" I asked him.

"I don't know . . . I get nervous. When things like that happen, I can't find my words. . . . But that guy stole my money."

The language barrier was not, in this case, the main problem; the cashier was Hispanic and apparently spoke or at least understood Spanish well enough. Yet, as French sociologist Pierre Bourdieu has uncovered, speech is a social act, enabled and determined by the speaker's sense of authority and entitlement to speak. You learn and exercise the practice of saying what you want to say. Santos, an uneducated foreigner who is self-conscious about his illiteracy, was made speechless by the cashier's brazen move.

I learned the details of this story about three months after it happened. Santos had called me shortly after the incident and given me a somewhat confusing account of the events. He believed that he had won a big lottery prize and had been robbed by a cashier. He said that he could remember the numbers on the ticket and that he needed "someone who knew how to defend himself," which I understood to mean a lawyer or legal expert. He was hoping I could help him contact one.

I could not help but feel some skepticism about the whole thing and, in any case, did not know of a lawyer who could take up his case. I offered to accompany him to the Texas Lottery Commission (TLC) headquarters—a step he had suggested himself at some point over the course of our phone conversation—but he turned down my offer. "God knows what could happen. What if I get in trouble? I don't want you to get embarrassed because of me."

I was busy then, preparing for a trip overseas, and so I did not insist. Before hanging up, I simply reassured him that contacting the police was not, contrary to his fears, "an offense." I also told him that the odds of obtaining help in this matter seemed rather slim to me.

Three months later, when we resumed our interviews, he showed me a copy of the complaint form a relative had filed on his behalf with the TLC. He told me about his attempts to report the incident to the police (who sent him back to the TLC) and described to me his two encounters with the investigator appointed to his case by the TLC. He explained to me how, in his memory, the numbers and corresponding prize had been displayed on the ticket. If his recollections were accurate, his ticket was indeed the winner of the grand prize of $1,000 per week paid out over twenty years. He complained, however, that the investigator was not responding to his requests and that, on the two occasions in which he had paid a visit to the TLC offices to try to meet with him, clerks had kept him at bay. He asked me for help with his case for a second time.

The facts, of course, remained dubious. Yet his efforts to recover his prize, against all odds and in the face of an overpowering institutional apparatus, were compelling.

A broader notion of justice also seemed to be at stake, one that extended beyond his personal struggle. Santos expressed outrage at the idea that a store clerk would "take advantage of the fact that I do not know how to read." Adding to the experience of abuse, there was the expectation of living a comfortable life on the part of someone who had more than paid his dues. "If I can retrieve my prize," he told me, "I could pay for my house. And you know what I have been wanting to do for a long time? Learn English. That money could pay for an English teacher."

Rehashing a recurring sentiment, he added, "If I spoke English, I wouldn't be working for others . . ."

Partly out of sympathy and partly because I felt intrigued, I decided to get involved.

Given our limited resources, we sought free legal aid with a local nonprofit organization. Santos had visited the nonprofit once before but had been required to fill out a check-in form before he could speak to a lawyer. On that occasion he had simply taken the form and waited on a bench near the check-in table. He had hoped that someone would talk to him or that something favorable or unexpected would happen as he waited. When neither came true after half an hour, he left.

When we returned together, during a near hour-long wait in line, Santos stressed what seemed to be a crucial point for him: he did not want to sign any document. He insisted that we had only come for an "orientación"—a Spanish word meaning something close to "directions" or "guidance."

When the doors finally opened and the line began to move, we were directed across a huge hall to a table where two rather serious-looking assistants were checking in clients. I handed the sign-in form to one of the assistants, who glanced over it, laid it down on the table, and put his finger next to the empty signature spot. I told Santos to sign it. He scratched his name in a few practiced, simple, and shaky strokes.

After a short wait, a diligent young lawyer who only spoke English called Santos's name and asked us to follow her to a table. I did my best to explain my companion's problems to the lawyer, noticing as I spoke how the bareness of the setting and the demands of the interaction—a short and to-the-point exchange that left no room for mistakes or digressions—had filled even me, the supposedly laid-back observer and educated interpreter, with a nervousness that was filtering into my voice.

When I finished, she explained to us what, over the course of my recount, had become all too obvious: our evidence was flimsy; it was unlikely that any lawyer would take the case without payment; suing the state of Texas, to which the Texas Lottery belongs, was doomed to failure; and our best bet was to try to get in touch with a TLC supervisor and request a formal response to the complaint filed by Santos six or seven months earlier.

Following a series of fortunate coincidences, I obtained from an efficient and highly cooperative TLC official an electronic log of all the prizes registered at the store where the incident took place within the one-hour time window that spanned Santos's visit. Among them was a four-dollar cash prize.

I gave Santos an oral account of those email exchanges, and I relayed to him a copy of the documents, but he was not convinced. He described to me one more time what, in his memory, the order of the numbers on the ticket had been. I told him that if I were in his shoes, I would let go of the fight. But Santos still believes, with the conviction of a man whose life has been defined by struggle, deception, and disappointment, that he was done wrong that day. Regardless of what the actual numbers on the ticket were, it is hard, knowing Santos's personal story, not to think that he has some grounds to feel that way.

Some readers could be tempted to dismiss the stories of a man who believes in unicorns as not credible. It is even likely that some factual details in the stories recounted by Santos are not accurate. Yet these stories are true in that they define the way in which Santos sees the world and his place within it. More importantly, the general facts, like his deportations, dismissals, and incarcerations, along with the physical structures that he helped build with his labor, such as the bridge and the hospital, are true.

These experiences had to be dealt with and made sense of by a man who does not understand the dominant language of the country where he has spent most of his adult life. His supranatural notions and beliefs are, in this regard, as much a cultural legacy of the land where he was raised as they are a window out of a reality that would otherwise be too hard to cope with on a daily basis.

Why and how Santos ended up in Austin, a city that he helped build "for others," is a question with no definitive answer. He says that he likes Austin, and that he somehow chose it. Of all the cities he has been to in the United States, he finds it to be the liveliest. "I've been to Tampa, Charlotte, San Antonio, but the streets there are . . . desolate, I guess," he once told me. "Here, the streets, the people . . . they feel warmer."

And yet, when I asked him about the places in Austin where he likes to go, he shrugged his shoulders. "I hardly ever go out," he said. "Going out is expensive, and I can't find the streets by their names. I only go out to visit a few friends, my compadres." Urban life is still trying for his rural soul. "Here, the town was imposed on me [*me vi obligado al pueblo*], but I'm from the countryside, the rancho. I'll never get tired of the rancho."

"Do you plan to go back to Mexico some day?"

"Well, I'd like to. But I can't, not until things cool down over there. Maybe in a few years . . ." Santos is afraid of the drug violence that is ravaging his homeland.

"And what about the adobe house that you built with your brother, for your mom?"

"It's now in the hands of an enemy of the family, a bad man."

The cornfields where he grew up are also gone. Corn is no longer the main crop in the area. The house now sits at the center of a large marijuana plantation.

Santos always seemed to enjoy our conversations. If anything, they offered him a break from his ongoing struggle for material stability and an enduring sense of purpose that, after a lifetime of hard work, continue to elude him. When our last interview came to an end under the porch overlooking his disheveled garden, Santos stood up to walk me to the front door. On the back of his baseball cap, an embroidered slogan read, "Success is no accident."

Recommended Readings

Bourdieu, P. 1991. *Language and Symbolic Power.* Cambridge, MA: Harvard University Press. An illuminating treatment of the intricate and obscured relationships between politics, power, and language.

Bourgois, P. 2003. *In Search of Respect: Selling Crack in El Barrio.* Cambridge: Cambridge University Press. A moving and disturbing ethnography of the political, economic, and cultural dynamics of one particular sector of the U.S. underground economy.

Smith, R. C. 2005. *Mexican New York: Transnational Lives of New Immigrants.* Berkeley: University of California Press. A detailed study of Mexican migration to the United States—and of the transnational lives at its center.

CHAPTER 3

Clarissa: "A Woman Who Fell on Hard Times"

KRISTINE KILANSKI

"It's inappropriate for a grown man to ask a woman for money," Clarissa says, leaning across the expansive wooden table that separates us. It is a Tuesday morning, and we are sitting in the 1886 Cafe & Bakery at the famed Driskill Hotel, located on Sixth Street in downtown Austin, sipping coffee and waiting for our breakfasts to arrive. On her walk to the restaurant, a man asked Clarissa to spare a dollar, and she is annoyed.

Jokingly, I ask, "Is it okay for a woman to ask another woman for money?" Clarissa debates her answer aloud before arriving at her main point. If you want to help the homeless, she tells me, you are better off giving to organizations like the Salvation Army than to a panhandler. People who ask for money on the street don't use it for what they say they will, she continues.

Clarissa could be any middle-aged white socialite commenting flippantly on an unknown "other." With her perfectly coiffed brown hair, edged with gray, baby-blue cashmere cardigan, matched accessories, faux-snakeskin purse, and long black coat, she certainly looks the part. But instead Clarissa is speaking from experience. It is hard to imagine, from inside this warm cocoon of dark wood, leather, marble, and soft light, that Clarissa will spend the night bundled up in a clean but used sleeping bag in a wingback chair in a storage unit that she rents in south Austin. And this is exactly what Clarissa wanted, I suspect, when she suggested we have our first meeting here—at one of the most luxurious settings (and her favorite spot) in town.

Clarissa makes it easy to forget that she's homeless, even though many of our conversations center on exactly how she arrived at and experiences this predicament. From her self-presentation (which she is aided in maintaining by a nonprofit where she is both client and volunteer, as well as by her innovative spirit—the purse, for example, came from attending a free giveaway at Saks Fifth Avenue) to her leisure activities, Clarissa both purposefully and unintentionally disrupts any stereotypes about what a "homeless person" is like—even those produced in well-meaning academic literature.

Clarissa's view of herself as a "regular person" who has found herself in unfortunate and often demeaning circumstances rubs off on me during the many breakfasts and lunches we share, and we are as likely to talk about the latest headline in the *Austin American-Statesman*, a new movie release, a recent debate in the state legislature, a community protest, or Clarissa's salsa recipe as we are to discuss the mechanics of living in precarity.

"A woman who fell on hard times"

Before I can turn on my tape recorder during our third meeting, Clarissa stops me. "I want to be portrayed as a woman who fell on hard times, not someone who is disadvantaged," she says. At the time, she isn't sure she wants this statement "on the record." However, Clarissa's insistence that I recognize "the good life" she has led for many of her fifty-odd years captures her perspective on the barriers she currently faces—and the perceived transiency of these barriers—better than a full reconstruction of our many hours-long interviews.

Most of the scholarship on people struggling to "make ends meet" focuses on people born into poor families in the inner city. Met with structural disadvantage from every angle, the story goes, there is little chance of making it out of the "ghetto." A combination of poor schools, neighborhood violence, widespread unemployment, deteriorated housing, daily police intervention, and government and social service neglect make it a miracle that anyone raised in a poor community achieves a middle-class lifestyle.

But this is only one face of poverty. There are other individuals who have fallen, rather than been born, into poverty. And while the reasons for such a transition are broad and varied, one of the most encapsulating explanations is the lack of a comprehensive social safety net for the working and middle classes in the United States. Jacob Hacker refers to the "great risk shift" to point to the fact that most Americans today—no matter how well off they may appear—are just a step away from falling off a financial cliff. And it is the most vulnerable people, those in low-wage jobs, who are the least likely to benefit from the very limited and frugal protections still available in this era of devolution and decentralization.

As an employee in one of the largest service sectors, the food industry, Clarissa is one of the millions of workers who have no access to health insurance, retirement plans, or basic job protections. When she was young and healthy, the risk she was carrying didn't feel so burdensome: "I didn't get sick. I didn't get sick. When I was younger I didn't get sick. Not ever. So [a lack of health insurance] didn't matter," Clarissa recalls. Nor was the cost of care always so high: when Clarissa gave birth to her only child, a daughter, during the early 1980s, it cost $385. Today a hospital birth costs an average of twenty-five times as much, while real wages at the bottom end have stayed flat or even fallen.

When an emergency struck, and, later, when Clarissa started to develop health problems, the burden of living at the low end of the wage spectrum—and the risk it entailed—started to become untenable. Fully unable to work for months after a bad car accident and faced with multiple forms of discrimination when she tried to reenter the labor market, an unemployed Clarissa could not cover her living expenses for more than a few months. As a result, for the past five years she has bounced around between short-term jobs, unstable housing situations, and homelessness as she has struggled to return to doing the work she loves.

Clarissa grew up in a stable working-class family in Midland, Texas. Texas pride runs through Clarissa's core: "When you're Texas, you're Texas," she explains. In fact, pretty much anything Clarissa doesn't like about Austin, her home base for most of her adult life, she blames (somewhat tongue-in-cheek) on Californians. Too much traffic on the freeway? Californians. Bad drivers? Californians. Drunk people on Sixth Street? Californians.

Clarissa holds tightly to her "southern values." In her five-plus decades, Clarissa has spent only one year living outside of Texas—relocating to Nebraska to live closer to family. Clarissa hated her experience up "north" because of the "rude" people. Men, Clarissa thinks, should always hold doors open for women.

Several months after we meet, Clarissa presents me with a bookmark that she picked up from her local bank outlining the "Unofficial Texas Code." It is a point of pride that, despite my childhood ties to the "pro-union" North, and my insistence that I can open doors for myself, Clarissa offers me this partial extension of Texas citizenship.

For the most part, Clarissa had a happy childhood. The oldest of five siblings, Clarissa was an accomplished student and musician. She played saxophone in the junior high school band and was "first chair" in her section. She sang in one of the top-ranked high school choirs in the nation, even traveling to Vienna, Austria, to participate in a singing competition.

Clarissa says that her mother pressured her to pursue a career in singing. Clarissa's desire to stay out of the limelight has been a long-standing point of contention within the mother-daughter relationship. When I express surprise at this revelation, Clarissa looks at me earnestly: "I was *that* good."

When she wasn't singing in the high school or church choir, Clarissa spent time caring for her horse, High Socks, a beloved escape artist who liked to eat dog food. Her childhood dog, she tells me with her signature grin and laugh, liked to eat her sandwiches.

Although she was one of five children, Clarissa was never particularly close to her younger brother or sisters growing up. She explains:

"I was the oldest, and it was kind of like I was an outsider with everybody. I don't know why that worked out. I was . . . everything I did was . . . I was good at everything I did, and it was hard to follow me. I made As in school without even trying. I was in choir. We did the competitions every year. I always made 1s. It was hard for them to follow me because everyone expected certain things, and it wasn't the same. So I was kind of like, apart from them. So when I left home . . . So we don't really speak that much."

Today Clarissa keeps in irregular touch with one sister and has minimal contact with her other three siblings.

Clarissa found love and acceptance from her father, a roustabout, or general field laborer, in the oil and gas industry, as well as from her paternal relatives. It was Clarissa's father who taught her how to garden and her grandmother who taught her how to cook—skills and interests that would lead Clarissa into a four-decade career in the food industry.

"When you work in restaurants you work all the time"

Clarissa was fifteen when she got her first job. She recalls, "My daddy said, 'If you want more money than I am giving you as allowance ($1.25), get a job.' I said, 'Okay.'"

Her first job was as a carhop at a local restaurant in Midland. From there Clarissa sought out a number of positions in the food industry throughout high school: "I was a carhop, then a busser, then a hostess, and then I was a waitress—when I was old enough to be a waitress. Then I made the *real* money, being a waitress."

A few days after her high school graduation, Clarissa moved out of her parents' home. She and her "high school sweetheart" set off to start a new life together five hours away from home in the bustling capital city of Austin, Texas.

Clarissa and her boyfriend, who later became her husband, took advantage of the amenities that their new home had to offer. Clarissa fondly remembers family hikes and swims, as well as frequent trips to Mount Bonnell. Most of the memories that Clarissa shares, however, revolve around work. She explains:

"When you work in restaurants you work all the time. You work holidays. You work Christmas. You work. You work. All the time. That's all I did. That's all I did was work. That's what I am used to doing. Our family was the people that I worked with."

At age twenty-eight, Clarissa and her husband split up. Clarissa recalls what happened next: "I fell in with the wrong crowd. I thought they were my friends, but they were not." Clarissa prefers not to talk about this tumultuous period of her life. Rather than defining herself through the difficult experiences she has gone through in the past, she reminisces on the parts of her life that bring her joy and pride: mainly, the more than four decades she has spent baking, cooking, and serving food to others.

Indeed, over the past forty years Clarissa has held an impressive array of positions in the food industry. She has been a busser, hostess, waitress, bartender, prep cook, line cook, catering manager, kitchen manager, banquet waitress, banquet bartender, head baker, dishwasher, and mobile food vendor, and she's worked in every type of establishment, from a fast food restaurant to a high-end steak house. In fact, Clarissa thinks it is easier to list the positions that she hasn't held in the food service industry instead of listing the jobs she has had.

Sociologists tend to conceptualize low-wage work as a "fallback" plan for those without other, better-paying job options. This is a mischaracterization of Clarissa's career in the food industry. She is proud of the jobs she has held and the skills she has developed. In fact, her work in the food industry is a central part of her identity, down to what she calls her "waitress personality."

In her own words, Clarissa describes the profound connection she

has to the food industry and what it has meant to lose that connection in recent years.

"I mean, I worked. Got home. Work. When you put in a double shift, that's a twelve-hour day, working in restaurants. You go out to eat a lot. That's what people in restaurants do. That's where my money goes. Going out to eat. That's what I did." She sighs. "Thought I'd be able to do that forever. When I got hit by a car, that took *my life* right there. I couldn't do what I do. It's been so hard because I am so used to working all the time. All the time. That's all I do. It's hard."

When I ask Clarissa to draw me a map of Austin and pinpoint the places that mean the most to her—an exercise that she clearly views as juvenile, though, kindly humoring me, does anyway—five of the eight places she pinpoints are restaurants: a fact that she notes and expresses embarrassment over. But I am not surprised. When Clarissa talks about her work, she glows. It makes sense, then, that restaurants are the places that hold so much meaning for her.

"You just had to do what you had to do . . ."

In the spring of 2009, Clarissa was hit by a car. The driver, who had run a red light, striking Clarissa in the middle of a pedestrian walkway, immediately stopped the car and got out to apologize. Clarissa recalls the woman's panic: "'I'm so sorry. I'm so sorry.'"

Still lying on the ground, Clarissa used her own cell phone to dial 9-1-1. When the ambulance arrived, Clarissa warned the paramedics that she was uninsured. She had just opened her own business selling homemade tacos and salsa to construction workers and, as has been true for most of her life, was not covered by a health insurance plan. The paramedics said that Clarissa needed emergency room treatment anyway: her foot and ankle had been badly mangled in the accident.

Clarissa was in the hospital for a week, several days longer than what was medically necessary. With no one to sign for her care, the doctors hesitated to release Clarissa to her third-floor apartment. In fact, when the doctors finally released Clarissa, at her own insistence, she was unable to make it up the stairs to her apartment by herself. Clarissa called the fire department, which helped her to her door using a special lift chair.

But once the fire department left, Clarissa was left largely to fend for herself. Even basic tasks such as getting groceries became onerous:

"I lived on the third floor, so getting downstairs was . . . a challenge. When I first got hit, the fire department carried me. But after that, then I had to just figure it out. . . . I couldn't put any weight on this leg, so I couldn't really walk unless I had my walker. You can't really use a walker on stairs. So I sat down on the stairs and kind of scooted, and going up I sat down on the stairs and scooted myself up. And that's how I got up and down. And that took a while. You just had to do what you had to do . . ."

At least one experience revealed Clarissa's vulnerability during this period. Several weeks after the accident, Clarissa fell in her apartment. Unable to put any weight on her left leg, she could not lift herself up into a standing position. Stranded on the floor, she was eventually able to scoot across the apartment, reach her phone, and call 9-1-1.

Clarissa made several visits to the clinic at Brackenridge Hospital to receive follow-up care for the injuries she had sustained in the car accident, relying on neighbors in her apartment complex to drive her to appointments. Clarissa does not feel that the appointments were particularly helpful: "It cost $2,000 for the doctor to look at the X-ray and tell me what I already know." Once the doctors said that she could start putting weight on her leg, Clarissa stopped attending appointments: "I quit going because I can't afford *$2,000 a visit*. I don't run up a hospital bill just because I can. Cause that's not right."

Clarissa didn't receive a boot, a cast, or pain medication to help her through recovery: "They didn't give me any of that." When she applied for physical therapy, she was told that the program was full, and she would be added to a waiting list. In an attempt to speed up her healing process, Clarissa concocted her own daily physical therapy routine. With time, her foot and ankle began to recover. Today, five years later, she can do jobs that require her to stand for multiple hours on end as long as she is given occasional breaks to rest her foot. The next day, however, she experiences soreness and pain—making it difficult for her to be able to work one shift after another. Had she received proper follow-up care, Clarissa believes, her injuries might have fully healed.

During the initial weeks and months after her accident, Clarissa relied on her small savings account to meet her basic needs. Although the driver's insurance company agreed to pay Clarissa $25,000 for the injuries she had sustained in the accident, this amount did not cover the nearly $60,000 bill for her hospital stay or the costs of her follow-up care. From the beginning, the hospital had accepted that it would bear a financial loss for treating Clarissa: her savings and income at that time had qualified her for free care. However, when Clarissa's insurance money came through, the hospital took nearly two-thirds of it as compensation for its services. In Clarissa's estimation, that still left a few thousand dollars to be used toward food, housing, and other needs during the many months it would take for her to recover.

When the check from her settlement with the driver's insurance company hadn't arrived several months after her accident, Clarissa phoned the lawyer she had hired to represent her during the legal proceedings in order to express her concern. The lawyer informed her that his office had in fact received a check from the driver's insurance company—some months ago. He explained that the insurance money had been applied toward his fees.

Clarissa remembers signing paperwork that entitled her lawyer to one-third of the settlement, but she hadn't understood the legalese when she'd placed her name on the dotted line. She thought the lawyer would get one-third of the money that came to her through the settlement, not one-third of the total amount paid out by the insurance company. It wasn't until this phone call to her lawyer that Clarissa learned that she was not legally entitled to a single penny of the $25,000 that the insurance company had agreed to pay her in compensation for her injuries. Out of pity, and after some cajoling, the lawyer eventually agreed to send Clarissa a $500 check—some money at least, but less than a month's rent.

For an office worker, immobility is an inconvenience. An injured foot and ankle would make life slightly more difficult, for sure, but would not interfere with most day-to-day job tasks. For Clarissa, however, whose work required spending long days on her feet carrying heavy trays through high-traffic areas, immobility equaled unemployment.

For the most part, Clarissa answers questions matter-of-factly, as if she's recalling someone else's experience. But anger, sadness, and disappointment are at the surface when she talks about the accident and how she was subsequently treated.

"When I got the insurance from the lady that hit me, the hospital took it. So basically they made me homeless. The hospital made me homeless. I mean, I understand people have got to get paid. *I understand that.* And it's not that I don't want to pay the doctor that fixed my ankle. It's not, but . . . when you haven't worked, you can't walk, you're recovering from something like that, and then they take all the money. I mean, it wasn't like, 'Okay, we'll give you this. We'll give you this. We'll give you this.' It was like . . . It's very hard to get back from something like that."

Clarissa wonders if the driver who caused her injuries ever thinks of her. Once, when giving a talk about her experiences with homelessness on behalf of a local nonprofit, she caught the woman's face in the audience. At first it seemed like the woman didn't recognize her, but after Clarissa's talk the woman got up and, looking shocked, left the room as quickly as possible. As we sit underneath the shade of several trees in the parking lot of the storage unit building in which she is currently squatting, Clarissa asks me how I think the woman, the name and address of whom she has committed to memory, might respond if she left a note on her doorstep:

"You made me homeless."

"It's very hard to get back from something like that"

Clarissa stayed in her third-floor apartment on Rundberg Lane until January 2010. Without any income, she could no longer afford the rent. She moved to an apartment complex in south Austin that required only a ninety-nine-dollar down payment. Still unemployed, Clarissa quickly fell behind on the rent.

Hoping to stay in her apartment, Clarissa turned to Travis County Health and Human Services (TCHHS) for help paying the rent. TCHHS issued Clarissa $1,500 in rent vouchers, a large enough amount to put Clarissa ahead on her payments. The apartment manager turned down the vouchers, citing the city's timeline for processing payments (thirty days). So Clarissa turned to Goodwill for help. Goodwill immediately issued Clarissa an emergency housing voucher. However, the apartment manager turned down Clarissa's second voucher, too. Again, she gave processing time as her reason—although, as Clarissa notes, Goodwill only took a few days to issue checks. The manager then started the process of evicting Clarissa.

Clarissa thinks that the apartment manager's refusal to accept her vouchers was a form of retribution. The complex's parking lot was one of the major exchange points for drugs and sex work in south Austin. An active member of her local neighborhood watch, Clarissa had called the police whenever she observed illegal or suspicious activity on the complex's premises. Clarissa suspects that the manager had been complicit in the illegal activity happening on the complex's grounds and thinks that she had angered the manager by placing her job and secondary income at risk.

Clarissa protested the eviction and, because of an error on the city's behalf in scheduling a repeal after the initial ruling, was able to continue living in the apartment for several months rent-free. Although the judge expressed confusion about why the apartment manager had turned down Clarissa's rent vouchers, what she had done wasn't against the law. As a result, Clarissa eventually ended up being evicted. In her own words, Clarissa explains what it was like to become homeless for the first time, joining the ranks of the 2,300 Austinites who live on the streets on any given night:

"I had moved most of my big stuff out into a storage unit, like my bed and everything. That was the furniture I inherited from my father and all my mementos and the sharpshooter medal from my father's uncle—he was in the marines, and he got a medal—all that type of stuff that I had inherited; and then I'd lived all my life and collected things. That was that. And I only had a few things, like a mattress, left in the apartment. Because I knew I was going to have to get out. Because [the manager] wouldn't take my money. So the constable came, and they put everything out on the lawn. And I stayed there with it for a while, and then when she [the manager] went for lunch I had somebody take some things and put it in their apartment. And then I just had to walk away and leave it. And I didn't really have any place to go, so I just tried to figure out where was I going to sleep. And they [Clarissa's neighbors] told me, 'Go to the Salvation Army,' and so I did. So I did, and they didn't have any beds, and they said, 'Come back at eight thirty in the morning.' So I didn't really sleep that night, went back at eight thirty. There were no beds."

Eventually the Salvation Army found a spot for Clarissa. While she was grateful for a bed, the adjustment from living independently in an apartment to living under supervision in dorm-like surroundings was difficult for Clarissa. "A lot of people think, 'Oh, the [Salvation Army], that's where you go.' But if you haven't lived there, and you're just a regular person, it's torture, absolute torture," Clarissa explains.

Clarissa's biggest complaint about living in the Salvation Army is dealing, on a daily basis, with people suffering from drug or alcohol addictions or mental illnesses. While she is adamant about taking "care of people that can't really take care of themselves"—frequently bringing up the city's laxity in providing mental health and addiction services—Clarissa is also indignant about what she perceives as the Salvation Army's revolving door policy toward people who "do not know how to behave." She explains:

"People who can't stop using drugs go in and out of the Salvation Army. And people that are . . . you can't put them in a hospital. And I'm not saying that people should go into a hospital. I'm not saying that. But we need to take care of the people that can't really take care of themselves. We need to take care of them in some way. And that's where they go, to the Salvation Army and stay there. And there's really no supervision for that sort of thing."

Even after moving to the more selective "workers' dorm," Clarissa spent most of her time at the Salvation Army feeling unsafe and avoiding common areas as much as possible. Other women residents tried to intimidate her. Often she'd skip dinner in order to avoid catcalls and come-ons from the men residents, who outnumber women residents (in Clarissa's estimation) by five to one.

"The homeless men come in, and they don't know how to act at all. I quit talking to strange men, especially there, because they want somebody to take care of them, and they want to ask you for money. And if you can't take care of yourself—if you're living at the Salvation Army, you can't take care of yourself—so there's absolutely no reason to meet somebody that can't take care of themselves either. It's like an anchor around your neck. You'll just sink to the bottom. But everybody's trying to latch on to somebody that . . . It's not a good thing. The men are just . . . [sigh]."

Living in the Salvation Army was hard on Clarissa for a second reason. Having worked in the food service industry for forty years, Clarissa is what I would call a full-fledged "foodie." She is quick to give me—an amateur and reluctant cook and baker—advice on how to improve my skills in the kitchen. As her frequent dining partner, I can attest that her excitement about food and the people who make it is intoxicating. During one of our first meetings Clarissa stopped mid-sentence to point out a favorite pastry chef. Grinning from ear to ear, it was almost as if she had spotted a famous celebrity.

Although a conversion from home-cooked and restaurant-quality meals to donated, and often leftover, food ("processed food," "burritos from this or tacos from this," "food from a can") would be hard on many working- and middle-class Americans, this shift took an especially difficult toll on Clarissa. For that reason, it is not surprising that one of the first things that Clarissa does upon receiving her tax refund in early March, a month after I first met her, is go to the 1886 Cafe & Bakery at the Driskill Hotel for lunch. After meeting me for dessert, she traveled across town to a hotel, where she could take a warm shower, sleep in a bed, and catch up on some of her favorite TV shows—three firsts in a long time.

"I'm still trying very hard to do what I do"

Since her first stay at the Salvation Army in 2010, Clarissa's housing and employment have remained unstable. A mixture of interlinking factors—including Clarissa's injuries, declining health, age, spotty work history, low credit rating, two previous evictions, and lack of personal transportation—have made it difficult for her to reestablish her pre-accident independence.

Although Clarissa tends to pinpoint the car accident as the cause of her current difficulties, over time and many hours of conversation, it became clear that Clarissa had been struggling long before the careless driver struck her in the pedestrian walkway. Clarissa's decision to start a business selling lunch to construction workers had been, in large part, a response to discrimination in the workforce that predated her accident. Well before 2009 Clarissa had sought work-related services from the nonprofit Dress for Success, hoping to overcome obstacles to employment she faced, such as being an older woman in an industry and city "geared toward the younger people." The accident, which might have been nothing more than a momentary stroke of bad luck to someone with a good job, health insurance, and a strong support network, was devastating to Clarissa. Prior to the accident, she had been holding on, but only by a thread.

However, despite the long-standing nature and the magnitude of the hurdles she faces, Clarissa has demonstrated continued determination to attain and maintain employment. At times traveling upward of two hours to access a computer from which she can apply for jobs, as well as to access a cold shower, Clarissa has succeeded in securing a number of jobs in the past five years. Among other things, she's been a Salvation Army bell ringer (a job in which she spent fourteen hours on her feet for four days a week), a greeter at a fast-food restaurant, a baker, a political canvasser, a waitress, and a timeshare salesperson. These jobs, however, have tended to be short-lived.

Clarissa explains, "A lot of places where I work, they'll use me, then they'll quit scheduling me so many hours. So I know my foot is part of the reason. I know that. But I'm still trying very hard to do what I do. It's hard. It's just hard. And I've been told I should go do something else."

"Who has told you that?"

"Oh, a lot of people. 'Oh, why don't you try this. Oh, you should try this. Oh, you should try this.' And I'm just going, 'Well, I don't have any experience doing that.' Like a call center. 'Oh, you'd be great at a call center.'"

The presumption that Clarissa can easily, or should have to, switch from a field in which she's built up forty years of experience to another sector is revealing about our society's attitudes toward low-wage workers, and the tendency to equate low-wage work with low-skilled work. Clarissa's reluctance to simply "go do something else" can be understood only from a perspective that values low-wage labor and recognizes the often high level of skill involved in even supposedly lowly jobs.

Most other fields that require a high school degree or less involve the same heavy labor as waitressing or busing tables, meaning "something else" is not as easy for Clarissa to come by as outsiders looking in may think. In 2011 Clarissa enrolled in a six-week course offered by Goodwill that certifies the un- and underemployed to work in the solar energy field. Clarissa was one of a few people to have passed the course, earning a higher score than the master electricians in her class—a fact of which Clarissa is, understandably, very proud and attributes to her years of experience as a waitress and the math skills she gained in that position.

Although Clarissa passed the course and received her certification to work in the solar energy field, the only jobs she could find required climbing on roofs—a task that is physically impossible for a woman who has memorized every bench in the downtown area so that she can take frequent breaks to catch her breath and rest her injured leg.

However, Clarissa, cocking her head and giving me a winning smile, is quick to show me that she could *sell* solar panels.

"What is it worth to you to have electricity when nobody else does? You still have your refrigerator. You still have a fan. And you *need a fan* in Texas heat. So what is that worth to you? Sometimes, that might be priceless. So it doesn't matter what the cost is, because it's going to pay for itself over time."

I laugh and tell her she's "almost sold me."

"Pretty amazing for an old woman, huh?" she responds in her typical quick-witted banter.

Even when Clarissa can find a job that doesn't rely on physical strength and stamina, getting there typically depends on an able body and private transportation. For example, Clarissa explains why she declined to follow up on a lead she was given for a call center in Round Rock, a city about twenty-five miles north of Austin's downtown center.

"I don't have a car. I can't get there. It's pointless to apply to a job when you can't show up for it. I'm on the bus system. I don't have a car. I have to be able to . . . It's got to be within a certain amount of walking distance so that I can get to it, because I can't walk two miles to get to work after I get off a bus. I can't do it. When I was younger it wouldn't have mattered, but I am almost sixty, and I have a hurt ankle, and I simply can't do it anymore. It's just hard. It's just hard."

But for now, at least, Clarissa has refused to give up. Her work in the food industry is too closely tied to her identity to let it slip away without a fight.

"I was thinking about filing for disability, for SS. But I want to work. I want to support myself. That's why I was thinking about doing the personal chef stuff. And doing the website. [A few weeks earlier Clarissa and I had used software she had won in a lottery held by a nonprofit to design a website advertising her chef services.] Because I should be able to do that. Even though I kept trying and kept trying and kept trying to do what I normally do with my ankle. I don't want to be taking disability. I truly don't want to do that. I probably should, but I don't want to. You know what I mean? I want to support myself. I want to work."

"So I was homeless again on my birthday"

Like her work situation, Clarissa's housing situation has been volatile since her eviction in 2010. Clarissa has met the Salvation Army's stay limits on several occasions in the past few years, forcing her to look for other housing alternatives. This has included living in a storage unit (as she has done for several periods of time during the past year) and relying on volunteers from her church to open up their homes to her for short-term stays.

Only once in the past four years has Clarissa been able to build up enough of a nest egg to get her own place: a bedroom she found listed for rent on Craigslist. The living situation, however, was untenable. Shortly into her lease Clarissa began to suspect that her landlord (who lived in the house with a female partner and child) was a drug dealer, a suspicion that was later confirmed when she saw the contraband. Clarissa couldn't afford to move but called a contact on the police force to inform him of the situation. She wanted to ensure she wouldn't get in trouble if the house became the object of an investigation.

The situation went from bad to worse when Clarissa suffered a hernia as a result of lifting heavy furniture on the job and was laid off after initiating a workers' compensation claim. After her hernia surgery, "I couldn't lift ten pounds. I couldn't apply for another waitressing job." Although she took what jobs she could find, they did not pay enough or provide enough hours to make rent: "So I was homeless again on my birthday."

One of the jobs Clarissa took post-surgery involved walking from door to door to ask for signatures on a petition. When I asked, partially in shock, how she could manage this so soon after getting out of the hospital, she gave me a surprised look, one that questioned if I had really been listening to her all these months: "Do what you can when you can."

Clarissa worries about what she will do even if she gets enough money together to rent her own place: "I'm not sure what I am going to do about a place to stay when I have enough money. Because I have two evictions. And I don't think anybody would rent to me."

On top of that, Clarissa's fallback plan of living in her storage unit is always uncertain—dependent on a lenient manager willing to overlook her presence. One manager was particularly kind, spontaneously offering Clarissa a temperature-controlled storage unit for only two dollars more a month, frequently lending her an extension cord to plug in her cell phone, and even on occasion offering his personal shower for her use. This manager left in the summer of 2013, just as Clarissa was transitioning into the Salvation Army. Now, on nights she needs to use the storage unit, she has to be extra cautious not to be seen, and she lives in fear that she will be discovered and kicked out with nowhere to go.

Clarissa daydreams about saving up enough money to afford a trailer and a small plot of land. All she needs, she says, is enough space to plant a small garden. To make ends meet, she would sell the produce that she grew to local restaurants. The "farm-to-market" craze is big in Austin, she assures me. And if there were enough room, she would install a hot tub: no more quick, cold showers. She looks at me and says, "That's possible, right?" We sit together, willing this dream into existence.

"It doesn't help to be depressed"

It is mid-March, and Clarissa and I are sitting in a booth at a McDonald's. I have just ordered her lunch—a double cheeseburger, a side salad with ranch dressing, and a soft drink—off the dollar menu. Having eaten lunch earlier, I order myself an iced vanilla coffee, which I sip in between asking Clarissa questions about her first stay at the Salvation Army.

Clarissa looks slightly bedraggled, a stark contrast to the first two times I met her, at the 1886 Cafe, when she was a picture of composure. Today her long black coat and snakeskin bag are sitting on the table, and she is resting her leg on the bench. There is significant dandruff buildup on the shoulders of her black blouse, and both of us are swatting at tiny gnats that seem to be centralized at our table. It is the first and last time I will witness Clarissa in a physical state that in any way hints at her vulnerability.

Clarissa has been sitting in the corner booth for some time before I arrive. Predictably, she is buried in her latest J. D. Robb thriller when I startle her by calling out her name.

Clarissa, I learned from our first meeting, *never* travels without a book. "People who are addicted to this," she says the first time we meet, pulling a book out of her cavernous purse, "don't do drugs." According to Clarissa, her love of reading and her desire to be educated helped her detach herself from "the wrong crowd."

It has been a particularly tough week for Clarissa, who was hired by a Mexican restaurant to help handle the influx of tourists in town for the South by Southwest music festival. Clarissa was ecstatic about the opportunity to waitress again and hoped that the temporary position would lead to a full-time job offer. The first two days of work went exceedingly well, Clarissa recalls. She made tips in the 20 to 25 percent range, and management expressed pleasure with her work.

Things went downhill on Clarissa's third day on the job. The restaurant staffed the bar only during the weekend, so five out of seven days a week, waiters and waitresses were responsible for delivering drinks to tables. This meant climbing a steep set of stairs to the bar, filling the drink order, and then balancing a tray of heavy drinks while going back down the stairs again to deliver them to restaurant patrons. Like climbing onto a roof, this was a job task Clarissa couldn't do.

After talking to the manager, Clarissa decided it would be best for everybody if she resigned from the job. The experience of having and then immediately losing a job that she liked and that paid well had a profound impact on her, and it's still visible in her demeanor as we talk. But having known Clarissa for even just a month now, I am sure she will come through the disappointment soon.

For the most part, Clarissa lets incidents like losing a job slide off her shoulders, revealing a remarkable optimism in the face of what—to outsiders like me—often look like insurmountable barriers. Clarissa herself recognizes this aspect of her personality, once turning to me well into a five-hour discussion to ask, "I should be more depressed about my life, shouldn't I? I should be more depressed."

Clarissa says that she doesn't understand what it's like to be, or why people might allow themselves to be, in a state of depression—a state that she considers to be analytically distinct from being temporarily depressed as well as unproductive.

"Sometimes I get depressed. But I get over it because I don't have time to be depressed for very long. It doesn't help [laughs]. I don't understand people that get *in* depression. Well, what is it helping you do, you being in depression? It doesn't help. It doesn't make things better to be depressed. Things don't magically happen when you get depressed. Things happen when you think, 'Oh, this is going to happen.' In fact, I'm waiting to find that bag full of money on the ground, because I keep seeing it in my imagination. Every day I'm walking around, 'Oh, I'm going to find a bag full of money.' I'm kidding, but you know. It doesn't help to be depressed."

Clarissa is far from delusional about her current circumstances. She is well aware of the challenges she faces, for example, in getting and keeping a job. However, she prefers to look at the bright side of things, and to focus on her dreams for the future, rather than dwell on what went wrong in the past.

When necessary, she modifies those dreams to better match the reality of her circumstances. For example, when I ask her about her dream job, several months after meeting her, she responds:

"I want to be Clarissa's Kitchen. Well, what I would like to do is be at a really busy restaurant waiting tables and having the best time and be like the head waitress. I would love that. That's not going to happen. That's not going to happen. Because I'm almost sixty. It's just not going to happen. And I have to be realistic. So we will just change dream jobs. Just change it around. So now my dream job is, I'm working for myself. I am creating food at people's houses. And I help them clean it up. And if they need me to, I'll do some laundry. That's my dream job. We'll just change it."

Clarissa's obstinate refusal to give up is one of the many reasons—along with the cocked grin and the laugh lasting two seconds too long that accompanies her jokes—that I quickly come to appreciate being in her company and find myself thinking more and more of her as a friend.

"Queen Clarissa"

Despite having spent the past few years living at the Salvation Army, in a small storage unit packed so tight that she is forced to sit upright to sleep, and at other people's houses under other people's rules, Clarissa still manages to find ways to, in her words, "escape."

For example, Clarissa daydreams about what it would be like to spend a night in one of the luxury suites at the Driskill Hotel. Drawing from her conversations with hotel staff and information from online virtual tours, Clarissa is able to describe her three favorite hotel suites in remarkable detail—down to the chocolate left by housekeeping during turndown service. During one of our first meetings, Clarissa pulls out her cell phone—which, at eight years old, is threatening to split in two—to show me pictures of the hotel that she has downloaded from its corporate website. "Do you know who this is?" she asks me, pointing to a picture of President Johnson sitting in one of the Driskill's luxuriously decorated rooms. I have seen that photo album multiple times since then, expanded over time with pictures of the lobby decked out in various holiday decorations. When the hotel's ownership changed, resulting in hotel renovations, Clarissa complained to management that the 360-degree virtual tours of the rooms had been taken off the website.

Other attempts to escape take a more material form. When she can, Clarissa buys books to add to her personal library. She loves going to the movie theater and maintains a loyalty card to earn points toward free viewings. On occasion she'll splurge on an expensive ingredient at the grocery store or a meal at a sit-down restaurant.

With her friendly demeanor, Clarissa has befriended the waitstaff at a number of local diners and cafés. She is lovingly referred to as "Queen Clarissa" at one local restaurant. Once, we had our meals paid for by a restaurant manager—a gesture of thanks to Clarissa, who had baked the staff a cake and brownies in her church's kitchen and dropped them off a week before.

However, when Clarissa "treats" herself she is sometimes met with harsh criticism from others. One Valentine's Day, Clarissa used her SNAP card (food stamps) to purchase the ingredients for quesadillas, which she made in the microwave set out for customers' use. Hoping that a fancy meal would make the holiday feel less lonely, she purchased high-end cheese and mushrooms to fold between the tortillas. The cashier, Clarissa reports, looked her up and down with a sneer that said, "You're using food stamps for *this*?"

But Clarissa rarely dines like a "queen." Instead, a typical dinner consists of a hoagie roll, an avocado, a slice of cheese, and a tomato, bought at her neighborhood grocery store. I have been beside Clarissa as she constructed a meal out of grocery store samples. I have watched her expertly construct a salad to maximize calories while limiting ounces. Even when paired with a bottle of vitamin water and two handfuls of free saltine crackers, there is no way that small mound of lettuce, cheese, and dressing could quiet a hungry stomach. If we listen to Congress, the three-and-a-half dollars Clarissa spent on that night's dinner should be enough to purchase almost three meals—a disjuncture from reality that overwhelms me as I stand behind Clarissa, waiting for my turn to check out and avoiding the derisive stare of the young woman behind the counter.

The U.S. Congress and the occasional judgmental cashier aren't the only ones who devalue the worth of people in Clarissa's shoes. Employers assume that because she works in low-wage work, Clarissa is easy to exploit and manipulate.

However, Clarissa is not willing to accept mistreatment. Clarissa walked off a waitressing job in which tips were two to three dollars an hour. She refused to do a free eight-hour trial at a call center and called the state to file a complaint against a bakery chain that did not pay her for what the manager claimed, after the fact, was an "interview shift." "I do not work for free. In Texas, you do not work for free. Anybody who works for free doesn't know about Texas laws."

When a restaurant manager refused to require the cook to keep the door to the kitchen closed, meaning that pigeons made the kitchen their free range, Clarissa knowingly risked her job to file a complaint with the health department. Although she wasn't fired from her job for reporting the health violation, she received such a chilly reception from her co-workers in the aftermath that she eventually quit.

This is not the first or last job Clarissa has lost because she decided to follow her moral compass rather than concede to her immediate needs. Clarissa, a strong supporter of the Austin Police Department, lives by their tagline: "If you see something, say something."

Clarissa is consistent in her desire to be respected, in her commitment to her friends, and in the maintenance of her ideals around what it means to be a good person and citizen—even when, and though, other "needs" often go unmet.

The first time we meet, Clarissa says she has one request of me: if I write a best seller about her, she wants half the cut. I don't know how to tell her that I'll be lucky if the book I am coauthoring gets published, let alone if anyone buys it. My discomfort is written all over my face, and Clarissa immediately picks up on it. When I applaud her for this later, she humbly attributes her ability to read people to her "waitress personality." The next few times we meet, she teases me about my "best seller":

"I know I'm not going to be a best seller. I'm teasing you. I *know*. I might be a paragraph or two."

"Actually," I say hesitantly, "you'll be a chapter."

"Yay, I'm a chapter. I am a chapter."

Later, with me leaning against the metal frame of her storage unit, we talk more about the mechanics of the book-writing process, and I remind Clarissa that I'm working as part of a collaborative. Clarissa is looking up at me from her pink antique wingback chair, which, upon first seeing it, I nicknamed her throne. She asks me if the group reads my notes, and I respond in the affirmative: yes, we discuss you.

Clarissa, for her part, responds in her characteristic fashion, full of humor that belies the fact that she is about to spend the night in the equivalent of a one-car garage: "They probably think my story is so interesting that they want to drop their characters and just write a book about me, and we'll have a best seller."

As I walk away to return to my car, and in minutes the warmth of my home, Clarissa notices a Band-Aid on the back of my foot and asks how I got hurt. I tell her the cut on my foot is from wearing high heels. She wants to know why I dressed up, and I say that I had gone to a friend's house for a party the night before. "Aw," she says, looking genuinely concerned for my well-being.

Recommended Readings

Boushey, H., S. Fremstad, R. Gragg, and M. Waller. 2007. *Understanding Low-Wage Work in the United States.* Washington, DC: Center for Economic Policy and Research. This policy paper provides a comprehensive overview of low-wage jobs and the condition of low-wage workers in the United States.

Ehrenreich, B. 2001. *Nickel and Dimed: On (Not) Getting By in America.* New York: Metropolitan Books. Journalist Barbara Ehrenreich goes undercover to shed light on low-wage jobs in the United States and to examine how people making minimum wage make ends meet.

Hacker, J. 2006. *The Great Risk Shift: The Assault on American Jobs, Families, Health Care, and Retirement—And How You Can Fight Back.* Oxford: Oxford University Press. This groundbreaking book sheds light on increasing economic insecurity in the United States, which Hacker argues is as important in the lives of Americans as growing economic inequality.

Paules, G. F. 1991. *Dishing It Out: Power and Resistance among Waitresses in a New Jersey Restaurant.* Philadelphia: Temple University Press. Paules's ethnography of a roadside restaurant in New Jersey illuminates the strategies that waitresses draw on to increase their power and autonomy in the workplace and attain respect for their labor.

Snow, D., and L. Anderson. 1993. *Down on Their Luck: A Study of Homeless Street People.* Berkeley: University of California Press. A classic study of homelessness, *Down on Their Luck* centers on the experiences of people living on the streets in Austin, Texas.

CHAPTER 4

Inés: Discipline, Surveillance, and Mothering in the Margins

JESSICA DUNNING-LOZANO

My first conversation with Inés occurred over the phone. I was working as morning security personnel at the Disciplinary Alternative Education Program (DAEP) her daughter, Araceli, had been forced to attend following her removal from a regular public high school in Austin. Araceli had arrived at the DAEP that morning wearing "skinny jeans," a style of jeans that was universally abhorred by DAEP administrators for being "too tight." She was instantly marked "out of compliance" with the program's mandatory dress code.

Inés's name and number were the fourth entry in a long list of parents whose children were out of dress code compliance for the day. My job was to call and inform each parent of their son's or daughter's dress code status and request that they bring an appropriate change of clothing to the DAEP.

"It's the skinny jeans again?" Inés confirmed over the phone. I responded "yes" and asked if she could bring a new pair of jeans to the DAEP for her daughter. Cordially, she told me that she was "already at work" but would try to bring jeans to the DAEP during her lunch break.

There was nothing distinct or special about my first conversation with Inés. Like most of the other parents I spoke with over the phone that morning, she immediately recognized the DAEP phone number and was not surprised by my request. What made this occasion unique in hindsight was the regularity with which Inés received similar phone calls and requests for her presence at the DAEP over the year and a half that followed.

In total, I spent three years getting to know Araceli and Inés while

I worked and collected data at the DAEP as part of a separate research project. It wasn't until a formal interview in 2013 at Inés's apartment in the northeastern part of Austin that we had our first interaction outside of the DAEP.

Inés lives in a suburban, nondescript sienna brown apartment complex isolated by freeways and empty farm-to-market roads. The complex is eerily quiet and encircled by a tall metal security fence. Inés has been sharing a small, spartan two-bedroom apartment there with her fifteen-year-old daughter and her husband, Fernando, who is not Araceli's biological father and has had limited involvement in her upbringing.

Upon entering the apartment I was immediately struck by the security camera Inés had mounted at the top of the wall and aimed at the front doorway. The apartment furnishings were minimalist: a plain brown sofa set and a television in the living room and a wooden dining table in the adjacent kitchen nook. The walls were decorated with several multi-picture frames and photographs that depicted joyous events from the family's past. Inés guided me to images from a trip to Disney World she took with Araceli and her sister-in-law's family. In one photograph Araceli was hugging her cousins and in another was posing happily next to Disney characters.

Inés thanked me for showing up and apologized for the last two times we had had to reschedule our meeting; she explained that she is often on call at her job as a line cook at a downtown Austin restaurant and eager to pick up additional hours. In the case of both missed meetings, she had finished eight-hour shifts and been offered last minute opportunities to work extra hours. She informed me that such an unpredictable schedule was quite common. "I'm sorry," she reiterated, "but it's work, and I really need the money." Inés works full-time at the restaurant and is typically scheduled for thirty-seven-hour workweeks.

Inés is a short and stout woman, standing about five feet tall, and is in her late thirties. Her hair is thick, wavy, and dyed an auburn color, and she typically keeps it pulled back in a bun to accommodate the hairnet or visor she wears for her job. In fact, prior to visiting her home, I had only seen Inés in her work uniform.

From the moment I first met her in person at the DAEP, I was struck by the resemblance between Inés and Araceli; they have the same oval face shape, heavy eyelids, high cheekbones, and warm smiles. Unfortunately, smiles were scarce most of the times I saw Inés.

Mothering in the Margins

Inés's story is about life and mothering in the margins. Her narrative is situated at the intersections of low-wage service work and the work she performs as a mother under the scrutiny of the punitive state. Inés, like many other undocumented workers, exists in the shadows of a booming Austin that thrives off of her labor but fails to acknowledge her marginalization. Inés's work, however, does not end with her shift at the restaurant: she also toils as the single mother of a child who has been drawn into a web of zero-tolerance school policies and the juvenile justice system.

Contemporary mothering is generally undervalued, unpaid, and often unrecognized labor. Mothering in the margins adds on enormous emotional and financial tolls. Inés's hourly job is physically taxing and laced with uncertainty. Yet, unlike that of middle-class mothers, her labor as a mother often does not involve cultivating her child's talents and enjoying the rewards and recognition that come with this. Instead, like her daughter, Inés is drawn daily into the punitive exercises of the DAEP, and her precarity as an hourly wage earner is compounded by the financial penalties and demands on her time by the punitive state.

Importantly, Inés's story sheds light on how one segment of Austin's population, made up primarily of low-income black and Latino families, experiences the cityscape, the promise of public education for their children, and the state-induced pains of parenting. As a mother in the margins, the version of Austin that Inés traverses is hidden to most. Inés's Austin is a crisscross of daily trips by public transportation or car between her residence in northeast Austin, her job downtown, and the centrally located DAEP. It also includes monthly court appearances at the Travis County Juvenile Court on South Congress Avenue and occasional visits to the Gardner Betts Juvenile Justice Center when Araceli is locked up.

Disciplinary Alternative Education Programs in Texas

DAEPs in Texas were implemented in 1996 following a national trend toward "zero-tolerance" school policies. The mid-1990s in the United States bore witness to several isolated, but severe, acts of school violence. These brutal events were followed by predictions of an impending wave of so-called juvenile super predators, generally characterized as urban, black, male, and sociopathic. In response, public school districts across the country enacted zero-tolerance policies that imposed harsh consequences for rule breaking and misbehavior in schools. As a consequence, the juvenile justice system and public schools began to coordinate their efforts to reduce school violence. Since then, public schools have never been the same.

George W. Bush passed zero-tolerance school legislation to create DAEPs when he was the governor of Texas. These "alternative" programs were designed to isolate, punish, and remediate—in the governor's words—"youths who terrorize teachers and schools." Students can be removed from their regular schools to a DAEP for serious offenses such as assault and weapons possession; however, 80 percent of current DAEP students have been removed for nonviolent, discretionary reasons. The violation of a given school's "code of conduct" is a common reason for a discretionary removal to a DAEP, but codes of conduct vary across public schools in the state. Therefore, most removals to a DAEP are based on the local discretion of regular schoolteachers and administrators.

To date, every school district in Texas is required by law to operate a DAEP that serves students in the first through the twelfth grades. The majority of DAEPs are operated on a separate campus and isolated from other public schools in a given school district, and there is still minimal state oversight of their operation. Although a set of uniform standards was created for DAEPs in 2009, there is still no standardized system in place to enforce or evaluate its application.

Eighteen years after the DAEP system's creation, some troubling statistics associated with DAEP enrollment in Texas have emerged. Black and Latino boys, low-income children, and students diagnosed with emotional and learning disabilities are disproportionately referred to DAEPs. Students at DAEPs in Texas are more likely than their mainstream school peers to face severe disciplinary actions, such as expulsion from the public school district. In addition, DAEPs also have a school dropout rate that is five times higher than the rate for regular public schools in Texas.

Inés's Arrival in the United States

Inés was born on a small ranch in Chavinda, Michoacán, Mexico, to a family of modest means. Now thirty-eight years old, she tells me,

"I'm old but I never had a childhood! I always had to work, since I was eleven." Fourteen years ago, at the age of twenty-four, Inés made the decision to leave her native Mexico and embark on a dangerous journey to Austin, Texas. Her brother Paulino, along with one of his nephews, was the first to make the trek to the United States. Once Paulino's family was established in Austin, Inés left Chavinda to join them.

As a young single mother of two, the promise of economic stability in the United States proved to be a strong motivator. Inés didn't finish elementary school in Mexico and viewed the move to the United States as an opportunity for her children to receive the education she had not.

Inés recalled for me that brutal trip across the border, which she undertook with her two-year-old daughter "strapped" to her back. "You couldn't imagine how long we walked to get here! Araceli was just two at the time. She was *really* pretty." A smile graced Inés's face, and she laughed warmly at the memory of Araceli as a baby. Her voice gradually returned to a serious tone. "Pero, los solazos [but the sun], the hunger, the thirst. . . . They would give me something to drink, and I would save it for her, for the walk. Everything that they gave me I would save for her."

A few years after Inés crossed the border with Araceli, her older son, Hector, who was twelve years old at the time, crossed with Inés's older brother, Rogelio. Hector survived the trip, but Rogelio was injured along the way, and the group had to leave him behind. A wave of sadness overcomes Inés, and her tone lowers: "They left him along the way, and he died." She adds somberly, "He left a one-year-old daughter, a three-year-old, and a six-year-old." Inés led me to a picture of Rogelio on the wall that was taken at his infant daughter Amelia's birthday shortly before his fateful trip. He proudly holds Amelia on his left hip while standing in front of a wooden table decorated with pink and white balloons and a birthday cake. Inés lingered over the photo for what felt like minutes, but surely only a few seconds had passed. She eventually perked up a bit and told me that she and her brother Paulino now fund the middle child's education in Mexico. "He is in a really good school in Chavinda. And we are very proud of how he's doing. Sometimes I don't know how he does it, where he gets the energy, because what he is studying is really hard!"

The Four-Year "Battle"

When Araceli got to middle school, Inés told me, something changed. "Oh my God, they called me every day. 'Araceli did this, Araceli was behaving badly, Araceli, and Araceli, and Araceli.'" Araceli started to use drugs, developed a violent temper, and was getting into physical fights with other girls. "She was angry, very angry." Araceli began to hang around with friends who were engaged in similar behaviors and eventually found herself in trouble at school. "Estaba en la mera edad de las loqueras [she was at that age when they are crazy]. . . . They arrested her. She robbed houses, she did really heavy things like that. . . . I would tell her, 'I don't know what happened to you, what got into you. What was it that made you do all this?'" By the seventh grade Araceli was regularly being sent to the DAEP to complete sentences of ten, twenty, and thirty days at a time. By the ninth grade Araceli was working off a year-long sentence at the DAEP. During her bouts in and out of the DAEP, and as many before and after her, Araceli had become enmeshed in the juvenile justice system, transitioning back and forth from the DAEP and regular public schools in Austin to stints in the local juvenile detention facility. At the time of our last conversation, Araceli had been on juvenile criminal probation for three consecutive years and had spent a year of that time wearing an ankle monitor that was checked regularly by her probation officer (PO).

"They [POs] show up unannounced wherever she is. They don't warn her, they only show up! . . . She was under the surveillance of like three or four people. . . . Almost every week they were looking for her. They would check the [ankle] apparatus, and if she didn't come home by 6:00 p.m., they were out looking for her. It got that bad, I'm telling you. It was something very painful for me."

Inés let out a deep exhalation and told me that watching her daughter's downward spiral was the hardest thing she's had to endure in her life. "I tell you, God is great, but he didn't listen to me. I would get on my knees and ask him for something different for Araceli."

What Inés referred to as her "battle" with Araceli lasted the better part of four years. But by Inés's account, Araceli has now transitioned to a new, more positive stage in her life, due in large part to her frequent referrals to the DAEP: "They helped her so much, so much you couldn't imagine." Thanks to the DAEP, Inés asserted with gratitude, Araceli's change has been total and dramatic. "I am very grateful because my daughter arrived there down here"—Inés hovered her hand close to the floor—"and since the day she left she is here." Inés shifted her flattened hand upward to convey improvement. She said that these were in fact "the principal's words" and shared the praise Araceli was accorded on her last day of classes at the DAEP. "The principal said, 'Araceli, you're leaving, and we are very proud. . . . It's incredible what you did, how you've changed.'" Araceli is scheduled to return to a regular high school in the district next fall to begin her junior year.

Inés rejoiced in the "clean" drug test results Araceli has had over the past three years—always randomly administered by her probation officer at home, at the DAEP, or at juvenile court hearings. For three years, Inés shared with an air of accomplishment, "Salió limpio, limpio, limpio [the test came up clean, clean, clean]." However, the process of coming up clean for Araceli has been at a hefty cost to both mother and daughter. Inés and Araceli have become entrenched in a penal web of DAEP regulation. Their four-year relationship with the DAEP has exposed them to hyper-surveillance, ensnared them in the criminal justice system, required regular court appearances, and placed a financial and emotional burden squarely on Inés's shoulders.

Inés's complex sentiments and relationship to the penal web she is embroiled in are an example of what sociologists refer to as sociological ambivalence. Inés and Araceli, as targets of punitive zero-tolerance policies, have become enmeshed in the criminal justice system—exhausting Inés's finances, compromising their physical freedom, and increasing employment insecurities for the entire family. However, as a low-income single mother with limited resources, Inés is forced to rely on the punitive functions of the state to achieve a sense of safety for Araceli and control over the family's circumstances. The complex mix of gratitude and disdain expressed by Inés for the DAEP, the financial and emotional strain of Araceli's involvement in various facets of juvenile punishment, and Inés's own application of surveillance strategies in their home convey this ambivalence well.

Follow the Rules and Pay the Costs

Inés recalled that Araceli's transition to the DAEP was difficult at first because "she wasn't adapting, and, well, it's a different world over there. That school is very different from a normal school. Mainly because of the rules. They have to follow all of the rules—*us* [parents] as much as them."

The DAEP "rules" are numerous. They include a strict student dress code and rigorous behavioral standards: students must walk in single-file lines, constrict their bodies and movement, and avoid contact of any sort with students from other classrooms, whether that be physical, vocal, or visual. A student's ability to successfully follow all of these rules is recorded daily on a disciplinary student point sheet, with three potential outcomes for the status of the day: "unsuccessful," "pending," or "successful."

These point sheets are considered legal documents and are retained by the school district for seven years. For students who are "on paper," local parlance for being on juvenile criminal probation, the point sheets are frequently collected by probation officers. The point sheets inform their assessment of a child's progress while on probation, and they are drawn on directly by juvenile court judges during court hearings.

When I asked Inés to estimate how much she has spent on clothes for Araceli to meet the DAEP dress code, she responds with a boisterous, "¡Híjole! ¡Ni pensarlo! [Oh my! I don't even want to think of that!] I spent like a $1,000 all this year!" She explained that meeting the DAEP dress code was a constant issue for her in terms of both her money and time.

"The clothes issues were daily, for an entire year, and they didn't want their pants like this—tight—they didn't want them with holes in them, they didn't want them dirty. And the shoes, they had to be black. Black socks. These [grabs at her shirt], their shirts, white. Their underwear, white. And you know that you won't find anything, as cheap as it may be, for under five or ten dollars. And I became very, very tense."

Araceli often received "unsuccessful" point sheets, primarily due to dress code infractions, but also as a result of breaking the behavioral rules. When students are "out of dress code," they receive an "unsuccessful" day on their point sheet and "lose" their day at the program, which means that this particular day will not count toward the completion of their sentence. Dress code infractions are typically determined within the first ten minutes of a child's arrival at the program, during the morning security check and pat down. Therefore, a student will know before they have even started the first period of the school day that they are out of dress code and have lost their entire day. This often spurs frustration in students and leads to what the DAEP considers rule-breaking behavior.

When Araceli breaks the rules, Inés is subjected to the consequences as well. When Araceli is out of dress code, it is program policy that someone contact her mother or another family member to request that they bring the correct clothing item to the DAEP. If Araceli receives an appropriate change of clothes, she has another opportunity to keep her day; Inés received daily phone calls at work and requests that she bring new clothes to the program for Araceli. If Araceli was suspended for misbehavior in the classroom, Inés would be required to meet with the high school principal before Araceli could return to the DAEP. As a consequence, Inés frequently received phone calls from DAEP staff that forced her to take time off work to meet one-on-one with the DAEP administrators. This, Inés explained, caused her a tremendous amount of frustration and compromised her employment, especially as an hourly wage worker.

"The principal would get angry and tell me, 'I understand that you work a lot.'. . . Because sometimes they call me and say, 'It's that she did not bring the right clothes,' and I say, 'It's that I don't have time, and I'm out of money.' Last time, they suspended Araceli for a week because she was wearing a white T-shirt that had a small logo on the pocket. And I told her, 'I don't have any more money. This time I'm really out.' I told her, 'The money is all gone.' And they suspended her. Later they told me to try to find cheaper clothes, and I told them, 'But there are no cheaper clothes!' . . . If there were, then I wouldn't be spending the money that *I don't have* [chuckles]. That's obvious."

Inés described numerous instances in which she confronted staff about Araceli's dress code infractions. They typically focused on the long-sleeved T-shirts with prohibited logos her daughter would wear to cover the tattoos on her arm, skinny jeans, and Araceli's shoes, which were deemed out of dress code for having more than 3 percent of any color other than black, gray, or white on them. Inés would bring receipts to the high school principal to show her how much money she had spent on Araceli's clothing to meet the dress code. On these occasions, the high school principal would respond with a critique of Inés's spending habits and refer to her parenting of Araceli as "spoiling her." The principal would suggest that she "go to a Goodwill" instead. Inés balked at this advice:

"At the Goodwill they have good and cheap clothes, but it's all colorful. It's impossible to find a shirt that doesn't have a stain. . . . I'm telling you, they had to wear the same thing every day, and it had to be clean, because even if it had a little stain, they won't have them [stay at the DAEP for the day]; if their clothes are just a little white, or if it's a little faded, or if there is a bleach stain, they won't have them."

The constant calls and trips to the DAEP became an issue for Inés at work. Her supervisor began to warn her about not meeting the demands of her job, reiterating that although they knew Araceli was her daughter, "You have a job, and your job brings obligations, and these are rules too."

Clothing costs, however, account for only a fraction of the total amount of money Inés and her extended family have spent to meet the rules and demands of the DAEP. Inés has lost hours at work, and her husband and her brother Paulino have had to take time from their own work schedules to bring Araceli clothing or to drive Inés to the program to meet with DAEP staff.

Sleepless Nights

As a child, Araceli was so engaged with school that Inés was sure that she would be successful. She dreamt of Araceli one day becoming a teacher.

"When Araceli was a little girl, and I can show you, they gave her more than one hundred awards. She was a little girl who was focused; if she missed one day—she would almost die if she missed one day of school! Se lo juro [I swear]. I have all of those awards, including [from] that former president, Bush, something like that; he mailed her a certificate, although you might find it hard to believe."

Inés's son, Hector, had arrived in the United States at an older age than Araceli and was very successful in school sports and well liked by his teachers. This perplexed Inés even more. "I felt that if he as a guy—since Araceli is a girl, they would praise her even more! [She laughs.] I felt that! I think that's why I was so affected by her situation. I was really affected; I would spend entire nights without sleeping."

Inés has raised Araceli without the help of her daughter's biological father, Juan, who now lives an hour and a half away from Austin. Despite the close proximity to Araceli, Juan has no desire to have a relationship with her, which she is well aware of. "Her father never wanted anything to do with her. . . . He's always rejected her."

This isn't the only trauma that has burdened Araceli and drawn Inés deeper into the criminal justice system. In 2011 one of Araceli's best friends died under mysterious circumstances while in police custody.

"They killed a friend of hers right in front of her. Araceli was even in treatment for that; it really affected her. She was really traumatized by that. . . . She spent about a month without being able to sleep. . . . She wouldn't eat. . . . So eventually her probation officer got her some help with the doctor because I didn't have any money. And they still see her, over by Congress [Avenue]; the doctor there sees her every month. Because she couldn't focus on anything. Her mind went completely blank."

Starting at the DAEP

When Araceli first began to attend the DAEP, the family lived on the outskirts of Austin, where there was no access to school district buses. Araceli had to take three different city buses to get to the DAEP every day, which clocked in at a two-hour travel time in each direction. In an annoyed tone, Inés recalled the route Araceli had to take on public transportation to arrive at the DAEP: "She'd take the 33, and then the 114, and then the 12, the one that would drop her off in front—and not even so 'in front,' because she then had to walk all the way up that hill."

As the parent of a child at the DAEP, Inés is expected to follow and meet many of the rules and standards required of her daughter. When Araceli broke the rules, Inés was likewise subjected to the repercussions, and she was often forced to endure lengthy bus rides.

For Inés, it was difficult to not be able to drop her twelve-year-old

daughter off at the DAEP and to pick her up at the end of the school day. "You've seen that that neighborhood is something serious." Inés described witnessing people doing drugs and loitering around the nearby bus stops and *los proyects*, a large housing project located next to the DAEP campus. She reflected on Araceli's first removal to the DAEP, which is described as a "lock-down facility" by program staff during new parent-student orientations.

"The pain was killing me when they sent her to that school. And I . . . I would hear that that school—¡ay, no!—that school is where all the 'crazy people who do this and [that] go.' . . . I felt that I wanted to die, really. And I went. It was something very different—everything, the rules—and I'm telling you to see all that, and to see those people, to see those huge people next to her, people who have done horrible things, that's how I saw everything. . . . Leaving her there would make my chest hurt."

Despite eventually moving to a neighborhood with access to a school district bus that could transport Araceli to and from the DAEP, transportation was still uncertain for Inés. Over the years Inés has spent much of her income on gas and bus fare, while also suffering lost wages at work. Sometimes Inés would make up to three trips a day to the DAEP in the family's only vehicle:

"I would spend about forty dollars in gasoline because the truck that they would lend me was an eight cylinder. That's why I tell you that everything in life has a price. . . . I would go in the morning and come back then at one or twelve forty. I had to be over there with her lunch. Then I would come back home, and then at four forty I had to be there to pick her up."

Every morning, along with all of the other DAEP students, Araceli was subjected to a physical pat down by security personnel and passed through a metal detector or waved with a security wand. As a female student, she was searched by a female employee; however, this didn't make the process any less invasive. "You have to believe that when they get there, they check them from head to toe. They check the shoes, their underwear. . . . [Security] checks everything. All of their underwear. Everything, they make sure it's white, *everything white*."

Araceli is an opinionated girl, quite vocal when she disagrees with another person's actions or statements, and she doesn't think twice about using profanity with other students or with staff when voicing her discontent. Inés acknowledges Araceli's rough exterior and involvement in criminal activity but stresses that this doesn't make her any less vulnerable or sensitive to pat downs by security personnel.

"I felt bad because Araceli—although she's been this way—but she's never had a boyfriend. So Araceli has been very, very—she doesn't like people touching her. She didn't like when this security would check her. She would get really frustrated, and she would get angry and scream at her! She told her, 'Don't grab me like that, you're only supposed to be checking here!' And I was there, standing right in front of them since I would take her in the mornings, and it felt really bad to watch all that, but those were the rules."

"Regular" School

At the start of Araceli's freshman year Inés attempted to enroll her in a regular public high school in their new neighborhood, which happens to have one of the better-performing high schools in Austin. When Inés and Araceli arrived at the registration office to start the enrollment process, the high school secretary asked them for their social security numbers. A wave of indignation came over Inés as she discussed this; she was stunned and felt shamed by the school officials. She and her daughter are both undocumented and do not have social security numbers. "I wish I would have had a tape recorder to record the person who said that to me. Just like that, I swear to you, just like I told you. Como que era-mos de otro mundo [as if we were from outer space]. Since we got there that's how they saw me and her." They left the school, and Araceli was very upset.

"We both felt bad. When she got home, she sat there thinking to herself. . . . And I told her, 'Hija, tu no te preocupes, hija [don't worry, hun]. We know that we are 100 percent Mexican, . . . but you don't have to feel bad about that.' And she tells me, 'But you saw how they treated us.' . . . And that's something that has really stuck with her."

Inés called the high school the next day and spoke with the principal about the incident. "They told me, 'Oh, well, that was our mistake.' But she thought that I was going to keep my mouth shut." Inés issued a complaint to the school district, and they told her that they would investigate the event, but "to this day there has been no investigation."

The high school principal pulled up Araceli's file through the district system and told Inés that she was doubtful that her daughter would be successful at the high school: "'I've already looked into it, and she's been having problems since she was in middle school.'" This made Inés defensive. "I said, 'So what? She's human, we all make mistakes, nobody is perfect.'" Despite expressions of doubt made by the principal, Inés was able to complete Araceli's enrollment. However, Araceli remained at the high school for less than a week before she was removed to the DAEP for a discretionary offense.

As Inés tells it, "There at that school it's almost completely Anglos instead of Mexicans, and Araceli said that they looked at her almost as if they were scared, and she felt bad." Inés recalled that during Araceli's removal hearing from the regular high school, the principal and the referring teacher claimed that Araceli "had been really mean to her teacher" when she began to talk about how the registration office had mistreated her and her mother. "Araceli les habló muy fuerte [screamed too loudly at them]. That's what the principal said."

When Inés discussed the referral during Araceli's removal hearing, the referring teacher told her that Araceli was not academically prepared for her class. Inés shot back, "'You have not even had her in your class for four days, how are you going to be able to know if she is prepared or not? . . . I don't think that from one day to the next you can tell that about her.'" The high school vice principal told Inés that he understood her sensitivity as a mother but flatly stated, "'Araceli doesn't want to follow our rules.'" Inés confided that she believed they were looking for any reason to send Araceli back to the DAEP.

Return to the DAEP

When Araceli advanced from middle school to the ninth grade in 2012, she was transferred to the high school side of the DAEP, which is run by a different set of staff and teachers. In high school, Inés notes, the rules were enforced more intensely, and her daughter was suspended almost every day. In contrast to the DAEP middle school principal, whom Inés described as more lenient and willing to take the time to "get [Araceli] to see his logic," the high school principal was swift in her judgment of Inés and Araceli.

Inés informed me that there were days when Araceli didn't even last an hour at the school, and she felt as though the high school staff were focusing an inordinate amount of their attention on her daughter. Inés started to get upset.

"I know that she too sometimes—she was at fault, but it's not always only her. . . . When I knew that they were right, and that it was her, then that's it, it was her fault. But when it wasn't, I was over there knocking on doors as soon as I could. . . . You can ask anyone over there at the school. I've always been there for her. Since she has been at that school, I've always been there for her, during the good times and the bad."

She requested that the high school principal find a mentor to work with Araceli. "I said, 'What she needs is someone to understand her . . . to guide her.' Not that she be getting punished every day. I don't even punish her. I talk to her. I get her to see things, which is different." Inés told me that the principal agreed to provide Araceli with a mentor since she was on juvenile probation. The principal directed her to a female teacher who was one of the few DAEP staff whom Araceli felt treated her fairly and expressed genuine interest in her well-being.

Inés cited the intervention of hands-on mentoring as one of the major factors in the improvement and "life change" Araceli experienced by the end of the school year. One is thus forced to wonder if close-up mentoring, instead of zero-tolerance punishment and surveillance, is in fact what truly made a difference in Araceli's life.

While Inés appreciates the DAEP for simply being a space where Araceli could attend school and earn credits toward her high school diploma, she worries about the quality of education Araceli received there. "Not being in a normal school. Having other types of friends, being involved in other classes, *that* would benefit her. Because in the future she's the one who is going to be at a disadvantage because of this." Inés warns Araceli that without a good education, "You're going to end up like *us*, washing dishes and mopping floors."

Time in the DAEP, Time in Juvie

The last four years of Inés's and Araceli's lives have been a revolving door in and out of the DAEP, juvenile detention, and juvenile court and have been marked by ongoing criminal surveillance by probation officers. Araceli's long-standing enrollment at the DAEP has brought her into close contact with the juvenile justice system, where records of her behavior at the DAEP are utilized by POs and judges in juvenile court to determine whether she has improved enough to be removed from probation. Inés told me that she has gone to juvenile court "more times than I can count." At one point they were going to the courts at least once a month, especially when Araceli had the ankle monitor.

Over the past four years Inés has spent all of her savings to meet the rules and mandates of the DAEP, settle juvenile court costs, and pay "tickets" associated with various types of violations, driving her to claim, "I'm left without a dollar in my pocket." When I asked Inés to recall the total amount she has paid toward court costs and tickets, she struggled to remember everything she spent and decided to tell me about Araceli's most expensive transgressions instead. One time she had to pay an $800 ticket in $100 monthly installments; at another time she paid $1,850 in court costs and penalties, which also had to be paid off in installments.

Inés told me that she paid these costs not only because of her love and sense of responsibility for her daughter, but also because of the threats of criminal prosecution if she did not.

"They [the court] would tell me, 'If you don't pay this, then they are going to arrest you. They won't do anything to her. It's on you. Everything that your daughter does goes against you, not her, because she is underage.' And I would say, 'But I haven't done anything!' And they told me, 'Well, you are her mother, you're her custodian, you're the person in charge of her.'"

For Inés, the time eventually came when she considered moving with Araceli back to Chavinda. With her eyes watering and her voice trembling, she confided, "I'm tired of the courts, the phone calls." A return to Chavinda, in Inés's eyes, would be tantamount to failure. She not only considers Texas to be her home and her future, but also conceives of the return to Mexico as an affront to the mortal sacrifice her brother Rogelio made to relocate her family to the United States.

The last time Araceli was sent to the local juvenile detention center, Inés was broke and at her wits' end. She left Araceli locked up in the facility for a month. "I told the PO—I told them, 'You know what, leave her in there for two or three weeks. I can't anymore.' At least there I know she is safe. If she's there, she can't be out on the streets."

While Araceli had been scheduled to finish her three-year criminal probation within a month of our last conversation, Inés told me that she could have been off of her probation five months earlier, but she had requested that the judge extend Araceli's probation for six months so they could continue to monitor her sobriety:

"Last time, she was about to get off of probation, but I asked the judge to give her another six months. I asked for that. And because maybe, if she does happen to make another mistake, she'd have to go back and do it all over again anyway. That way they see, and they can observe, how she is improving, getting better, and that is really good for her."

"Everything I do, I do for her"

Living as an undocumented single mother of a child caught in the nexus of the public school system and the punitive state has not only drawn Inés into the disciplinary system that her daughter is routinely subject to, it has also become one of the few resources at her disposal to meet their most basic needs. Whether it be grief counseling following the death of a friend, drug rehabilitation, or mentoring, problematically, Araceli and Inés's entrenchment in the penal web provides them with the only semblance of safety and control available to families in their situation.

Popular discourses that would construct Inés and Araceli's situation as the result of deficient mothering, a "culture of poverty," or laziness fail miserably to help us understand the social and material condition of their lives, especially in the context of extreme policing and zero-tolerance policies. Inés is not an absentee mother; in fact, she has met every demand placed on her at each level of the juvenile justice system. She has even incorporated disciplinary tactics typically employed at the DAEP or Gardner Betts Juvenile Justice Center into her own home, such as video surveillance and frequent reliance on POs to monitor Araceli's behavior and movement in and out of their apartment.

Inés's story and her use of these penal resources, however, should not be read as an argument touting the success of zero-tolerance policies. That would be a facile reading. As a mother in the margins, Inés relies on the DAEP and the juvenile justice system as her *only* sources of support. Rather than obtain mental health services and a public education through nonpenal sources of public assistance, Inés and Araceli's only access to these services is facilitated through the punitive arm of the state, driven by the regulative force of the prison and judicial system. The punitive allocation of resources and support comes with financial and emotional costs to Inés that, while beneficial in the short term, compromise her current and long-term economic stability. Inés is resourceful and committed to her daughter, so she avails herself of any opportunity to meet the needs of her family.

Moving On

We transitioned to the dining table to eat the pozole and *frijolitos charros* Inés had prepared earlier. She pulled up her iPad to show me the Facebook pages and pictures of her friends and family back in Chavinda, in particular Rogelio's son, whose education is supported in part by Inés. She took on a cheerful demeanor as she showed me pictures of her grandchildren and of her son, Hector, playing the keyboard for one of my favorite Norteño bands at one of their Austin shows. Landscaping and yard work are Hector's primary sources of income, but during the weekends he plays as a musician in many Spanish-language venues throughout Austin and the surrounding area.

The mood was quite relaxed, and I motioned to the surveillance camera monitoring the front entrance of Inés's apartment and asked her if the camera actually worked. Inés responded that it did indeed work and that she had installed the camera to monitor Araceli and to see who was coming in and out of her home. I nodded my head in an effort to convey my understanding.

Inés told me that Araceli's plan is to join the military and get a permit to work in the United States through the Deferred Action for Childhood Arrivals program, or DACA. However, she will have to hire a lawyer to help expunge her juvenile record when she turns seventeen. Inés exclaimed, "I imagine that it's a lot of money. You see that just one appointment [with a lawyer] is $500!"

Despite the steep costs that may await Araceli, Inés focused on the positive.

"She got past that, that stage, and now, thanks to God, she changed; she stopped everything, she changed her ways, and now she regrets, and she tells me crying, 'I don't know why I did that.' . . . Because she saw that she is in another stage now that she's sixteen. And now she regrets having done all that. And she tells me, she says, 'Vas a ver, mama [you're going to see, mama].' Her dream is to go into the army. She tells me,

'Everything that you suffered and that you struggled with to pull me out of all of this, your tears,' she says, 'you'll see that everything you hoped for is going to come true. You're going to see me succeed.'"

Inés paused for a few moments, as if remembering all that she had been through, and said, "Yes, the truth is that it's very difficult—more, I would say, in these schools. I would never wish all of this on anybody."

Recommended Readings

Comfort, M. 2008. *Doing Time Together: Love and Family in the Shadow of the Prison.* Chicago: University of Chicago Press. An insightful ethnographic study of the effects of prisonization on the female partners of men behind bars. The punitive power of prisons transforms these women's bodies into extensions of their incarcerated partners and subjects them to "secondary prisonization."

Cortez, A., and J. Danini. 2009. *Disciplinary Alternative Education Programs in Texas: A 2009 Update.* San Antonio, TX: Intercultural Development Research Association. A report assessing fourteen years of DAEP implementation in the state of Texas, including demographic shifts in DAEP student enrollment, analysis of academic performance, and suggestions for DAEP reform.

Fowler, D. F. 2007. *Texas' School-to-Prison Pipeline. Dropout to Incarceration: The Impact of School Discipline and Zero Tolerance.* Austin: Texas Appleseed. A comprehensive study of the history of zero-tolerance school policies in Texas, the long-term impact of policies on students, the state of public schools, and the funneling of students into a school-to-prison pipeline.

Reyes, A. H. 2006. *Discipline, Achievement, and Race: Is Zero Tolerance the Answer?* Lanham, MD: Rowman and Littlefield Education. A critique of the extension of zero-tolerance policies, originally designed to prevent crime, into disciplinary school practices and the uneven enforcement of school punishment on racial minorities, low-income students, and boys.

Rios, V. M. 2011. *Punished: Policing the Lives of Black and Latino Boys.* New York: New York University Press. A rigorous ethnographic investigation of the experiences of low-income black and Latino youths and the social effects of policing and criminalization on their lives. These youths are "hyper criminalized" and live in a web of punitive practices and surveillance experienced through a "youth control complex" comprised of community centers, schools, juvenile justice structures, and families.

Wacquant, L. 2009. *Punishing the Poor: The Neoliberal Government of Social Insecurity.* Durham, NC: Duke University Press. An in-depth study of the shift in U.S. poverty governance over the last three decades. Under neoliberal capitalism, the poor are doubly regulated through "prisonfare" and "workfare." Mass imprisonment, the police, and other repressive forces have replaced social relief agencies to achieve the punitive management of the most economically and socially marginalized sectors of society.

CHAPTER 5

Chip: The Cost(s) of Chasing the American Dream

ERIC ENRIQUE BORJA

"We're not starving," Chip said to me in our last interview. "We're still going. They're not knocking on the door or anything." Chip wouldn't call himself working class, but in many respects he is.

Chip is white, just under six feet tall, and has light-colored hair that he keeps buzzed. His face has some wrinkles around the eyes and forehead, but despite his fifty-seven years he still maintains a youthful look that is partially offset by his thin-framed glasses and a barely visible hearing aid. We always met on campus after Chip got off of work, so I usually saw him in his work clothes—a fading red button-down and a pair of gray work pants—and with his hands perpetually covered in black ink.

Chip is a contractor who has been fixing copiers in the Austin area for three decades, but his hard work has not translated into a secure financial future. Over time his labor has taken a toll on both his physical health and his finances—making retirement seem increasingly improbable. "I figure I probably won't retire," he told me once. "I mean, just the way things are now. I don't know how that's going to work out." Like many people, Chip is chasing the American dream, but often that chase has felt more to him like running on a treadmill, going nowhere fast.

Recent studies have shown that the United States lags behind other major developed countries with regard to economic mobility. A child born at the bottom in the United States has about an 8 percent chance of making it to the top, whereas in Denmark, for example, the odds are twice that. In fact, people raised in the United States are more likely to stay in the same class as their parents—both those born at the bottom and at the top—than are people raised in Pakistan, France, Japan, and Canada. Among the major developed countries, only in Italy and the United Kingdom is there less economic mobility.

Moreover, income inequality in the United States has widened—with the top 1 percent taking 22 percent of the overall income in 2012, which is more than double the share they took in 1980. This widening inequality only further exacerbates the issue of social mobility here in the United States. And according to a study conducted by the Pew Charitable Trusts, more than 40 percent of Americans raised in the bottom quintile of the family income ladder remain stuck there as adults. Chip's story is about this "stickiness" at the bottom and top of the income ladder.

In 1984 Chip enrolled at the Southwest School of Electronics, which has since become the Southwest School of Technology. Similar to ITT Tech, the Southwest School of Electronics is a vocational school where students learn the skills necessary to become electronic technicians. At age twenty-seven Chip earned his associate's degree and began working for a local Austin business, fixing copiers. He's been doing it ever since.

Chip and his wife of thirty years live in an aging double-wide on the outskirts of Austin with no gas and no sewage. Chip's car, like his body, requires constant maintenance. Hard work and perseverance are supposed to be the only ingredients needed to achieve the American dream, but the truth is much more complicated. You can see it in Chip's hands, his failing eyes, and in his car that doubles as his mobile office. Something is about to give.

"It's just one of those things"

Every time Chip and I met he told me a story about something he had to fix. Chip and his wife, Mary, own two cars, both of which have over two hundred thousand miles on them, and they live in a seventeen-year-old double-wide trailer. Both cars and their mobile home require constant upkeep.

Chip was born in Louisiana and moved to Austin in 1976 after graduating from high school in Houston. Both of his parents were in the air force and worked at Bergstrom Air Force Base, which closed in 1993 and was converted into what is now Austin-Bergstrom International Airport. His mother was in the reserves and his father was an aircraft mechanic.

Chip has three brothers; one was born in Ohio, and the other two were born in Louisiana. As the children of military parents, they traveled a lot growing up. Chip lived overseas in Okinawa, Japan, and also spent time in California and Arizona. He has a close relationship with his three brothers, who all work "in basically the same business," as mechanics. Growing up, Chip said, they "always had somebody's car in the driveway, torn down—rebuilding the motor, doing something to it. It's what we did."

In this respect, Chip and his brothers take after their father, who, as

far back as Chip can remember, did all of the family repairs. Because Chip's father worked in the area of equipment maintenance on the air force base, he became an expert at fixing all kinds of machines. Thinking back on his childhood, Chip said, "You know, anything breaks, we were fixing it." Now that Chip is an adult, he is the one who must do the day-to-day maintenance. Between having to maintain his home, his vehicle, his wife's vehicle, and his son's and daughter's vehicles, it's a never-ending and often expensive job.

For instance, in 2012, between August and November, Chip had to repair a water line that had snapped within his wall and flooded his home, fix his refrigerator, spend an entire weekend and $1,500 in parts to do a "mini-rebuild" of the engine in his wife's car, buy two new tires for his daughter's car, buy a whole new set of tires for his wife's car, and fix his son's car; he did all of this while also working his full-time job.

But having to constantly fix the things in his life never seems to overwhelm Chip, because for him it is "just one of those things that happen." Fixing things is what his family does—and it is engaging in this day-to-day maintenance that keeps the precarious threads in Chip's life from unraveling.

"Everything runs my way"

For the last seventeen years Chip has been living in a mobile home community located in the city of Cowboy Ridge, just south of Austin. He moved there in 1999 because he found living in Austin to be too expensive—an issue that has plagued Austin's working class for decades and that has been exacerbated by the city's aggressive gentrification of affordable neighborhoods such as the East Riverside corridor.

According to a report by the National Low Income Housing Coalition, Austin is the most expensive city in Texas for the working class. High rent makes it impossible for most renters to afford a two-bedroom apartment without a second job or roommates. But it is not just rent that makes Austin too expensive for the working class—utilities are also high, and they are on the rise. The cost of living index for the Austin–Round Rock area is 14 percent higher than the state average. Therefore, Austin's working class is being pushed outside of the city limits and into new peri-urban areas such as Cowboy Ridge.

In 2000, according to the U.S. Census, Cowboy Ridge had a population of 724; by 2010 it had grown to 861. Peri-urban areas like Cowboy

Ridge are typically comprised of self-built, low-cost informal or mobile housing and are populated by people like Chip—people who are dependent on the city for employment but whose incomes don't allow them to live there.

Cowboy Ridge "used to be a nice place," Chip told me. In fact, at the time they moved in, Chip thought it was the perfect place—it was "out in the sticks" yet relatively close to the city, and it was affordable. In Cowboy Ridge Chip was able to purchase a three-quarter-acre lot, something that would have been impossible for him to do in Austin proper. Having a sizable lot gives him the space he needs to carve out a little tranquility in the midst of his demanding daily routine.

At the end of the week Chip loves to tend his garden and care for his birds. He lights up every time he tells me about his purple martins— the largest North American swallow—and garden. But the one peaceful spot Chip has found in the greater Austin area is now in danger of being submerged by a river of "crap and urine," as Chip put it.

What often happens in these peri-urban spaces is that someone purchases a large tract of land and subsequently divides it into smaller parcels. Once the land is divided up into these parcels, they are sold to subdevelopers. When Chip first moved to Cowboy Ridge there was a subdeveloper that enforced housing regulations in Chip's subdivision.

"They had all these restrictions: no junk cars, no cars on jacks, you must keep up your lawn. But then the developers went out of business in two years, and Cowboy Ridge wouldn't take over enforcing the restrictions. It just went . . . [makes a fart noise and points his thumb down]."

Peri-urban spaces like Cowboy Ridge typically lack city services for sewage, gas, and trash. Residents have septic tanks, and gas is provided through large propane tanks. Not surprisingly, poor heating and septic tank issues, such as clogging and overflow, are major problems in such communities. But because of the informal nature of these areas and the lack of government oversight, residents survive through do-it-yourself maintenance.

Chip looks at other peri-urban areas he considers to be thriving and imagines what Cowboy Ridge could be: "It could be another Lockhart or San Marcos or something. . . . You have potential that businesses could pop up." As always, Chip sees the practical side of things and tends to direct most of his frustration at the city officials, whom he feels have failed to tap Cowboy Ridge's potential. But recently, Chip's frustrations have been directed more and more toward his neighbors.

Since no one is enforcing housing regulations in Cowboy Ridge,

Chip's neighbors can get away with housing practices that are typically prohibited. For instance, his neighbor two houses down convinced Chip's immediate neighbor to merge their backyards. This is because his neighbor wants more land for his horse, sheep, chickens, and goats to graze on.

Infuriated, Chip told me, "I lost it yesterday when I found out." Before, Chip was okay with the animals because only occasionally would the goats graze into his garden. But now that the animals can come right up into his yard, it is too much for him. On top of that, Chip realized that the animals would be grazing over his neighbor's main septic line, which could cause serious problems for both of them.

As he explains, "Everything runs my way. All that crap, urine, all that stuff, is going to run into my garden and kill everything. And if they get a good heavy rain, the river that runs back by my garden is going to overflow and kill my garden." If his neighbor gets his way, Chip will lose his one tranquil spot in Austin.

But just because these areas lack formal housing regulations doesn't mean that the residents do not pay taxes. In many cases, they must pay a number of taxes in order to get services such as firefighting and trash pickup. There are so many that Chip has a hard time keeping track of them all. "Oh, we have—dang, I'm trying to think how many . . . I mean we got Travis County, Cowboy Ridge, ACC [Austin Community College], hospital district, fire district, and Deer Valley schools. And I think there's one or two more for the property taxes."

Chip originally moved out of Austin because, like so many people across Central Texas, he was priced out of the city. And now Chip faces the same issue in Cowboy Ridge.

Smooth Operation

When I was first introduced to Chip's work I was reminded of Mike Judge's 1999 cult comedy classic, *Office Space*, an Austin-filmed satire about white-collar work in the 1990s. The scene I always recall is the one in which three disgruntled employees destroy their office printer to the gangsta rap song "Still" by Geto Boys. This scene is the climax to a recurring joke where the machine continually frustrates the character Michael Bolton with error codes he cannot understand and paper jams he can never fix. While humorous, it illustrates the importance of copying and printing technology in today's offices and the critical role of people such as Chip in ensuring the machines' smooth operation.

Thinking about the nature of Chip's work, I asked him if there is a rhythm to his job. Chip responded, "Well, you know, at UT, the first week of class they're going to get run hard, and you're going to typically get more service calls. Then, of course, you have midterms. Then you have finals, and what're they doing? They're standing in line running their finals and all that." How a client "runs" a machine—meaning how the client uses the machine on a daily basis—establishes the ebb and flow of Chip's work.

In fact, the conditions that Chip describes mirror the circumstances under which he and I first met two years ago. It was finals week, and I was standing in line, waiting to make two hundred copies of a final exam. Then, as if on cue, the copier broke. "It's just like that scene from *Office Space*," I thought, and just as I was about to hit the machine, Chip came. He was able to resolve the issue quickly, saving us all a great deal of stress and frustration.

Chip is always traveling from one part of the city to another—being tossed around from one client to the next, forced to try to balance his clients' needs with his own while simultaneously searching for newer, faster, and more creative routes. Chip drives an average of 80 miles every day for work, sometimes even driving up to 120 miles, which over the years has added up to well over two hundred thousand miles on his car.

Moving Faster than Ten Miles per Hour

At Copy Co.—one of the world's largest manufacturers of office technology and the company Chip works for—technicians, or "techs," are assigned a geographic area to cover based on their expertise and the amount of copy volume they are expected to service.

The areas Chip covers are downtown, the university, and a handful of Austin Independent School District offices located on the East Side of the city. These areas cover a copy volume of nine to ten million copies per month. To service these clients, Chip must drive all over the city, through some of its busiest streets and highways.

Austin traffic, which is among the worst in the nation according to a study conducted by INRIX, a company that collects real-time traffic data worldwide, is a daily source of stress and frustration for Chip. To do his job well, he must traverse the city efficiently and quickly.

A typical workday for Chip begins at six in the morning. He wakes up and turns on his "device," a computer about the size of an iPhone that is the main organizational tool for Copy Co. techs. He then hops into the shower and prepares himself for his day while the device is logging in to Copy Co.'s servers.

After showering and getting dressed Chip checks his device to see what service calls he has to complete that day. His calls include any that are left over from the previous day as well as any new ones. Every time Chip receives a new call, his device "chimes" to notify him. When this happens, he is required to call customers within the hour to notify them how long it will take him to reach them.

Once Chip has a sense of his clients for the day, he prioritizes them by the severity of the problem and by the proximity to his location. For instance, if an office has only one copier, and that copier is "hard down"—meaning the copier is completely broken—he prioritizes that call over another one from an office with two printers. Then he works his way down the list, responding to calls he can get to quickly.

Before heading out the door, Chip brown-bags his lunch, which is typically a ham sandwich, some potato chips, an apple, some peanuts, and a half-gallon jug of water. He then hops into his car. Before leaving his home, he records his starting mileage into his device; all Copy Co. techs are required to record the number of miles they drive throughout the workday. He hits the road, puts on KLBJ News Radio, and typically arrives in the parking lot of his first client by 8:00 a.m. When he arrives, he clocks in using his device.

Chip lives about twenty miles south of Austin, but because of traffic it takes him an hour to an hour and a half to get into the city. Over the years Chip has found his own route using what he calls "back roads" to avoid main thoroughfares and highways. "I do a lot of zigging and zagging," Chip told me, "through McKinney Falls [Parkway], to Burleson [Road]; I cut through Pleasant Valley [Road]—Riverside [Drive] to Pleasant Valley—and then I go across the East Side, wind up onto MLK [Martin Luther King Boulevard], which takes me straight into UT."

When I asked him why he takes these back roads, he chuckled and said, "I'm moving faster than ten miles per hour."

A Good Day of Work

A good day of work for Chip is a day when he completes all of his calls, which happens when all the conditions are just right: traffic is light, he finds parking next to the client, machines are easy to fix, his knees aren't swollen, and other techs are getting their calls done. But these ideal conditions are almost never met, especially during events such as South by Southwest, one of Austin's major music and media festivals.

During the festival, traffic is worse, parking is impossible to find, downtown Austin is transformed into one huge concert, and the streets become clogged with thousands of festival attendees. All of this exponentially increases Chip's stress level. But even on ordinary days it's a struggle for Chip to maintain control over his schedule when he has to respond to service calls on the University of Texas campus.

Chip told me, "Out here in UT, it's a lot of stairs, a lot of walking from parking, because out here parking is hard." UT's main campus is 350 acres, and most of the parking is located on the outskirts of campus. On top of that, between classes Chip must navigate "the human traffic on campus. . . . It's like ants." For the majority of college-age students, walking across campus is at worst a minor inconvenience. But for Chip—who has had three knee surgeries—traversing UT's campus, and especially climbing up and down stairs, gets harder and harder as the week progresses.

When other techs take vacation, Chip's job gets even harder, as he is required to pick up the calls from other techs' service areas. Chip told me that one of his worst days of work was during one of those times, a particularly busy week he had in late December. He described it this way:

"I was the only Canon mid-volume tech for the whole city of Austin for like a week. I mean, that's back when we didn't have these [picks up his device] to keep track of all of our calls. We had a pager, and it would only hold like twenty pages, maybe thirty pages. But it would only lock in ten. So it would hold those, but if my pager got full, it would . . . you know, when the one come in, one had to go. So I had to start writing everything down and scratching them off because I was getting so many calls. And then I got in trouble for telling 'em [the customers] that it was going to be like four days."

Instead of anticipating the volume of demand at what is known to be a hectic time of year, Copy Co. placed the burden of absorbing the consequences of its labor shortage on Chip alone.

"Go ahead and die, battery"

Once Chip arrives at the client's office, he records his mileage; by this time he has driven twenty to twenty-five miles, depending on how long it takes him to find parking. For Chip, parking can be difficult, but over the years he has become an expert on Austin parking lots. However, he can only do so much.

In early 2014 Austin's city bus system, Capital Metro, began its MetroRapid service, adding two new routes and creating "transit priority lanes" through downtown. Contrary to what city planners had anticipated, Chip says, parking downtown is getting worse since they added the bus lanes. "They took out both sides of parking on Lavaca and Guadalupe [two major streets]," Chip explained to me. "Mostly all the way down. So people who were parking there are parking in other spots, and everything is full." As a result, Chip has been forced to drive around looking for parking, extending the time it takes for him to service a client. The irony is that city officials are attempting to make parts of Austin, such as downtown, more accessible through such projects.

Once Chip parks, he walks into the client's office. He asks for the contact person for the account, who then takes him to the machine. When he finally arrives at the machine, he zaps the machine's barcode with his device. This records his arrival time and gives him the error codes and jam codes. After zapping the machine and figuring out what is wrong with it, he "gets into the machine," as he put it. He checks every section. Looking at each part, double-checking that they are still functional, he tries to resolve the problem.

In Chip's line of work, like jobs in most service industries, it is important to have a good relationship with the client. "It makes my life easier if I have a good relationship with the customer," he said. "If I can't fix it, I mean, they know I'm trying. . . . It just makes it a lot better, it really does." Good relationships with the customers are important because the clients have the power to complain about a tech and generally make a tech's life difficult.

Chip told me a story about a tech who was servicing a copier for a client at a dive shop. The owner of the dive shop became so fed up with the tech that he pointed a speargun at the tech, demanding he fix the copier. When I asked him if anything like this had ever happened to him, Chip responded, "I have some strange ones."

One time, he told me, he dealt with a woman who was trying to scan an important document to send to her head office, but the document feeder kept jamming. Chip fixed the problem in an instant and vividly remembers the woman's effusive expressions of gratitude. "She started jumping up and down, and she goes, 'I love you! I love you!' And she took her hands and went [makes a kissing noise]." The woman was so happy she kissed Chip right on the mouth.

"Basically I'm the hero in that office now," he said. In Chip's line of work, a little recognition goes a long way.

Once Chip completes the call, he zaps the barcode again to record his time out. He then fills out a form with all the details of the call—what the problem was, what he did to the machine, and how many parts he used—and has the client sign it. He then packs up and heads back to his car. He then does it all over again, usually six to eight times a day, eating here and there between calls.

By the end of the workday Chip has driven 60 to 80 miles—which adds up to about 350 miles a week. By Friday afternoon Chip is so tired and fed up that in a small act of rebellion he maniacally allows his device to die—and doesn't plug it in to charge until Sunday evening. "I turn it off, and I don't even plug it in," he told me. "So I say, 'Go ahead and die, battery.'"

"If you want to work, that's just what you gotta do"

A tech is only as reliable as his or her car, but techs at Copy Co. are not provided with company vehicles. Instead, Copy Co. offers them a per diem that is rolled into their paychecks each month. The per diem is intended to offset the costs associated with techs driving their own vehicles, which include paying for premium insurance, maintenance, and wear and tear and compensating them for mileage. However, the way the per diems are calculated means that techs often end up covering additional costs that accrue from driving their personal vehicles. With the decline of unions and the rise of deregulation in recent years, many businesses have employed similar strategies, shifting financial responsibility to workers wherever possible in order to enhance the corporate bottom line.

At Copy Co., per diems are first calculated based on the age of the car—the newer the car, the more money you get. Next, the per diems are supposed to cover the cost of paying for business-class car insurance, but in the state of Texas there is a law that requires employees to also purchase premium insurance for every vehicle registered at their home address. So when Chip's son and daughter were living with him, this meant paying for premium insurance on four different vehicles. That additional expense was not covered.

Next, the per diem covers the cost of gas and wear and tear, both of which are calculated based on the number of miles a tech drives. But instead of using the tech's actual vehicle to calculate how much they need, the calculation is done using a company-wide car. For Copy Co. that's a Ford Fusion. The Ford Fusion has a combined fuel economy of twenty-five miles per gallon—ten miles more than what Chip's 2004 Ford Free-star van gets, which costs him $500 per month in gas.

Chip admitted that the per diem is hardly enough to cover all of the costs he incurs to do his job. "But if you want to work, that's just what you gotta do," he said.

Dealing with the per diem is not the only thing Chip puts up with in order to work. Since each tech must carry all the necessary parts to complete a call, Chip's van has essentially become his office. In addition to parts, Chip's vehicle holds a number of what are called PM (periodic maintenance) kits; these are essentially "repair kits" that are tailored, by the manufacturer, for specific machines. He also carries a number of personal items to help him maintain himself throughout the day—particularly to deal with the aches and pains he so often experiences. "I have Tylenol, I have allergy stuff. . . . It's almost like a medicine cabinet." Chip's van is so well stocked it is almost like his second home.

For instance, on one occasion somebody asked Chip for a Band-Aid. When Chip got the Band-Aid, the individual was shocked to see how well stocked he was, even making a joke that all Chip was missing was a TV. In response, Chip pulled out his three-inch color-screen portable TV and asked, "What do you want to watch?"

Perhaps the only thing Chip's car lacks is a time machine. I say this because each time we meet, he tells me how many miles his car has. The last time I spoke with him it was well over two hundred thousand miles. Chip is constantly shoveling money into maintenance because he simply cannot afford a car payment.

Most recently he spent $4,000 dollars replacing the transmission in his car. When he told his friends, they did not understand why he didn't just invest in a new car instead. "Everyone said, 'Oh, you're stupid! You could put that down to get a new car.' But it's like, then I have a car payment. I can't do a car payment right now," Chip told me. He charged half of the transmission on his credit card and wrote a check for the other half.

This car is Chip's fourth vehicle in his thirty-year career. He essentially runs his cars to the point where either he can't fix them anymore or they cost him too much money each month. But how much is "too much" remains unclear to me. During the time I have known Chip, he has spent countless hours and thousands of dollars on maintenance, re-

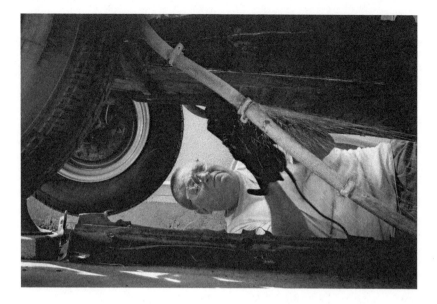

placing tires and transmissions and rebuilding engines. Chip always speaks with so much pride about how he learned to fix things from his father. Maybe, I decided, it's not only about the money, but also about Chip's desire to be a good man, a responsible father, and a reliable provider. After all, fixing things is what his family does.

It's Not Only His Car That Is Breaking Down

As the needs of the postindustrial office evolve, so too does the copier and its technician. This means Chip is constantly training to keep up with new products and innovations. Currently, Copy Co. is expanding its services to include building and maintaining wireless networks. Copy Co. made it mandatory for all of its techs to acquire both A+ and Network+ certifications, which teach techs computer basics and how to set up and troubleshoot networks.

During our interviews, Chip was in the midst of a lot of online training. At Copy Co., techs have one full workweek to complete their training, which is held at Copy Co.'s main offices. In this week they are not required to answer any service calls.

For Chip, completing all the training in one week is virtually impossible. This is because Chip has been diagnosed with macular dystrophy—a rare genetic eye disorder that damages the cells of the macula, an area of the retina that is responsible for central vision. As the macula degenerates over time, daily activities such as reading and driving become progressively more difficult. Even looking at a computer screen becomes problematic.

"Driving at night is . . . it's not impossible, but it's real tough. And it's like your keyboard . . . you've seen the keyboard that's ergonomically, or whatever—the ones that go up. I was looking at my keyboard today, and it's just a flat laptop, and it looks like it goes like this [makes a hand gesture to illustrate a bubble]. My computer screen bubbles out. . . . It's getting tough, and I'm sitting there trying to read. . . . It's getting tough."

Chip's eye disease affects not only his daily activities but also the kinds of work he is able to perform. When I first began interviewing Chip, he was servicing both color and black-and-white copiers, but he has since been moved away from repairing color copiers. When I asked him about the change, he told me he was having trouble repairing the color copiers because he could not tell the colors apart.

"I mean, I could see the colors, but I couldn't tell if they were fuzzy or not or if they were the right colors or not," he told me. This is because color copiers work by putting down one color on top of another color, and if one of these colors is off, then you get what he calls a "3-D effect." But for Chip, that was what he always saw, no matter if the color copier was working properly or malfunctioning. "When I see something, it's not like lines. It's like, no—they're all crooked."

Copy Co.'s expansion into information technologies has opened up new roads for advancement in the company, but these opportunities don't seem to interest Chip, even though in the long run an IT job might be better suited for him, since it would involve less walking. Chip has had a total of three knee surgeries—two in his right knee and one in his left.

"They hurt," he said of his knees. "They pop. Getting up and down, you can actually hear it—pop pop! Or if I squat down all of a sudden, it'll catch, and it's like, 'Oh no,' and then all of a sudden—snap! [He snaps his fingers.] And then it's like having a knife stabbed in your knee, and then you stand up, stretch out. It's okay, and then you go on."

Fifteen years ago doctors told him he would need a knee replacement in ten years, but they also said he was too young to have a knee replacement. What the doctors meant was that if Chip were to get his knees replaced, he would need another replacement before he died. When I asked Chip what he had said to the doctors after his diagnosis, he said he told them, "Well, okay. We'll just keep them going for as long as we can." He's now had three knee surgeries, but those surgeries have created new problems. At this point the cartilage in both of Chip's knees is so thin that if they were to operate on his knee again, he would be left with bone on bone, which would make walking excruciating.

As it is now, after work Chip ices his knees, and twice a week he goes to the gym to do his own physical therapy; otherwise his knees would make his job unbearably painful. But if Chip were to move to the "IT side," his knee pain would be less of an issue. "Moving up to the IT side, you don't carry a tool case. You're not down on your knees all day. You just sit in front of a computer screen." But he is not interested in moving to the IT side of things. "Just leave me to the hardware," Chip told me.

Despite Chip's reluctance to move to the IT side, Copy Co. is clearly moving in that direction. I asked Chip if he's worried about his job security over the next ten years, and he responded, "Nah. I'll be, like one of my managers said, the last technician to leave."

"That's when I'm retired"

Chip is about ten years away from retiring.

"I don't know if I want to stay doing the copiers or not. I've done it for twenty-seven years," Chip once told me. His nearly three decades of experience fixing copiers have made him one of the top technicians at Copy Co., but being good at your job doesn't always translate into a secure financial future. In fact, it has been shown that manual laborers typically stagnate in their careers due to a lack of career development.

"I've been with this company for twenty [years], and I was expecting my gold watch—retired, you know. I got a jacket. That's fine. It's a nice jacket. But, you know, back in the olden days you worked twenty to thirty years at a company, they'd give you a gold watch, a pension, and you go on your way. Not anymore."

From 1990 to 2009 corporate pension plans in the United States fell dramatically. In 1999 there were ninety-two thousand single-employer defined benefit plans. By 2009 that number had dropped to twenty-nine thousand. This trend has shifted the burden of paying for retirement to individuals, which has made personal savings and investments the primary source of retirement income. According to financial experts, one must save eight times their ending salary in order to retire and maintain their same lifestyle. For instance, if you have an ending salary of $50,000, you should have $400,000 saved by the time you retire.

But in the case of low-income earners, like Chip, is maintaining the same lifestyle really what a person wants when he or she retires? Most advice about retirement is reserved for those who are financially secure, not for people like Chip. And the retirement advice given to the working class is simply to postpone retirement. But is that an option for Chip?

For Chip, the amount of money it would take for him to be financially secure in retirement is unattainable. When I asked him about saving for his retirement, he said, "I should be on a schedule, but there's no way I can dump any more money anywhere, because I have too many bills." With his knees and eyes failing, his vehicle busted, his home falling apart, his daily and monthly expenses adding up, and the student loans unpaid, retirement seems to be an impossibility for Chip—and an impossibility that he always seemed hesitant to admit to me. Still, Chip doesn't know if he'll ever stop working.

"When they close the lid on that box and put me into the ground," Chip said, "that's when I'm retired."

Recommended Readings

Ehrenreich, B. 2001. *Nickel and Dimed: On (Not) Getting By in America*. New York: Metropolitan Books. Journalist Barbara Ehrenreich goes undercover to shed light on low-wage jobs in the United States and to examine how people making minimum wage make ends meet.

Howell, R. 2000. *One Hundred Jobs: A Panorama of Work in the American City*. New York: New Press. Looking at New York City, Ron Howell interviews one hundred workers to find out what they do all day, how they do it, how they are compensated, and how they view their working lives.

Pew Charitable Trusts. 2012. *Pursuing the American Dream: Economic Mobility Across Generations*. In this 2012 report, the Pew Research Center illustrates current trends in economic mobility in the United States.

Purser, G. 2012. "'Still Doin' Time': Clamoring for Work in the Day Labor Industry." *WorkingUSA* 15 (3): 397–415. Gretchen Purser presents an ethnographic case study of an industry that actively recruits and makes profitable the labor of ex-offenders, revealing the pliability and exploitability of such labor.

Sullivan, E., and C. Olmedo. 2014. "Informality on the Urban Periphery: Housing Conditions and Self-help Strategies in Texas Informal Subdivisions." *Urban Studies*: 1–17. The authors describe in detail two informal subdivisions in Central Texas, shedding light on the issues these communities face and how local policymakers can help address these issues.

Uchitelle, L. 2007. *The Disposable American: Layoffs and Their Consequences*. New York: Vintage. Louis Uchitelle offers an eye-opening account of layoffs in America, their beginnings, their questionable necessity, and their devastating psychological impact on individuals at all income levels.

CHAPTER 6

Raven: "The Difference between a Cocktail Waitress and a Stripper? Two Weeks"

CAITLYN COLLINS

By many accounts, Raven Edwards is a typical Austin transplant. A twenty-three-year-old aspiring chef and music lover, she moved to Austin because of its reputation as a music and entertainment mecca for open-minded young people. Having visited the city every year while growing up, Raven had always thought of Austin as a place she'd like to live one day.

Dallas, by contrast, was too fast paced, too pretentious, and too Christian for Raven. She loves that Austin is laid-back, she says, and that people don't feel the need to impress each other here. She was also chasing a fresh start and seeking to break from a tumultuous past in Dallas. To Raven, Austin is a place that feels like "I can actually be okay with being me."

Since moving to the city in 2010 at the age of nineteen, Raven has worked at many of Austin's most iconic businesses. She has plated prepared dishes at the flagship Whole Foods store downtown, catered for Mandola's Italian restaurant on North Lamar, prepped cold dishes at celebrity restaurateur Sandra Bullock's Bess Bistro on historic Sixth Street, and made salads at the health-food restaurant Snap Kitchen.

However, Raven's career hasn't panned out the way she had hoped when she first dreamed of moving to Austin and starting anew. She started working in the service industry at age fifteen in Dallas, and estimates that she has held sixteen jobs in the past eight years (half of those in Austin in the past three years), working in each position for only two to twelve months. She earned from $5.15 to $10.00 an hour. Some of these positions she quit; from others, she was fired. She worked back-to-back shifts for unreasonable supervisors. She put up with back talk from customers and endured sexual harassment from coworkers and bosses. Her employers' promises of promotions and raises never materialized. Guaranteed transitions from part-time to full-time work that would have provided benefits were ignored. And she had little to no control over her work schedule, often learning of her shifts with only a few hours' notice.

Raven has always worked at least two jobs in order to support herself, and despite this, she still often cuts it dangerously close to broke at the end of every month. Facing an uncertain future with low wages and little autonomy, Raven turned to another line of service work in Austin: stripping.

During our first meeting at a local coffee shop, Raven tells me, "There's a joke: What's the difference between a cocktail waitress and a stripper? Two weeks."

Raven tilts her head back and laughs. "I literally went two weeks. It was my two-week mark after my new cocktailing job that I first showed my tits for money. And man, do you make a *lot* more money than being a waitress." But it is not only "for the money" that she dances and strips. Raven at times finds more appreciation, stability, enjoyment, and independence working as an exotic dancer at a gentleman's club than she does waiting tables in some of Austin's most famous restaurants.

"I'll tell you everything; I have nothing to hide"

I met Raven through an online forum where she discussed her life as a stripper here in Austin. I introduced myself via email in January 2013 and asked whether she would be willing to let me interview her about her work. She replied enthusiastically and agreed to meet me in person the following week. Raven and I met at a cozy coffee shop in central Austin, where we had the first of many conversations.

I felt nervous meeting Raven in person for the first time. But my worries proved ill founded, and Raven's light take on dark aspects of her life and her habit of interspersing her stories with laughter and sarcasm quickly put me at ease. She is gregarious, articulate, and self-reflective. I've come to look forward to our time together, often leaving with my sides aching with laughter from her witty jokes, casual profanity, and colorful anecdotes.

Raven's Italian heritage shows in her olive skin, shoulder-length thick brown hair, and long eyelashes. Occasionally she smokes cigarettes at our table. She orders a coffee if she has had a long night beforehand or a stout beer if she's in a good mood. Raven always shows up eager to fill me in on what's happened in her life since I saw her last—new boyfriends, workplace drama, and fun nights out with friends topping the list of topics. Many of her sentences start something like this: "Didn't I tell you about—? What! I didn't?! Girl, okay. You won't fuckin' believe this . . ." I am a captive audience. She brings her focus intensely to me when she tells these stories. When she recounts sadder memories, her eyes usually comb our surroundings rather than meeting my gaze.

Although Raven often dresses femininely to show off her petite 5'4" frame in tight-fitting T-shirts and jeans or flowing sundresses, she carries herself with the toughness of someone accustomed to standing up for herself. Raven's classic beauty also contrasts with her frequently dirty stories, love of swear words, and brusque laugh. She is a self-proclaimed tomboy and sports several tattoos with pride. Her most recent one is the logo of her favorite video game series, Assassin's Creed, on the inside of her forearm.

Despite our lively meetings and intimate conversations, I sense that Raven has a sort of defensiveness, a wariness that becomes more intelligible to me over the months as I get to know her better and hear the many tales of heartache that pepper her past and present.

Growing Up Lonely

Raven was born five days after her mother turned nineteen. She was the result of an affair with a thirty-two-year-old married man—a man who, Raven tells me, is in the Italian Mafia. Raven didn't meet her biological father until she was sixteen, and today he calls her occasionally from jail, begging her to post bail for him. "I'm like, 'Fuck you.' I told him I can barely pay my own fuckin' rent. I'm not going to bail you out of jail."

She has three half-siblings but has never met them. "God knows how many other kids he's brought to this Earth," she says with a shake of her head.

When Raven was two, her mother married a Dallas police officer ten years her senior. The family of three lived in a series of crumbling neighborhoods in east Dallas: "We were living in the ghetto, with crack dealers across the street, with cops going up and down all the time. We'd hear gunshots in the middle of the night. It was bad."

Raven remembers her childhood life as turbulent:

"My parents are fantastic for each other, but they were not meant to be parents. . . . My mom abused me until I was sixteen or seventeen. Like physical and mental. My mom would beat me, but my dad knew he couldn't beat me. . . . I honestly think that my dad is way too much in love with my mother, so he could never lay a hand on me."

Raven has a congenital heart condition and has undergone four heart surgeries as a result. A light craggy scar runs up and down the center of her chest, starting just under her collarbone and descending beneath the neckline of her T-shirts—the pale white stitch marks are still faintly evident. She recalls her mom slapping her across the face in their kitchen at age nine when she balked at the epinephrine shot her dad administered to build up her blood cell count between surgeries: "I remember it like it was fuckin' yesterday. She told me to fuckin' grow up."

Raven had many lonely years in school, an experience she traces to the fact that her mother had raised her as a Jehovah's Witness—an evangelical Christian denomination with roughly 1.2 million followers in the United States and more than eighty congregations in Dallas alone. Her parents forbade her from making friends with anyone at school because they were "worldly friends," or non-Jehovah's Witnesses.

As the victim of her mother's abuse and strict religious demands, Raven isolated herself. She withdrew from her peer groups at school and thinks of her younger self as a loner: "I was that silent Christian girl walking through school." Her parents encouraged her to attend therapy for being antisocial.

Raven tells me that in retrospect she feels as if her parents robbed her of a childhood. Through forbidding her from having school friends or attending school functions like homecoming and prom, Raven's parents have become the objects of her resentment.

When Raven was growing up, her mother also criticized her regularly about her weight. This is despite Raven being slim, by all accounts, at 5'4" and 125 pounds. "'Why are you eating that much? Don't eat that.' It was all around body image with her." Raven became anorexic in junior high after watching her mother obsessively count calories and purge her food as she grew up.

Raven also resents her mother for being a "part-timer" when it came to religion. Even though her mother attends church three days a week, she "has fake tits and cusses and drinks and wears slutty little outfits. I was never allowed to do that shit—are you kidding me?" She remembers:

"As soon as I got my driver's license [she would make me] drive her around to bars and shit, and [she would] flirt with men, and tell everybody that me and her were sisters, and beat me in the car on the way home, and tell me to pull over so she could drive even though she was drunk. I came home with black eyes. I locked myself in the bathroom one time because she was so angry."

"I had to find a way to block it all out"

Raven started rebelling during her junior year of high school and dropped out when she was sixteen. She homeschooled herself, received her diploma, and then started looking for work in the food industry. As a teenager, her jobs included cooking meals for a family she knew through church, working as a chef's assistant at the upscale cooking store Sur la Table, and serving as a hostess and waitress at several Dallas-area restaurants. When she turned eighteen in 2009, Raven renounced her religion, the few religious friends she had, and moved out of her parents' home.

With her newfound freedom, Raven became deeply involved in the music scene in Dallas. She met her first boyfriend at a concert. It was the "worst mistake of my life," she admits, her voice filled with anger and grief. She lost her virginity to her boyfriend a few months after they started dating and moved in with him shortly thereafter. They had a tumultuous, unhappy relationship that lasted several years.

Much like her parents, her boyfriend forbade her to have any friends. He told her she was stupid and would never amount to anything. "We were horrible to each other," she tells me. He was sexually and mentally abusive to her, forcing himself on her when she wasn't in the mood for sex and telling her she needed to be on medication because she was "fucked up," "too anxious," and needed help. Raven tells me that during this time she developed acute social anxiety and experienced frequent panic attacks.

Since Raven's parents had encouraged her to go to therapy since she was seventeen, she reluctantly agreed to see a psychiatrist. Raven's mother had moved up the ranks at work and become an IT consultant; she was willing to pay for the $180 sessions. Raven despised her doctor, who would listen distractedly and then prescribe her clonazepam to treat her anxiety and panic disorders. These prescription pills opened up a new world for her: "I took one, and then I took another one. And then I took another one. . . . It numbed everything out." She quickly became addicted to them. As she explained, she took "everything—anything I could get my hands on," primarily Xanax, Ritalin, and hydrocodone. Raven received medication from both her doctor and her psychiatrist. And when they balked at giving her more drugs, she would buy them on the street instead. Black market pills are available everywhere in the music scene, according to Raven. "And it's never the people you think—little tiny girls would pull shit out of their purses like you wouldn't believe."

Her part-time jobs as a waitress paid eight dollars an hour, and she was using roughly $500 worth of pills a week. Raven needed another source of income to fund her addiction. "What can I do to support my addiction and make a lot of money at the same time?" she remembers desperately asking herself.

High-End Companionship

When she was eighteen Raven waitressed at a local Dallas diner. There she worked the "deep night shift," 10:00 p.m. to 5:00 a.m. One night a middle-aged man caught her attention. They chatted while she served him his food and filled his drinks. She mentioned that she'd wanted to start her own business as a personal chef. He said he'd like to hire her, saying how beautiful she was, and gave her his business card.

She called him the next day, and the man asked her out to dinner. Raven agreed and met him at a nearby sushi restaurant. She recounts to me in a flat tone, "I knew right away. I knew the look in his eyes. I knew what was going on."

"One thing led to another, and he asked a price. I told him." They began to drink heavily at the restaurant, and the man agreed to pay Raven $500 to go back to his condo with him. Nodding her head slowly, with wide eyes and pursed lips, Raven tells me, "That was the day I started having sex for money."

Raven remembers waking up the next morning to find five one-hundred-dollar bills on the nightstand.

After that night she started working as an escort. Raven told me, "Sometimes you can work for escort companies or get prostituted out. And I don't want to say that escorting is a higher class, because it's not, but I was not on the street asking people [to have sex]." I ask her how she learned how to escort: Where do you go? What do you wear? How do you avoid the police? She tells me she was entirely self-taught and was highly selective and cautious about her clients. With a police officer for a father and because Texas, with 350 workers currently in prison state-

wide, is one of the few states that incarcerates sex workers, Raven was obsessive about ensuring that there was no written or recorded evidence of her work.

When she went out to meet men, Raven would dress expensively, with her hair in curls, makeup done nicely, and "sexy lingerie" and high heels. She went to the most upscale bars and restaurants in Dallas during happy hour. Men were usually just getting off work and having a drink to wind down for the evening.

Raven crafted a careful appearance while looking for clients: "I made sure I was just a lady having a drink by myself." At the restaurant bar, she targeted older, "lonely-looking men" and sent them over a drink. The men would usually invite her over to their table or come join her at the bar. She laughs and tells me that men would "kinda get the hint. I'm eighteen years old. You're fifty. You have a lot of money, and that's all I want. I'm eighteen, and I'm sitting at the nicest restaurant in Dallas.

Who can afford that?" She would never discuss pricing or go home with a man on the first night. Instead, she would exchange numbers with him and agree on another time to meet. Raven says this arrangement made her feel more comfortable, like she was able to connect more with her clients rather than feeling like she was, in her words, "fucking strangers for money."

Not all men paid her for sex, though. Some of the older, "less energetic" men sought Raven out solely for her companionship. They paid her to share meals at their homes, talk to them, and act like their girlfriend, if only for a short while. Sociologist Elizabeth Bernstein notes that this type of sexual commerce—"temporary intimacies" available for purchase in the marketplace as the "girlfriend experience"—is an increasingly common dynamic in sex work. This arrangement is appealing for professional men who say they are overworked and too busy to meet women. Raven was able to fill these clients' desires for a temporary intimate connection in the context of a paid sexual transaction. She said this scenario was more desirable and authentic than what she considers the more alienating, exploitative forms of sex work. This helps explain why Raven refers to her work as "escorting" and not as "prostitution."

Raven's clients were wealthy men, and in the first few months of work she quickly became accustomed to a lavish lifestyle. She estimates that she had forty or so clients over the year she escorted in Dallas, some of them married, the oldest one around fifty-five years old.

Raven typically escorted three evenings a week, charging clients $500 a night. Those who wanted her company for a whole day paid her $1,000 to $1,500. She was quickly earning between $1,500 and $4,000 a week, and some of her clients would also supply her with pills.

Raven's need to self-medicate increased significantly when she began escorting: "I started realizing that I need to not think about what I'm doing. . . . It's weird to realize that I actually did all these things." All of the money she earned from escorting went to pay for pills. "That's it. I would just waste my money away," she says.

"I'd make that $1,000 last to where I'd have seven bottles sitting in front of me, and I'd decide which type and how many [pills] I was going to take every day. I would spend hundreds of dollars on any pill I could get my hands on. There was no time that I was sober. I would wake up in the middle of the night and take a hydrocodone just to go back to sleep."

Her dealers came to depend on her as a reliable source of income, calling her to ask if she could buy something when they were short on rent or when their cars broke down. "Once you're in the drug deal business, you are fuckin' in it. Your dealers count on you to not eat ramen every day. Especially with me, because I had the money to do anything I wanted." She kept her waitressing job at the diner as a cover story for her boyfriend and parents and made up excuses to justify her absences. Her boyfriend traveled with his band, making it easy to hide her activities. Other times, when she and her boyfriend fought, she would storm out, saying she was going to stay with her parents or friends for a few days. Instead, she used that time away to escort without arousing suspicion.

Raven's job as an escort ended abruptly, and violently, on a cloudy evening in the winter of 2010, shortly after her nineteenth birthday.

The Dark Side of Escorting and a New Start in Austin

Raven tells me that after escorting for about a year, she met a man at a bar who slipped something into her drink while they were talking. She vaguely remembers waking up in a haze, frightened and groggy, and tied to his bed. She recalls being knocked out again.

The next time she regained consciousness, Raven found herself sitting alone inside her car in the garage at the man's apartment complex, with no recollection of what else had happened to her or how she had gotten there. She didn't seek medical attention because she didn't think anyone would believe her.

After that, she says, "I didn't go back. That was it."

Raven told me this story the first day we met, but it took many months for her to share the details. She refers to this experience nearly every time we get together. She tells me that this client "legitimately" raped her, and I get the sense from how she talks that others did not believe her when they heard this account. I can only imagine how Raven must feel when, after gathering the strength to share this story, she is told that someone who offers sex for a living can't be the victim of sexual assault. But Raven is not alone: somewhere between one-half to two-thirds of sex workers report being the victims of rape while working. Because the sex trade is one of the United States's largest unregulated industries, these crimes are difficult to trace or prosecute. In addition, victims fear getting entangled in the criminal justice system if they report their attack. Raven was no different.

After she was assaulted and raped, Raven decided she had "nothing to lose" and moved to Austin in the spring of 2010 following a rocky breakup with her abusive boyfriend. "I didn't want my past to be my present anymore. . . . I needed something different. I just was tired," she recounts. "I didn't like remembering the things that I've done, or the people that got me where I was. So I moved here—no friends, I didn't know anybody."

Raven's mother encouraged her to move away from Dallas—to go anywhere else—in order to stay away from her ex-boyfriend. Her mom learned of her pill addiction but not the escorting. She paid for a sobriety therapist when Raven arrived in Austin, since Raven had no health insurance through any of her new jobs. In Austin Raven came to trust and respect her therapist, and with her help over the course of many months she is now proud to be free from pills. It was a long and difficult struggle.

Raven's move to Austin, unfortunately, was not the end of all her worries. Despite finding positions as a line cook and waitress at popular establishments like Whole Foods, Snap Kitchen, and Bess Bistro, these jobs were not ideal. Every position Raven could find was poorly paid, had unreliable hours, and provided little stimulation. Employers assigned her positions that, according to her, didn't require much skill or talent, so Raven was never pushed to excel. Because she didn't excel, she didn't get promoted to better positions that she would find more en-

gaging and challenging. She hated juggling several of these tedious jobs just to survive every month.

Raven started dating the manager of the restaurant where she waitressed, and he encouraged her to apply for a cocktail waitress position at a strip club in south Austin. She was hired right away. Once there, she donned the standard cocktailing uniform for her shifts: a bustier top, tightly fitted shorts, and fishnet stockings with high heels.

Although a welcome change from her escorting in Dallas, this new line of work had its own appeal for Raven that would take her down a different sort of rabbit hole.

"Once you show your tits to everybody, you're done"

At the strip club Raven befriended one of the dancers, who goes by the stage name Ginger. Raven recounts to me, through peals of laughter, the story of her unexpected transition from waitress to exotic dancer.

One night, two weeks after she had started working at the club, Ginger and Raven were drinking together, and Raven confided in her new friend about her financial worries. Ginger urged her to get onstage, where the money is better. Raven remembers being nervous and intimidated about the prospect of dancing, but, fueled by several cocktails, she ultimately decided to give it a try and go onstage. She remembers, "I was scared shitless. I was terrified. . . . You get onstage, and everyone's looking at you, and I didn't know how to do pole tricks. Now I know how to fuckin' flip myself upside down and crawl up and do all sorts of stuff."

After Raven's first time onstage in front of an audience, her job title suddenly shifted to dancer instead of waitress. She jokes when she tells me about this transition: "Once you show your tits to everybody, you're done. It's impossible. It's the rule: you can't go back. You can go to another club and apply for a cocktail job, but you can't be a waitress anymore unless you get pregnant. . . . Once you expose yourself, you're done. Then you're on the dark side." These were club rules: if Raven wanted to keep a job at the club, she could no longer waitress. Besides, she earned much more money as a dancer. Raven and her new boyfriend had moved in together, and he quit his job as restaurant manager when she started making good money. Raven supported them both. She needed the money she earned from stripping more than ever now that she was supporting two people on her earnings.

Working at the Club

Raven says that dancers have to be eighteen to work in strip clubs, but dancers under twenty-one have to wear a wristband signaling that they are too young to be served drinks. Raven finds this rule absurd: "Everyone can see your titties, because you're old enough for that. But you can't drink? Sorry. I think it's bullshit. It's ridiculous. You can shoot a gun, and you can show your titties, but you can't drink?" Raven explains that because her club is more upscale than many in town, the workers there tend to be quite normatively attractive. They are all fit and slim women, ranging in age from eighteen to mid-forties.

Raven agreed to bring me to her club so that I could see where she worked, meet other dancers, and understand more about her job.

I met her in the bright foyer of the club on a balmy weeknight in mid-May of 2013. Raven walks me back through the double doors and into the club, explaining that there are three main stages, with a VIP section in the back. A gold pole stands in the center of each stage. The place is decorated to look chic and high-end—black velvetlike curtains hang lushly from high ceilings and pool around columns, and the DJ spins popular music from a small alcove next to the main stage. The lights are low and red-tinted, and music blares so loudly that it's difficult to hear anyone talk. Comfortable armchairs surround small pedestal tables, and dancers walk seductively from table to table to flirt with and dance for customers.

The VIP section is cordoned off with a rope and features swanky leather booths, small sofas, and wraparound chairs. White gauze curtains can enclose each booth to increase privacy. The VIP room has its own bar and separate staff from the rest of the club. Seats in this area range from $100 to $1,000.

On a slow night, only the main stage is used, and each of the thirteen women working dances to three songs before she is rotated offstage to perform lap dances for customers on the floor. On a busy night, the club holds several hundred customers, and sixty to eighty women may be working at once, with all three stages in use. Dancers perform two songs on each stage for their rotation, perhaps only dancing onstage once over the course of a particularly busy weekend evening. If a worker wants to dance onstage more than once, she has to tip the DJ twenty dollars to rotate her back into the lineup. This can be especially lucrative later in the night, when customers are eager to see their favorite dancers onstage.

Clients can approach the stage while a woman dances and put money into her bra or underwear to receive personal attention, ranging anywhere from provocative dancing in close proximity to clients touching and caressing the dancers while they perform at the stage's edge in front of the rest of the club.

In the back of the building, the dancers have a dressing room that looks and feels completely different from the club itself. It is extremely bright, with several mirrors surrounded by lightbulbs reminiscent of those in theater dressing rooms. Dancers come here to apply makeup, change clothes, shower and shave in the grimy corner stall, or get a quick fake tan in the tanning booth (five dollars for five minutes). In the dressing room the women seem uncomfortable as they stand or lounge around in their impossibly tall high heels and lingerie, sitting alone or sometimes chatting with one another. Under the fluorescent lights, the dancers all seem exhausted and deflated, and many look like they are high. Some stare aimlessly around the room, and others slur their words and stumble a bit as they move around, picking up a pair of heels here, donning a different negligee there. One woman bounces a crossed leg nervously as she applies makeup in a rush with shaking hands, dabbing concealer at the dark circles under her eyes.

Onstage and amongst the tables in the club, however, the women come to life under the seductive dim lights. They appear energetic and natural, at ease strutting, dancing, and performing for the night's customers. All eyes are glued to the dancers, and customers' faces are a bit dazed and wide-eyed—soaking in the flashing lights, blaring music, and undulating bodies that dance only feet, or inches, away them. Men's eyes light up when a dancer approaches them, big smiles spreading across their faces, heads tilted upward with pleased looks that range from adoration to hunger, pleasure to reverence.

When I see these interactions at the strip club, I slowly come to understand why stripping has an appeal for Raven. After a lifetime of isolation and hurt and powerlessness, sex work like escorting and stripping makes her feel in control of her own body for the first time. This sense of agency can be both alluring and enjoyable for Raven.

"I have my boundaries as a dancer"

Raven enjoys working at her current club because it is close to her house, and she can afford the ten-dollar "house fee"—the cut given to the club—at the end of her night. She dances more rarely at a gentleman's club in Round Rock that is an hour's drive from her house and requires a twenty-five-dollar house fee up front. This steep fee, on top of the gas needed to get there and back, means she doesn't go there very often. But she says, "Sometimes you just need a change of scenery. I've just seen *way* too many of these girls *way* too much this week, so it's kind of nice." Her main club in south Austin has a clientele that is, according to Raven, roughly 60 percent black and 40 percent white. "It's a little more ghetto, unfortunately, since it's closer to the East Side," she explains, referencing its location and the predominance of African American customers. Other clubs in Austin are fully nude; Raven refuses to dance at these because she finds it unsanitary and "gross." At her club Raven likes to dance to rock music and to wear lingerie dresses while she works. She prefers to be "at least somewhat fully clothed." One of her favorite tops is a black bra studded with silver spikes.

When she works, Raven tries not to imbibe more than four drinks, in order to prevent herself from becoming too uninhibited. Despite these precautions—a response to her past assault—Raven has still been "roofied" (drugged with Rohypnol) several times on the job. As a result, she tries to be careful about the people from whom she accepts drinks.

Just as she did when she escorted, Raven establishes strict rules about what clients can and can't do: "I'll cut the line at creepy dudes—too touchy. They can only touch certain places. . . . You let them be fully aware: this is what I will and will not do, period." The club sets rules about touching, but dancers are allowed to set their own boundaries as well. Raven avoids men who seem too enthusiastic, who have dirty clothes, or whose gazes makes her feel uncomfortable.

Lap dances at the club are twenty dollars per person per dance. Raven especially likes dancing for couples because she then gets paid double for the same amount of work. She tells me about a couple who are regular customers of hers, a "super sweet" husband and wife in their early forties with three young children who come in once a month, rent out a cabana, order bottle service, and tip generously. Other nights she recalls fondly are those when she makes enough money to carry a coveted beer bucket to hold all her tips—a symbol of a particularly talented dancer. "Sometimes there's like $200 in one-dollar bills flying through the air because a guy will like me, and I'm like, 'Bring it!'"

Dancing during the day also has its benefits, because it's less of a club-like atmosphere, attracting a different clientele—usually men on their lunch breaks who "want to spend money on you." As a result, Raven can make fast money working these day shifts. However, there is an exception to this rule: oftentimes car mechanics and construction workers come in during their lunch breaks to eat and watch the dancers, but they rarely pay for dances. When they do, Raven says, they often tip poorly and expect the women to sit on their laps, even though they are still "sweaty and smelly" from work. Raven says the dancers avoid such customers because of this reputation.

I ask her about the worst night she recalls, and she tells me that a man once urinated on her while she was giving him a lap dance. She remembers angrily the time a man exposed himself to her and demanded that she perform fellatio. She refused and said that he either needed to give her one hundred dollars or she would get him kicked out of the club. He demanded that she find another girl for him, and she told him, "I'm not your pimp." Instances like this show the very fine line Raven and other dancers must walk between creating the illusion of power and pleasure for their customers while maintaining their own safety and sense of control.

Raven likes some parts of the job. Dancing is a great workout; she is covered in sweat after performing several dances onstage. The lights overhead radiate a lot of heat, especially when she climbs to the top of the pole and flips herself upside down and performs tricks. She takes pride in the athletic nature of her work, saying that most men couldn't perform the way she does: "You try to get on top of that pole, motherfucker. It's tough!"

Unlike her waitressing jobs, she says she enjoys stripping because she is her own boss. She comes and goes when she wants and doesn't need to report regularly to a supervisor. Depending on her financial situation, Raven has danced anywhere from four times per week to only once in a few months. Reflecting on her work over a beer one afternoon, Raven tells me, "I do it for the money, not for the lifestyle or the men. I don't go there to show my tits because I feel like I have to. It's enjoyable. I love dancing. I love meeting new people, and I've met some friends there too. It's actually kind of nice."

Research on exotic dancing finds that people who frequent strip clubs go not only for sexual excitement but also for attention, for the possibility of interacting with the women workers. Not only do patrons pay to watch women strip but they also pay to be seen by women, to receive their recognition. The best-paid dancers are usually those who are best at creating and conveying feelings of interest, intimacy, and desire for their customers. Conveying these feelings may be a desirable part of the job for Raven, given that many of her past relationships have not been marked by intimacy or mutual recognition. Engaging in a broad spectrum of service work—dancing, escorting, and waitressing—may be Raven's way of connecting with and being recognized by others as a valued, helpful, and appreciated individual.

Raven is sometimes cheerful when she talks about her job, and at other moments she seems distressed and embarrassed by what she perceives as exploitation.

In February, she tells me, "I had one of those moments yesterday where I was actually disgusted with the place where I work. I like to push emotions away, and I don't like to face things. I would just ignore the fact that I was naked in front of everybody, you know what I mean? And then yesterday it just popped in my head. It occurred to me as I was dancing for this customer, 'What the fuck am I doing? This is not what I need to be doing at all.'"

Raven is clearly ambivalent about stripping—she simultaneously loves and hates this job. The passages above highlight the everyday pleasures she gets from dancing but also the disdain and shame she feels for being an exotic dancer. Given the structural factors and social location that have inclined Raven to engage in this kind of labor, her ambivalence, to me, is perfectly logical.

"I'm not dirty like that"

Raven feels no ambivalence, however, when describing herself in relation to the other dancers. Raven is adamant that she is nothing like the other women who work alongside her. She describes the other dancers mostly as shallow, fake, and backstabbing. She takes pride in avoiding hard drugs, even though she works at a club where most of the other girls do crack. Raven is especially proud of herself for not slipping into sex work at the clubs like some other dancers.

While it is technically forbidden, Raven says she sees strippers accepting money to perform sexual acts every night. "In the cabanas," she says, "if you pay the managers off enough, they'll shut their mouth. Anything goes." Some women workers stay in the VIP section of the clubs (Raven calls them "hustlers"), looking to make more money than dancers. Raven says she learned to "get out of their fuckin' way," because these women aim to "make money off of coke and sucking dick and fucking their clients."

Whereas Raven makes roughly $500 a night dancing, she claims hustlers can make $2,000 to $3,000 having sex with people at the strip clubs.

Stories of career strippers across the country with expensive cars and houses circulate amongst dancers. "There was one girl who made like $3,000 one night in Miami," Raven tells me. "I was like, 'What the fuck? I wanna make $3,000.'" At most, Raven tells me, she earned $1,300 for spending time with a man for thirty minutes at the club. Hoping that a big payoff is right around the corner, workers are often kept in the business by these stories of dancers making big money quickly.

Dancers are in constant competition with one another for clients, and drama ensues when dancers disrespect one another. Raven's girl-friend Ginger once got angry at another dancer, so Raven and her friend took revenge on the other woman by flicking quarters at her from their seats at the bar while she danced onstage:

"Bink! Bink! Oooh, this girl got mad! . . . I was like, 'Dude, I'm going to get my ass beat.' It's like, 'Don't fuck with me, or I'll fuck with you.' You gotta hold your own in that type of environment. If somebody starts talking shit, there's always drama, and I try my best to stay out of it. You are competing against different women every single night to make the most money."

Raven works hard to morally distinguish herself from the other dancers—a task that seems logical, and even necessary, in an industry generally considered disreputable. She tells me that there's no such thing as a classy stripper, "except for me. I'm the exception, which is awesome. Because I know myself well enough to know that I'm not like them."

Workers in other bodily trades, such as the boxers Loïc Wacquant documents in his book *Body and Soul*, also use this distancing logic to decry the brutal exploitation of those around them while claiming that they are not working under the same inhumane conditions. Like Raven, they accept this exploitation by convincing themselves that a "big pay-off" awaits them.

This distancing logic also explains the substantial efforts Raven makes to maintain her place in the social hierarchy at work. Raven laughs as she explains that some dancers perform past their prime and are looked down upon by the younger, more attractive dancers. She describes, for example, a Hispanic woman in her forties who tried too hard to look young. According to Raven, the woman had stringy hair that she tried to tease up, and she donned cheap-looking makeup. Raven swears she had "ass implants," since "no one's ass actually looks like that!"

Just as there are hierarchies amongst dancers at a given club, there are also hierarchies amongst clubs in Austin. Customers often choose clubs based on where they live, Raven explains. The nicest bars, according to her, are Perfect 10 up north, Yellow Rose in central Austin, and Palazzio down south. Similar to the racial segregation of the city, Austin's strip clubs are also largely segregated by race. Relying on widely shared racial and ethnic stereotypes, Raven gives me her take on Austin's strip clubs:

"Exposé, always ghetto. Oh man, ick. You walk in, and it smells like sex. It's disgusting. It's small. Yellow Rose, pretty classy, pretty cool—it's a better one. Ecstasy, fully nude, disgusting. . . . I've never been in Chicas Bonitas. I don't have *any* urge. It's this little rundown hole-in-the-wall. I mean this—you'll probably get herpes if you walk in there. It's disgusting. Perfect 10, it's a warehouse. It's bigger than Palazzio. It's fucking ginormous. Rick's, don't ever go to Rick's. It's also very, very, very ghetto. Like, if you look at the person the wrong way, you'll get shot."

Raven tells me that mostly younger white women work in Austin's upscale clubs with slightly better working conditions, while older and racial and ethnic minority women work in the more hazardous establishments. At Raven's upscale club, all the women I saw were young and attractive, and the Hispanic and African American women were dancing to seductive salsa or hip-hop music. In this privileged space, it is likely that dancers who are racial and ethnic minorities are compelled to play up or exoticize their hybrid or mixed-race physique in order to gain attention.

Despite being marginalized herself, Raven still benefits in this industry from being white, young, and beautiful. These features allow her to traverse the boundaries between low-wage service work in the licit and illicit economies with more ease than other young women. She often seeks more socially respectable service jobs during the day, while working at the strip clubs by night. The proportion of time dedicated to each line of work depends not only on how she's currently feeling about dancing but also on her finances and her love life.

In and Out of Dancing

In 2013, at age twenty-two, Raven was hired as a secretary at a luxury spa that belongs to a major resort in town. "My first really stable job," she tells me excitedly. Since Raven was hired at the spa four days a week and with the promise that she would transition to full-time work, she goes back to dance at the club only intermittently. She is thrilled about this new position: "I get my own desk, and my own computer, and my own phone! I am like a *real fuckin' adult!*" Raven explains that she is required to dress "business casual," and she therefore usually chooses to wear Ann Taylor pencil skirts. She tells me she is "the face of the spa" since she sits in the foyer to greet customers and schedule appointments.

Anthropologist Philippe Bourgois suggests that for those like Raven who are adjusting to work in the professional service sector context, "subtle badges of symbolic power" (1996, 161) like one's wardrobe become paramount markers of respectability. For Raven, working at her own desk with a computer and being required to dress formally are visible signs of having "made it." Her joy is palpable to me: this job means that she has a concrete, stable alternative to dancing.

Raven is proud of herself for "getting out of it" and feels bad about herself when she is compelled to go back to dancing every once in a while: "I don't need to be fuckin' bringing myself down. It sucks." A month or two into her new job at the spa, she explains:

"Once you're in it [stripping], it's really tough to get out of [it]. . . . Going from being a dancer to having a normal job and not really dancing as much, I took a *huge* pay cut—I'm talking *huge*. I'm losing $1,500 every two weeks. I made $1,000 a week dancing four days a week, and now I make like $250 a week working four days a week. *Huge* pay cut. It's bad. . . . I can't live like I used to, you know? My lifestyle has changed drastically. I'm broke every other week. . . . I'm not used to not having money."

Raven admits that she returns to dancing when she is running perilously low on cash or has plans and needs money for something fun, like for a recent trip to Dallas for a friend's birthday or for a wristband to attend the South by Southwest music festival in Austin. She tries to pay for groceries, rent, and other necessities solely on the $250 she earns weekly at the spa but often finds that it isn't enough to cover her basic expenses. Raven went to the club one night during the music festival and came home with $250 for four hours of dancing.

This financial safety net continued to come in handy, given that the spa's promise to bring her on as a full-time employee never materialized. In late fall this past year, Raven reported happily that she had moved to a different job at the resort, working as the administrative assistant to the head repairman. This job is finally full-time, and she is making $12 an hour.

At times she dates men who are able to loan her money to replace a dead car battery or give her enough gas money to get to her job at the resort. She is distraught over the few times she has decided to ask for help from her boyfriend. For a partner who is "well socialized," she reflects, it can't be easy for them to take it lightly that she dances at a strip club. Those boyfriends over the past couple of years who can afford to, she says, have been willing to help her out rather than have her "go show [her] tits to old men for forty dollars." At other times her partners have been in financial straits as precarious as hers, so she can't turn to them for help when she needs it. Raven tends to enter into romantic relationships quickly and enthusiastically but moves on to new partners as she looks for someone who has "a less fucked-up life than me."

Slipping Back

After Raven and I had known each other for eight months, we met up on a boiling-hot afternoon in August 2013 at our favorite café after a three-month hiatus. We cheerfully caught up with one another, and I asked if we could start trying to record her employment history. We'd previously talked about her employment in detail, but I was always confusing the timeline, duration, and location of her many jobs. She laughed her sharp laugh and said she didn't blame me, since she had a hard time keeping track of them too. She wrote me a long list, telling me funny, sometimes shocking stories about various bosses and coworkers as she went. Raven then paused for a moment and looked away from me.

She frowned and told me in an uncustomarily quiet voice that she had briefly returned to escorting since moving to Austin in 2010. She'd escorted roughly fifteen times shortly after moving here, a job she'd declared adamantly to me on several occasions that she'd never do again after leaving it behind in Dallas.

Raven says she went back to escorting because she hadn't fully kicked her pill addiction yet, having recently survived sexual assault and a traumatic breakup and having not yet begun therapy. She had been tired of asking her parents for money. So she turned once again to relying on men. She needed money—and, I would guess, the affirmation she got through her evenings spent with her clients—as a way of survival, financially but also emotionally. "I didn't have anybody. . . . These guys were lonely. It was what I was used to. I didn't know anything else, you know?" she explains.

Raven says that escorting in Austin was similar to escorting in Dallas. However, the men in Austin were younger, more respectful, and more accommodating. She took the same approach to finding clients: she would dress up and go to the landmark Driskill Hotel on Sixth Street, Sandra Bullock's bistro where she used to waitress, or to places on the East Side to attract customers. She sometimes went back to their downtown lofts with them but most often stayed at the Omni or the Driskill. Raven says that the W is "*the* place to go" for escorts to seek out and conduct business: "Oh my God, there's so much escorting that goes down there! If I was in the business right now, I would be making thousands of dollars a week at the drop of a hat."

Looking Forward

To date, Raven has worked as a chef's assistant, restaurant hostess, waitress, back-stock manager, pastry chef, line cook, storehouse coordinator, retail assistant, escort, exotic dancer, secretary, and handyman's assistant. Since I have known her, Raven has expressed determination to exit the service sector and embark on a new job path. She still loves to cook. Her interests range from a career as a veterinarian's technician to, most recently, a mechanic.

She toys with the idea of beginning night courses at Austin Community College this year but also dreams of living outside of Texas, somewhere close to the ocean, one day. She rarely attends the music shows that attracted her to Austin in the first place, given their high cost.

Raven lives on the precarious edge in Austin between morally respectable, low-paying work with little autonomy and what some might call immoral, but highly paid work with a great deal of independence. Both are degrading in their own ways.

Raven, like others involved in the sex trade, grapples with both the liberating and oppressive aspects of her work. Sociologist Elizabeth Bernstein suggests that many sex workers see their jobs as both participating in as well as challenging broader structures of class and gender oppression. Bernstein urges us to question "whether engagement in commercial sexual activity always and inevitably constitutes a further injury to those concerned, or whether it might sometimes (or simultaneously) constitute an attempted means of escape from even more profoundly violating social conditions" (2007, 2). Stories like Raven's give us reason to pause and reconsider the moral divides between different body trades like stripping and prostitution—for people who have little but bodily capital to sell—and other working-class jobs. Given the economic options available to a young woman like Raven, what makes one job more or less morally troubling than another? How do we understand ethical issues like coercion and consent for a dancer, or for a waitress? These are questions with no clear answers.

Despite her best efforts, Raven is routinely drawn back to stripping, and even escorting, because of the financial stability it provides. A night of dancing can mean the difference between keeping her apartment in south Austin and being evicted or can enable her to afford gas to get to her administrative assistant job in west Austin. It may also provide her with the interpersonal recognition she has lacked throughout her tumultuous life. Raven recently tells me with pride that she hasn't returned to dance in the past several months because her current job is full-time and, for now, stable.

Over the past year, one of the traits I've come to admire the most about Raven is her unflagging optimism. She is a remarkably "glass-half-full" kind of woman despite what many would label a "glass-half-empty" kind of existence, given her years of hard work and heartache. She refuses to dwell on the precarity or frustrations of her circumstances and tells me, "I *love* Austin. I can't think of a better city to live in." And without a hint of irony, she adds, "I guess I was more privileged than most. I guess it could have been worse."

Recommended Readings

Barton, B. C. 2006. *Stripped: Inside the Lives of Exotic Dancers.* New York: New York University Press. Barton spent five years visiting strip clubs across the United States to paint an intimate picture of the lives of exotic dancers. She gives us a helpful long-term perspective on not only what inspires women to begin stripping for money but also what keeps them in the job year after year. She chronicles both the everyday dangers and rewards of this line of work, depicting a more complicated, nuanced vision of sex work than is usually portrayed in current "sex wars" debates.

Bernstein, E. 2007. *Temporarily Yours: Intimacy, Authenticity, and the Commerce of Sex.* Chicago: University of Chicago Press. Bernstein explores the changing landscape of sexual commerce through an ethnographic study of sex workers, clients, and state actors in San Francisco, Stockholm, and Amsterdam. She maps the ways that postindustrial economic and cultural formations have spurred changes in the meanings, types, and spatial organization of sexual labor.

Price-Glynn, K. 2010. *Strip Club: Gender, Power, and Sex Work.* New York: New York University Press. Price-Glynn conducted an ethnography of one strip club where she worked as a cocktail waitress for fourteen months. Price-Glynn uncovers the intimate working lives of the dancers, owner-manager, bartenders, doormen, DJs, bouncers, and house moms in order to highlight the power dynamics and intersecting inequalities that constitute daily life in a club.

Stoller, R. J., and I. S. Levine. 1996. *Coming Attractions: The Making of an X-rated Video.* New Haven, CT: Yale University Press. This text takes us inside the making of a porn film to reflect upon our puritanical culture's beliefs, fears, and fantasies surrounding sex. By using interviews with people involved in every aspect of the film's production—from performers to producers and directors—we learn about the motivations to create and consume pornography and to pay money for erotic excitement.

Wacquant, L. 2004. *Body and Soul: Notebooks of an Apprentice Boxer.* Oxford: Oxford University Press. Sociologist Löic Wacquant immerses himself for three years in the world of amateur and professional boxing at a local gym in a black neighborhood in the South Side of Chicago. This text is insightful for its illumination of Pierre Bourdieu's concept of "habitus," highlighting the importance of corporeal experiences—"the taste and ache of action"—in the study of social lives and labor.

Zelizer, V. 2007. *The Purchase of Intimacy.* Princeton, NJ: Princeton University Press. Zelizer argues that intimacy and economic activity are closely and routinely intertwined: money not only accompanies intimacy but also sustains it. She demonstrates that everyone uses economic activities to create, maintain, and negotiate intimate ties with other people.

CHAPTER 7

Kumar: Driving in the Nighttime

KATHERINE JENSEN

"What is weird? Why should we keep Austin weird?" Kumar asks me. I don't remember how I defined it—unusual, strange, out of the ordinary, unique—but I remember his response. "But I'm not weird. I'm usual."

In his home country of Nepal, Kumar was an attorney and a college professor. There he taught political science for almost twelve years. He has a BA in law and education, an MA in political science, and a law degree. Now, in the United States, he works as a taxi driver. "The way of life is not like a straight line," he says one day. "It is like the way a snake moves."

The first time I went to his apartment in north Austin near Parmer Lane and North Lamar Boulevard, he answered the door in his pajamas, a soft cotton long-sleeved button-down with matching drawstring pants. He had just woken for our 4:00 p.m. meeting. He works the twelve-hour night shift, from 7:00 p.m. to 7:00 a.m.

During our weekly meetings, incense burned near the cracked balcony door while Kumar's wife, Manu, prepared me Nepalese coffee. I sat on the couch while Kumar sat cross-legged on the floor across the coffee table from me. There we sat, editing Kumar's writings, reading American short stories aloud, and discussing U.S. slang, until it was time to move to the dining room table for my dinner—his breakfast. Kumar's family was always excited to introduce me to new dishes—from *momo* dumplings to *panipuri*, from *papadum* to fresh fruit sprinkled with steak seasoning—or to a variety of foods all called "pickle."

Kumar has a warm, deep laugh that echoes from his belly. A stout, brown-skinned man in his early fifties, he has thick cheeks and a round cleft chin. He wears glasses with rectangular wire frames, and his expression is usually gentle and joyful. His eyes mark him as an inquis-

itive, reflective man. Most of the time he wears loose-fitting, short-sleeved button-down shirts in relaxed prints. He is an attorney and a poet, a professor and student, a devoted father and lover of languages—he speaks Nepali, Hindi, English, German, Urdu, and Maithili—and now, he is a taxi driver.

Driving a Big Van

Kumar asks me, "What does gentleman's club mean?" "Is there any word, night queen? Like that? . . . [For] the girls who are willing to be hired in the nighttime?" "And what is gay?" "And how about woman who dressed like a man?" "Why is bullshit so vulgar word? That is nothing, right? . . . Bull is bull and shit is shit, right?"

Kumar's drive to continue his English training emerges not from an objective need per se—he more than manages to communicate—but from his passion for learning. However, his work as a taxi driver also provides a particular impetus. The English he learns from drunks is very bad, he says, and he often finds it hard to understand drunken speech.

Kumar started as a taxi driver in March 2012. Before that, he worked as a convenience store clerk. "Many taxi drivers used to come to buy coffee, to buy soda, and to get gasoline, and at that time I asked them about the taxi driver's income and the profession of taxi driving." They told him it was better paid and less dangerous than working at the gas station and that there would be "more freedom."

When I ask him if being a taxi driver is everything the other drivers promised, he responds, "The true thing is that as a cabdriver we can earn more than as a cashier at gas station, but this is not less dangerous. . . . But freedom, yes. Nobody can compel me to drive the cab at night."

Kumar believes his job affords him more independence because no one dictates his shifts. Yet the realities of taxi work are bleak. The average Austin taxi driver works twelve hours a day, six or seven days a week, 360 days a year. In spite of this, in 2010 drivers earned on average $800 a month before taxes. That's $2.75 per hour—$4.50 less than the federal minimum wage and roughly $9 less than a recommended living wage in Austin.

Kumar drives a six-seater taxi van, which is a "little bit heavy, and long too," but that makes it safer to drive, he tells me. During the night the drunks "drive very rough," but when they see a "big van, they control themselves; if they see like sedan car, they don't care." It also means he can earn a little bit more money. From 9:00 p.m. to 4:00 a.m. taxi drivers can charge one dollar extra per additional passenger—more seats means more customers.

Between midnight and 3:00 a.m., Kumar drives around downtown or the Rainey Street neighborhood looking for customers. His passengers then take him all around Austin—to the Ramada Inn or Motel 6, to the airport or Chicas Bonitas strip club, or to people's homes near and far from downtown Austin.

The rest of his twelve-hour shift he sits and waits for calls. He and other drivers wait together at transportation hubs, like the Greyhound bus station; at gas stations; at large discount department stores, like Wal-Mart; at grocery stores, like H-E-B; and at big hotels, like the Hilton.

Since "we don't get customers continuously, we have to wait. At that time [we] relax, we read, we surf the Internet, we talk someone." Kumar uses that time to read books and use his phone to "search some news," mainly "political news in Nepal" but about "America too."

Kumar also uses that time to write short stories and poetry in his notebook. He writes poems in English sometimes, but finds it difficult to achieve the rhythm and meter he wants. He has spent his adult life writing ghazal poetry, Urdu-style poems, in Nepali. "I wish I could translate them into English. Nothing is impossible in human being's life."

"The luckiest child in the universe"

"Fifty years ago I was born without any help of a nurse, in a hut in a rural village in eastern Nepal, as the second son of my parents. . . . I was born healthy with the help of nature." In one of the essays he writes for me to practice his English, Kumar remembers his youth in Nepal.

The child of a farmer, Kumar walked three miles barefoot to school everyday. He only wore shorts because his parents couldn't afford long pants. In the summer there, he tells me, it's hot like in Texas. He would run to school across a dry creek as his feet burned from the hot ground. Sometimes he would faint due to the heat, and his friends would revive him by sprinkling him with water they had collected from the manual water pump onto a large taro leaf. That was the way of life. All of his friends were from villages like his, so he didn't think anything of it.

"I was born in a small remote village where there was no electricity, no road, no school. . . . Although it was an undeveloped area, I liked it very much. There wasn't anything to play the popular games like soccer, cricket, volleyball, or basketball. . . . That was why we generally used to play with small sticks. . . . I used to feel that I was the luckiest child in the universe."

"It was an amazing time," he writes.

As a legal asylee with permanent U.S. residency, Kumar cannot return to Nepal. He can't go back until he becomes a U.S. citizen. Since fleeing Nepal in 2006, he has only been back to Asia once, to visit relatives at the India-Nepal border.

Kumar misses a lot about Nepal. He misses relatives and friends. He misses where he was born, where he was raised, and where he played as a child. He misses the woods he used to visit. He misses the school where he used to teach and the college where he used to study. He misses the ground where he used to play. While reminiscing about Nepal, he tells me, "Soil is the same, but importance of the soil is different." He tries to explain to me what he means.

"The water in a bowl, and the water in a river are same—H_2O. . . . But when you put a fish from a river out and take it in the water of the bowl, the fish is not happy. It wants to go to the river, not in the bowl."

He continues, "I was like a fish in a river in Nepal, because of culture, because of language, because of importance. Everybody used to know me as professor or as attorney—it was little bit high[er] profile than cabdriver in the nighttime. . . . I used to pass my time by doing some good job, right? But here I think I am the fish in the water . . . in the bowl."

"But you know," Kumar adds, "at that time we have to forget where we are. If you forget where you are, then you can be happy, right?"

"The stomach is something"

When Kumar and his wife, Manu, came to Austin, they stayed first with friends until they found their own apartment at Manor Road and Cherrywood in east Austin. But Kumar didn't like the area. Though his portrayal is objectively inaccurate, Kumar draws strong moral boundaries between himself and those who live in east Austin: "Most of the people who live there are unemployed, and they have got leisure time to hang [around], from here to there. They walk on the road, they struggle, they fight, they use drugs, they get mad sometimes."

When Kumar and Manu first arrived in the United States, they didn't have work permits, social security numbers, or green cards. But they "had to work for survival." What savings they had brought lasted only two months. They walked the city on foot, looking for places they could apply for work, while being honest that they had no work permits. Finally a Pakistani man offered them jobs at a convenience store, Manu as cashier and Kumar as cashier/stocker, but he paid them less than he paid other people. They didn't have a car, and they didn't know how to drive. It was horrible waiting for the bus late at night, Kumar tells me. And Sunday there was no bus, so they had to walk three or four miles for work. It was "really terrible."

After four years on the East Side they moved to south Austin, where they worked as cashiers at a dollar store. There Kumar and Manu worked the same twelve-hour shift. "It was too busy . . . was too much." But "the stomach is something." They stayed in south Austin for almost a year, at Bluff Springs Road and William Cannon. After that they moved to the Rundberg area in north Austin, where Kumar worked as a convenience store clerk.

They moved again, farther north to where they live now, for their son and daughter. Now their eighteen-year-old daughter, Sobika, goes to a school she can walk to, and the area "is peaceful." When Kumar tells me what he likes about living farther north, he highlights how it differs from the ways he imagines east Austin. "We don't see any people walking, hanging outside with beer, smoking cigarettes." But west Austin, where the white and wealthy concentrate, is still his favorite part of the city because of "the hills, the windy roads, and [the] people who live [there]."

"I flew from my land"

"So when should we meet?" I ask. "Wednesdays are best," he says. Kumar explains: Tuesday and Thursday are physical therapy; Friday, Saturday, and Sunday are busy for driving; "and Monday I want to take rest."

"What's your physical therapy for?" I ask.

"For back pain," he says.

"For back pain, from the taxi?"

"Hmm, from the taxi, yes. . . . Not only for driving but also for physical torture in Nepal."

Even though Kumar had spoken publically of being tortured when I first met him when he served on a panel about refugees in Austin, I had fretted over how long I should wait before asking about that part of his life in more detail. And then, on only our second visit together, we stumbled into it.

"Did they hurt your back?" I ask.

"Hmm, yeah. I have been imprisoned three years and arrested by the police like four times, and each time they arrested me, they beat me up, severely. With sticks, with whips—whips for the horse, you know whips?"

"Yeah, for horses."

"They tied my legs in the rod of the window, you know? Window rod? We have got window with rod, iron rod. . . . And then tied my legs, both legs, and hanged, hanged me in the window rod, and they beat me in my feet."

Kumar motions to the soles of his feet, not knowing the word. They beat him there, he says.

He continues, "And they beat me with the whip for the horses, and it was dipped in water before two—two hours before—so that can be . . . could be thick and heavy to beat."

"So it absorbed the water?" I ask.

"Yes. If it is just water, it is soft. And heavy too, when it is—when they beat with that soft whips it hurts more. . . . They beat my belly."

Kumar was sixteen the first time he was arrested, younger than his daughter is now. When he was arrested the second time he was nineteen. The third and fourth times, twenty-seven. Kumar was the leader of the students' union and president at his university for two years. Kumar criticized "the activities of the king against the people, against the students." "It was long time ago," he says.

But Kumar did not experience torture and imprisonment only under the monarchy. With the rise of the Maoist Party, the violence continued. The communist party repeatedly petitioned him to serve as a judge for the Maoist court, but he refused. They abducted him and tortured him, but still he refused. "Especially, they threatened the teachers, lawyers, professors, doctors, to collect money, to make them [members]. . . . That is why they tortured me."

The experiences of torture suffered by Kumar reflected the larger political realities in Nepal. Over the last two decades, Nepal has seen rapid political changes. Nepal was a monarchy from 1768 until 2008. During the 1990s a communist movement challenged the absolute monarch. In 1996 a civil war began that lasted a decade. The Communist Party of Nepal fought violently to replace the monarchy with a people's republic. In a country with a contemporaneous population of twenty-three million, more than twelve thousand people lost their lives during the Nepalese Civil War.

In an essay, Kumar wrote,

One evening in 2003, I was returning from teaching at the high school and the Maoists stopped me. They beat me with bamboo sticks and stabbed me in my right palm. . . . [T]hey left me in the street bleeding. . . . I moved to the capital city of Nepal, Kathmandu, in search of a peaceful life. But the situation was not favorable. The Maoists found me in Kathmandu and I came to know that they had been following me the whole time.

In February 2005 King Gyanendra—recently instated after a massacre in the royal palace had killed the former king, queen, and seven other members of the royal family—dismissed the entire government in attempts to quash the violent Maoists.

Kumar continues,

One evening in 2006, when I was returning from . . . a rally . . . for multi-party democracy, a cadre of Maoists detained me. One of them gave an order to kill me and all the rest ran towards me with bamboo sticks ready to beat me to death. I ran fast towards a small village. . . . I was beat up heavily on the way. . . . Upon making it to the village, the Maoist cadre stopped chasing me. I had wounds, lacerations, and swelling all over my body, especially my face. . . . After that it was really a very hard time for me.

Under the weight of the 2006 democracy movement, the king agreed to relinquish power to the people. But the new state has been rife with political deadlock, and the Maoists continue to jockey for political power. No government in Nepal has survived for more than two years since 1991.

In 2013 Nepal ranked 157th out of 186 countries on the United Nations Human Development Index—the lowest of any country in Asia. Its ranking places it a few spots below Senegal and only a few above Haiti.

Confusing Questions

The following is an excerpt from Kumar's poem "Oh Mother! I Will Return" (March 12, 2013):

The midnight was dark
Like boiled black sour juice spilled all around
The peaceful and serene atmosphere
Was being speared and cut open
By the loud fires and furies of the cruel guns
To spread the kingdom of cruelty
And finishing the lives of so many helpless ones!
They were searching for me to put out the light of my life
Oh mother! When you said to me:
"At the time of confusion and fights save yourself
At the time of famine save the seeds of grains"
Saying so, you had sent me through the window
Up to the highest stair of our house
Sent me on an unknown journey

Kumar came to the United States in 2006 on a temporary visitor visa. But he had no plan to return. It was already too much, he says. "It was impossible to return to my land at that time, so finally I decided to apply for asylum," because "if I extended my visa, it would be another six month, but it would not be forever." In early 2007 he sent his application to the immigration office in Houston.

Kumar got a Nepalese interpreter to help with the interviews because at that time it was hard for him to understand American pronunciation. But while the Nepalese interpreter could speak English, he was "not the most educated." At Kumar's interview the immigration officer asked Kumar about the political condition in Nepal. Because he was a professor of political science, Kumar was expected to explain the "political culture, political ideology, and what I taught for the students at university." But the interpreter couldn't translate Kumar's explanation—he didn't know the words. Kumar told the officer that the interpreter was "not competent."

"And then what happened? What did the officer say?" I ask.

"Then officer gave me a letter telling me that they were going to decide the case. As soon as they decide case, then I'll get the reply. But it took like two to three years," Kumar replies.

"So then they didn't have another meeting with you?"

"No."

"With a better interpreter?"

"No, no."

When the interview ended, the officer gave Kumar no time frame in which his case would be decided. Two or three years passed, he says, and he tried to get information, sending email requests, only to receive again the same letter: "We are going to decide, and after the decision we let you know."

Three years went by. He contacted a local nonprofit organization, which he had heard about from Nepalese friends. The nonprofit provided him an attorney. Before that, he had struggled through the application process alone. Through the attorney, Kumar learned that by law if the U.S. government does not decide your asylum case within 150 days, then they must provide the asylum seeker with a social security card and a work permit. Kumar had already waited three years—over 1,000 days—without legal documentation when he found this out. He happily quit the dollar store.

Only after getting an attorney did U.S. Citizenship and Immigration Services (USCIS) decide his case. Kumar sees this as no accident.

He believes the pressure his attorney placed on USCIS was the reason they finally reached a decision. "So otherwise it would have taken longer?" I ask. "Yes!"

The decision was denial. Kumar appealed, with the help of a professor and students from St. Mary's School of Law, and went to the immigrations court in San Antonio. The state attorney asked some "problematic" and "confusing" questions, some repeatedly.

"They say, 'Why did you provide money to the Maoist?' Then I answered, 'I didn't provide any money to the Maoist.' 'But you have written something like that in your story.' 'If somebody grabs my money from my pocket and runs away, that's not my fault. I was not agreed to give them money, right? They stole my money! They captured my money. That was not my *will* to give them the money to support the people's movement of the Maoist.' And he repeatedly asked that question. There is one provision, if anyone has provided economic support to the rebellions he or she cannot get political asylum in the United States. . . . He wanted to fail me on that basis."

A month later Kumar received news from the judge. In total, it took Kumar roughly four years to be granted asylum. And only after that could he apply to be reunited with his children.

Reunited and Overwhelmed

Kumar has been lucky enough to be together with Manu, his wife of twenty-one years, for this whole American journey. But when they fled Nepal in 2006, their children stayed behind with family. When I first met Kumar, it had only been seven months since he had been reunited with his children.

"We missed seeing them grow from children to young adults," Manu tells me. Their daughter is now eighteen years old, and their son is twenty-one. When Kumar and Manu left, they were eleven and fourteen. Back then there was no Skype, and they had no computers, so they talked on the phone twice a week. But it was hard since daytime here is nighttime there. When people would fly back to Nepal, Kumar and Manu would give them letters to take to their children. One night while preparing *momo* dumplings, their daughter, Sobika, tells me that her mother cried all the time.

Once his case was approved, Kumar applied for his children to come to the United States. But immigration services misplaced his file for six months. So he applied again, but then they found the original file. It should have been done in three months, Kumar tells me, but it took almost a year. Despite the long delays in his asylum case, and the bureaucratic "hiccup" with his children's visas, he understands these experiences not as an integral aspect of the way U.S. immigration services functions but instead as forgivable mistakes.

"Everybody can do mistake. Mistake, error, is acceptable," Kumar tells me. "It happens sometimes. In my case it happened."

"I'm little bit cool guy, you know? I was not like this, but I'm cool now because of the practices in my life. My circumstances made me cool, so I was not frustrated because I didn't have any option. I couldn't do anything. . . . If you want to climb the mountain, or the Mount Everest, you have to cross many camps: base camp, first camp, second camp, third camp. If the weather is bad for the second camp, you have to stay in the first camp," he says, laughing.

"So U.S. Immigration was like bad weather?" I ask.

He laughs. "Yeah."

The day his children arrived "was extremely happy day for us." "They are overwhelmed, right? And almost me too! And yes, Manu!" Kumar remembers. "And I hardly recognized them as my children, since they were tall," he tells me amidst his laughter. "It was very happy moment."

As Kumar drove his son, Rabin, and his daughter, Sobika, to their new home, they were amazed by everything. When they opened the refrigerator they were surprised to find it full, like in a "restaurant," Kumar tells me, chuckling and reminiscing. When they first arrived, Rabin used to ask questions like "what is this wall made of?"

Now, reunited, morning time is very important in their home.

"My son is more talkative than my daughter, and he asks *a lot* of questions, you know? He is penetrating intellectual. . . . When I come in the morning, he sits there, and he starts asking twenty questions: 'How was the night? Was there any bad guy? How was the income? Did anybody escape from you without paying this time? How many customers did you get? Was there any particular story? What did you eat? Did you finish the [food] bag? Did you drink all the water? Biscuits?' Like that. And daughter has only two more questions: 'Are you okay? Might be tired, right?'"

Kumar laughs. He continues, "That is the natural power, you know? That is special nature of human being. Someone is penetrating, someone is okay, someone is dull, someone doesn't like to bother. My son doesn't care how tired I am. I must give the answers to him."

Where Are You From?

Throughout his life Kumar has been interviewed and questioned—by his son in the mornings; by law students, attorneys, and immigration officials during the asylum process; undoubtedly by those who tortured and imprisoned him; and now by me. But his job also offers him up as an object of intrigue and inquisition to his (often drunk) passengers.

Kumar is always ducking and dodging questions on the job. Sometimes he asks if they're going to pay for him to answer their questions. But he can't be silent "because they [keep] on asking question: 'Don't you like to talk with me? What's wrong with you?'"

The questions are usually the same. How long have you been here? Do you like Austin? But far more than any other—Where are you from?

Kumar has come to make a game out of it. He gives them four chances to guess where he is from, and after each wrong answer he gives them a hint. When you miss the fourth time, he says, "I will tell you my original country, after that you have to tip me one dollar more okay?" They always agree, because "one dollar is nothing, right? Just fun, right?"

His customers often guess he is from Pakistan, Afghanistan, Bangladesh, Bhutan, or India. Sometimes they guess he is from Morocco or the Philippines. The hints similarly vary. "My parents are neither Muslim nor Christian." "You have already read something very important about my country. . . . *Everybody* has read something about my country." I am not Bhutanese, but "all of the Bhutanese refugee speak same mother language as I speak." But the last hint is usually the easiest one: "I'm that small country in the world where most of the Himalayas and the Mount Everest lie." Then everyone gets it: "Oh, you're from Nepal!" "Then shake hands and be happy, that is the game," Kumar says.

Why does Kumar play the game? "Throw some piece of bone to the dog so that it cannot come to bite you," he says. "I want to engage them in that game so that they cannot talk like nonsense, vulgar words, [or start] any arguments."

It also allows him to maintain some bit of say in his work. Another way he maintains control is by not always answering honestly. Sometimes he concocts stories about his life. Other times he capitalizes on stereotypes against other nationalities.

"When the customer is like white but young, of like twenty-five year old, and they are drunk and with tattoo and they behave like differently," and they ask Kumar where he is from, he responds, "I am from Iraq."

"Because they scared from Iraqi. They never scared from Nepalese, because Nepalese are not like that. They are not violent like Pakistani, Iraqi," he tells me. "They afraid of Muslim. So I say, 'I am from Iraq' or 'Pakistan.' Then they kept silent."

"Why do you say that?" I ask.

"That answer saves me! So I invented those answer[s] by practice."

Customers also ask him incredibly personal questions, often of a sexual nature, "which I can't answer in front of my family." It makes him feel "very uneasy." His passengers make his twelve-hour shift all the more taxing as they force him to perform through conversation—marking him as their foreign entertainer and sometimes their verbal punching bag.

"Nonsense talking"

Kumar has been "mentally hurt" on the job. This is when someone "starts mistreating, telling this, telling that, blah blah, like that." This "blah blah," or what he also calls "nonsense talking" is code for profanities launched at him. "They say 'fuck you,' 'mother fucker,' like that, frequently." If "somebody is abusing me by words that is also abusing, right?"

On another occasion Kumar shares, "If I run after those words, then

I cannot work in the nighttime. . . . In Nepal there is one law . . . that prohibits you to speak those type of vulgar words. If you speak those type of vulgar words to someone, he can sue you! But here, is there no law? . . . Anybody can tell anybody like those type of words? . . . That is not the civilization. . . . Speaking like that type of vulgar words, without good mouth is not . . . the characteristics of civilization."

These passengers are so drunk, Kumar says, that they often forget their names and their addresses. And they not only yell profanities at Kumar, they also sometimes vomit in his cab. When a customer vomits in his cab, Kumar not only has to pay to have the cab cleaned, he also loses the rest of the night's earnings. He can't pick up any new customers. But when he asks for fifty or a hundred dollars to cover the cost of cleaning, his drunk passengers don't usually acquiesce. One woman yelled back, "But this is your job! You can clean it up. Why should I pay for that!?"

In his cab Kumar struggles to dodge prodding questions and pricking profanities. Sometimes he has to dodge bodies. In one essay, Kumar writes of how a teenage girl tried to commit suicide by running in front of his cab. Thankfully, "my cab was pretty new, and it has got hard brake[s]."

On another occasion, Kumar tells me of an incident when he drove six female college students. "They are like totally drunk, and one of the student girl, she was in the front seat . . . she came like this." He motions how she had pulled her shirt down to expose herself. "Hey, do you want to touch my booby?" she said. "What can I say?" Kumar tells me. "Relax, baby, relax. Please relax," he said to her. But she leaned over with her shirt pulled down and pressed her breast against his mouth.

"I told her, 'Relax, please. Please relax! I have to drive. I could hit something there. Don't disturb me.' 'Then touch my something,' [she said]."

Kumar sees this as abuse. "You don't have any right to abuse me, in any sense. I am from Nepal, I don't have that type of culture."

"Sometimes we meet snakes"

Not all of Kumar's experiences as a taxi driver are so seemingly innocuous. Kumar deals with a particularly "uncivilized"—a term he uses frequently in our meetings—version of Austin by working at night. His role as punching bag is sometimes more than metaphorical.

"One white, middle-aged guy was my customer one night," Kumar starts to tell me. Kumar picked him up from Bikinis Sports Bar, and the guy "was little bit drunk, and he had got the tattoos all over the arm and back and leg, and he was alone.

"I started driving my cab, and on the way he started using the vulgar words, expressions. And I react to him, immediately, so he punched me on my face, while I was driving. Then I thought he might hit me more than one time—he might harm me. That is why I immediately parked my car somewhere and opened the door, and he also opened the door and [came] out and started fighting with me. I was alone, and it was midnight. There wasn't anybody, and I did not get any chance to call the police. So he was little bit drunk, and he beat me one or two times, and I started beating him too. I didn't care about the law at that time because I had to defend myself. . . . I fought him up—I beat him well, okay? He was bleeding from his mouth, but he was not running away. He was still fighting with me. I knocked him down and kicked him well till he became little bit unconscious. And then I drove off. I did not [notify] the police."

Moments like this have led Kumar to explain that working as a cabdriver may provide more freedom, but it is not less dangerous than working at a convenience store—even though convenience stores are one of the most dangerous workplaces in the United States. While Kumar's adulthood in Nepal was marked by torture because of his belief in democracy, now in the United States violence is for him an unresolvable occupational risk: "That is a part of our life.

"It happens in the nighttime. Mostly in the nighttime."

"If we feel unsafe"

A taxi driver's ability to avoid these types of situations is limited. There is a difficult balance, which I could never quite grasp, between Kumar's obligation to accept certain customers—because otherwise "it is discrimination, and that is against the law"—and his rejection of others in attempts to safeguard his life and livelihood. Discussing one instance where he refused service, Kumar tries to explain: "We cannot discriminate people on the basis of skin color, on the basis of like female or gent[leman], or disabled, or the beggars. But if we feel unsafe with you, I can refuse you. . . . That's in my heart, what tells me the truth."

About once a week, Kumar tells me, someone runs off without paying the fare. When Kumar suspects someone "might flee from [his] cab without paying," he makes the customer pay the fare in the beginning. "That's okay, if you deny, but I can't serve you. You can call another taxi."

One night Kumar picked up a male customer, about twenty-five years old, and asked that he pay the fare in the beginning. But it turned out "he was gentleman, not the bad guy." But "I thought he might be bad guy. So I behaved him like that." In the end Kumar apologized to the man. But he still felt guilty, he tells me. "But I continue that. I have to continue that.

"If you close your eyes and grab something, it might be pain, it might be something else, right? So in the nighttime . . . we cannot recognize any people whether he or she is good or bad." While Kumar often takes calls that other cabdrivers won't—a transgendered customer or a destitute elderly black man from the hospital—he also tries not to drive those who make him uneasy.

"Collect honey even from the shit of human"

Kumar is thus not without preconceptions. He shares in and acts on local prejudices in order to protect his life and livelihood, oftentimes employing stereotypes of brown and black men, and any man covered in tattoos, as imperfect but necessary guides. Kumar's prejudices serve not only as a guide to staying safe but also have a particular relational purpose.

"Civilized freedom is better than uncivilized freedom."

"And what would uncivilized freedom be?" I ask.

"To speak vulgar words, to be prostitutes, to take bribes, right? . . . And homelessness is also uncivilized too. . . . Because they have not been evaluating the importance of their lives, right? They have been spoiling their life."

By embracing this narrative of "uncivilized freedom," Kumar affirms his own civility. He is civilized because he does not curse, or beg, or offer sexual favors for money. Kumar asserts that his life has not lost meaning even though he's not the activist and teacher he once was. He comes to believe he is not spoiling his life.

"I learn something from them," Kumar tells me.

"They have been doing that critical and unprestigious work to survive. Then why . . . should I not drive the cab to make my survival?

That's one type of strength in me, right? They have got the chance, they can speak English well, they have no problem, they don't need to learn speaking, writing, or listening. They are like citizen in the United States—they have got every privilege, they can get loan to study, right? . . . They can be teacher, they can be engineer, they can be professor. However, they are not going that way, and they are going that way to spoil their life to make some bullshit money, for survival, right? Then I am doing good job. I'm driving the cab. I am not doing prostitut[ion], right? That is one type of learning."

He continues, "The bee collect honey even from the shit of human. Yes! There is one particle in the shit of human—how do you say shit of human? Any word there in particular?"

Although Kumar dedicates himself to principles of tolerant acceptance, his construction and maintenance of a moral hierarchy of the civilized and the uncivilized mitigates his move from attorney and professor to taxi driver. Even though his work no longer provides the prestige it once did, these judgments help him locate himself in a stratified moral universe where he is not on the bottom rungs.

"With that hammer"

Taxi drivers in Austin deal with the challenges of the job in different ways. Kumar tells me that other Hindus will kiss Ganesh, the remover of obstacles, to protect themselves and stay awake. But he thinks that's silly (even though his kids put a Ganesh in his car) because "Ganesh isn't going to keep me awake. Only I can keep me from napping." Kumar doesn't believe in God or in heaven or hell. "Heaven and hell are here."

Since the fight, and over time, Kumar has learned more tricks to protect himself and his livelihood. For example, if a possible passenger doesn't tell him "the [exact] address," he suspects them. Or, "If they are like 75 percent drunk," then "I play the music in the radio" so "they forget to ask questions."

Not everything Kumar learns about the job—the tricks of the trade—comes from his own experience. Taxi drivers swap stories. "When we are out of downtown, we stay in one place and wait for the trips . . . for the safety. When we are like five or six, nobody can disturb us." In those moments, the drivers talk and share anecdotes.

Kumar recounts, "One driver told me a story: he has got an American gentleman, and . . . he started telling like nonsense, you know? And he tried to quarrel with him, and the driver was alone of course, and then he directed him towards . . . [a] dead end.

"The customer was about to punch him," Kumar continues. But "the driver has got a hammer underneath the seat in case of any danger. And he pulled out that hammer, and he was about to beat the customer with that hammer, but the customer opened other side of door and jumped the fence and ran away. He didn't get money, but he saved his life."

The driver had shared this story with Kumar to try and teach him how to be safe at night. "So he was teaching me, 'Try to keep something with you; in case of any danger it may [be] useful. Try not to hit any-body, but in case of danger you—you can use that.' And he showed me the hammer."

But Kumar doesn't want to keep something, like the hammer, with him.

In spite of the violent attacks Kumar has sometimes dodged—and sometimes suffered—he is unwavering in his perspective on bearing arms. He still holds to an ideal image of the state, despite being tortured and illegally detained—multiple times—in his home country. When I ask him in late February 2013 if there is any U.S. news story he finds particularly interesting, he brings up the renewed debate about gun control that emerged after the Sandy Hook Elementary School shoot-ing in Newtown, Connecticut. "In my opinion, all the citizens should not keep the gun for their safety, because our safety is the concern of the state. Why do we have police and the army—they have to save us, right?" He continues, "Gun is not one of the aspect of human right."

When I ask him if he ever worries about any of his clients carrying a gun, he shares that "sometimes they ask if you have gun." If they are "the drunk and the criminal people," he says he has an AK-47 hidden somewhere in the car to shoot anyone who tries to hurt him. And after that, he says, they keep silent.

Around His Neck

One incident shook Kumar more than any other. It challenged how he sees the state and how far the tricks of the trade can take him in main-taining his safety. Before sitting down cross-legged on the floor in front of the coffee table, as is his custom, Kumar disappears into the back bedroom. He comes back with his English-Nepali dictionary, which is blue but worn white at the edges from years of use, and with three small

pieces of paper he calls his "evidence": a list of his fares for the night, the dispatch information from the cab company, and the business card of an Austin Police Department officer.

He begins to write down slowly and purposefully for me all the facts: the date, time, dispatch trip number, client's name and phone number, cost of the fare, pick-up address, drop-off address, police officer's name, and case number.

It was 6:00 a.m. and the last trip of his shift. "I was about to stop driving, but I received a call from [the cab] company." When he went to pick up the customer, named James, Kumar was suspicious of him. Kumar thought he "might be bad guy," but since it was a "trip given by the [the cab] company . . . it won't hurt me, so let's try." "When we receive call from [the cab company] we don't suspect anybody because . . . they have got every information, like name, phone number, from which place to which place, like that." That was why, even though Kumar had a bad feeling, he let James into his cab.

Many small things made Kumar suspicious. Even though it was chilly out—fifty degrees—and Kumar was in a light jacket, James wore a T-shirt and shorts. And he didn't have any belongings with him. When Kumar asked for the address, James said, "Like I-35 and Rundberg." Using what he had learned after picking up the guy from Bikinis Sports Bar, he told James, "It doesn't work like that, my friend. You have to tell me the exact address." Following another one of his tricks to maintain his livelihood, Kumar asked James to pay the fare in advance. James paid the thirty dollars up front. But, unlike most passengers, James didn't speak to Kumar during the trip. James sat looking into his empty hands.

When Kumar parked his cab, James slid from the passenger's side to the driver's side to exit. "I suspected him and looked at the mirror, and he was about to go out, and then I realized myself that he is not going to harm me. He looked outside, and he was about to go outside.

"But all of a sudden he grabbed my neck." Kumar crosses his own arms over his neck, both of his elbows in front of his face, to demonstrate how the man grabbed him. "And he told me, 'Give me all the money. Give me all the money. I have gun and a knife. I can kill you.'" James held Kumar's neck so tightly that he couldn't move his head or even speak. "I could not save myself. . . . I was not free. He locked my neck with my seat.

"I just gave him all the money. He wanted to get more money, and I showed him two bags on the floor." One of the bags was his camouflage-colored lunch cooler. The other was a black bag with a book, his wallet, and his diary. In that stolen diary were all his jottings from on the job— short stories, ideas, poems, notes, and thoughts from life.

"[By] that time I was almost half unconscious," Kumar tells me. James was suffocating him.

When James grabbed Kumar's neck, Kumar lost control of the cab. The van went through a mailbox and toward someone's home. "Fortunately I jammed the brake, and there wasn't any accident," but dogs started barking from the commotion. The husband and wife who lived in the house came out just as James was running away.

The police arrived twelve minutes later. "They came and took pictures, fingerprints, and DNA." But, two months later, the case is still open. Kumar keeps calling and emailing the police officer assigned to his case. "He's a nice guy" who is "very responsive," but there has been no progress.

Kumar is disappointed. "The United States can find Osama bin Laden in Pakistan," he says, "[but] they can't find the guy whose name is there? Whose phone number is there? Whose voice has been recorded in [the cab] office?" Kumar expresses his surprise. "I used to think there isn't any discrimination in the United States. But I started revising my thinking. . . . I don't know what's going on.

"Because of insecurity, I moved from my land to the United States. But in the United States . . ." Kumar trails off. He does not finish the thought that weighs heavy on his heart.

After that experience, Kumar stopped driving at night. "I was totally nervous," he tells me. "It took almost one month to get back" to driving during the nighttime. "Slowly, slowly, I gained my confidence again."

Kumar talked to the president of the cab company about getting a partition barrier put up between the driver and the passengers. They could do it for $400, the president told him. But Kumar isn't worried about the $400.

"The matter is that if I get that barrier in my cab . . . whoever comes in [would] start asking, 'Why do you have this?' And then [I] answer him or her, and then they'll say, 'Was there any incident with you? Sorry,' and explain like six hours." Kumar lets out a chuckle. But it saddens me. He doesn't want to install the barrier because he knows it would open him up to a whole new series of prodding questions from his customers. Because he doesn't want to continue to relive the robbery in its retelling, he is unable to stop it from happening again. In spite of all he has learned by practice, there is no trick or barrier to protect him from both the mental and physical abuses of driving at night.

Not Responsible

I ask Kumar about the financial consequences of what happened. "Did [the cab company] give you any of the money [back], or is it just money lost?"

"No, no," he says. "They said, 'You are individual driver. You can contact the police and see what they can do.'" Even though they had been the ones to offer the trip to Kumar, the cab company said, "We are not responsible for any call."

In the late 1970s taxi drivers became classified as independent contractors rather than company employees. With this industry shift, all financial risks—accidents, slow business, illness, economic downturns, robberies—were transferred to the driver.

The income for cabdrivers can be meager and volatile, and it is often under threat from run-offs and robberies. But the expenditures are definite. In 2010 the average Austin taxi driver paid to a cab franchise every week: a lease fee ($190), a terminal fee ($153), credit card surcharges ($20), and an ad valorem tax ($5). Some drivers paid weekly driver's deposits ($35) and maintenance deposits ($40). Taxi drivers also paid for fuel ($183), cleaning ($15), and maintenance ($14). And because they are self-employed, drivers pay their own Social Security and Medicare taxes, or 15.3 percent of their earnings.

But even though cabdrivers in Austin are "independent contractors" and "self-employed," they cannot apply independently for the permits to operate a taxi. To alleviate the state's legal and administrative burdens, the city of Austin grants these permits not to individual drivers but to cab franchises. These franchises (of which there are only three) then re-sell them to drivers for a profit. Because the city regulates the taxi industry in this way, drivers can't hold their own chauffeur permits, nor transfer them from one franchise to another. Austin modeled its franchise system after the one in Los Angeles, as have other cities, like Atlanta, Pittsburgh, Denver, and Kansas City.

Always Student, Always Teacher, Never Expert

Kumar loves the rare moments when he still gets to teach. He has fondly recounted to me teaching mathematics to his children. He emphasizes that when the student attorneys came from San Antonio to his home, "they had been learning from me too. . . . They did my job, but they also learned from me. . . . That's good. I am very happy to explain something to the student so they can learn too."

But Kumar knows that is not his life anymore. "That is why I am not expert for anything. . . . For anything! Language, politics, law." He laughs. "Sociology." More laughter.

Another night, as we eat, I ask Kumar if he wants to go back to teaching political science someday. He seems determined that what matters now is his children's education, not his own. He needs to support them. He doesn't want them to be deprived of anything.

Kumar and Manu's daughter, Sobika, is in her senior year of high school. She is busy preparing for and stressing about the SATs, applying for college, and doing well enough in school to get scholarships. She works one day a week eyebrow threading at Lakeline Mall. Their son, Rabin, is taking classes at Austin Community College toward a degree in software engineering. He works on call as a stocker at a convenience store on South Lamar, just as his father did.

Anything but Usual

Though Kumar says he's not "weird," he is anything but usual. But while his particular life has twisted and turned, like the way a snake moves, in a most unique way, the great "exams" or "slaps" of his life—as he often calls them—are painfully real in their commonness. Much of Kumar's life confirms the usual state of affairs for immigrants—and asylum seekers in particular—in the United States, and for taxi drivers in cities across the country. The majority of Austin's taxi drivers are men who were not born in the United States, and the average driver is struggling to support two children.

Kumar doesn't know how often violent robberies happen, because "nobody tells." Maybe they are ashamed or embarrassed. Perhaps drivers prefer anecdotes that end well, with them outwitting their challenging passengers, as with the hammer story. Kumar has only shared his own robbery experience with his closest driver friend, Daniel. It had happened to Daniel too. "That is why he quit driving the nighttime."

Driving a taxi in Austin is precarious work. In the event of car accidents, even when they are not at fault, taxi drivers have no legal recourse or support. There are no regular pay increases, no benefits, and no insurance plans. There is no safety net in the event of poor earnings. There is no job security. Taxi drivers in Austin do not earn overtime or accrue vacation. They have no retirement.

And this precarity offers little promise for financial gain. In 2010, according to a local report, 12 percent of Austin taxi drivers faced eviction or foreclosure; 38 percent had utilities turned off or threatened to be turned off; and 43 percent of drivers had to borrow money to pay their bills.

But what does the future hold for Kumar? Once, he told me he wanted to move to New York City for a few years for the life experience—to "experience the beauty, the situation." He wants to travel through Mexico, Brazil, and Argentina someday and is picking up Spanish quickly—"necesito hablar poquito español." And for work? Maybe start a business, maybe a "convenience store," a "dollar store, or restaurant." When he is most taken away by his deepest desires, he tells me, "I think next job would be my writings." He hopes to write his own book about the United States. He wants to prepare future Nepalese immigrants for the realities of life in this country.

Recommended Readings

Bohmer, C., and A. Shuman. 2008. *Rejecting Refugees: Political Asylum in the 21st Century*. New York: Routledge. This book uncovers the many challenges asylum seekers face during the asylum application process in Great Britain and the United States.

Gambetta, D., and H. Hamill. 2005. *Streetwise: How Taxi Drivers Establish Customers' Trustworthiness.* New York: Russell Sage Foundation. The authors explain how taxi drivers learn to protect themselves by assessing whether or not to trust the strangers who are their potential clients.

Kenney, D. N., and P. G. Schrag. 2008. *Asylum Denied: A Refugee's Struggle for Safety in America.* Berkeley: University of California Press. The compelling first-person narrative of a Kenyan political refugee and his journey to find safe haven.

Legal Assistance to Microenterprises Project. 2010. *Driving Austin, Driving Injustice: A Report on the Working Conditions of Taxi Drivers in Austin.* Texas RioGrande Legal Aid. The majority of the statistics and descriptive data on taxi work in this chapter come from this study.

Mathew, B. 2008. *Taxi! Cabs and Capitalism in New York City.* Ithaca, NY: Cornell University Press. A grim account of the economics and exploitative nature of the taxicab industry, but also an assessment of what is possible when taxi drivers join together to improve their working conditions.

Ramji-Nogales, J., A. I. Schoenholtz, and P. G. Schrag. 2011. *Refugee Roulette: Disparities in Asylum Adjudication and Proposals for Reform.* New York: New York University Press. This study reveals the shocking extent to which the U.S. asylum system is a game of chance in which asylum case decisions are influenced by random factors relating to the decision makers.

Samarov, D. 2011. *Hack: Stories from a Chicago Cab.* Chicago: University of Chicago Press. A Russian immigrant and trained painter, Dmitry Samarov shares tales and drawings from his work as a taxi driver in Chicago.

CHAPTER 8

Ethan: A Product of the Service Industry

KATHERINE SOBERING

Ethan, thirty-four, is a tall man with brown skin, stylish, short black hair, and a trimmed beard. "My mom is black, my dad is German," he told me during one of our first meetings at a local coffee shop. A gay man active in Austin's vibrant queer community, Ethan described himself when we first met as being in a "limbo state": he was getting ready to go back to school to finish his bachelor's degree, working a couple of part-time service jobs, and "single, on the market, but not desperate!" Ethan told me all this in his deep voice, laughing, smiling, and exuding his characteristic down-to-earth confidence.

We met regularly for five months in the fall of 2013, spending hours talking about his life and work over coffee. When not meeting in person, we often exchanged friendly text messages: "Study study study!!!! Have all the confidence in you!!!!" he texted me the day before my comprehensive exams. But in early December Ethan stopped responding, and eventually my text messages stopped going through.

I began to worry about him and soon discovered from the public records that Ethan had been arrested and booked in county jail. "How are you doing?" I wrote in one of our letters back and forth. Ethan responded on paper I had paid for ($0.10 per page), explaining what had happened and why he was still there. He had been alone in a hotel room in Houston ("at an AA convention. . . . I know it doesn't make sense") when he relapsed on drugs. He spiraled out of control, taking methamphetamine and prescription pills until he was arrested weeks later when he was found asleep in his car. He clarified the incident: "I was parked in an intersection. Not a four-way stoplight but an intersection in the parking lot."

Almost three years before his most recent arrest, Ethan had moved to Austin and gotten a job at the W Hotel just months after it opened. How Ethan ended up in Austin managing the "talent" at the W is a journey through restaurants, resorts, and hotels in what could be called the "service capitals" of the United States: Orlando, Florida; Las Vegas, Nevada; and Dallas, Texas. For all of his adult life, he has struggled with addiction; not just to drugs but also, as he describes, to money, stress, and "the chase of the tip."

Luxury in the "Live Music Capital"

As you walk through the heavy glass doors at the W Hotel in Austin, you enter a world of twenty-first-century luxury and modern style. The reception desks are made up of silver-plated islands where "talent"— young staff who could pass as guests, save for the small W-shaped pins they wear on the lapels of their designer ensembles—stand ready to welcome you. To your right is a long wooden table with a single Remington typewriter placed at a chair in front of a wall covered in a patchwork of large framed photographs of quirky local landmarks: Leal's Tire Shop on the East Side, the BMX park in central Austin, and a man in a tuxedo perched on the tip of Red Bud Isle in Lady Bird Lake.

From the hidden office behind the podiums where guests check in and out, Ethan coordinated all the operations in the front of the house, from parking and reservations to the concierge and guest lounges. There, Ethan managed the very pinnacle of customer service at the highest end of the hospitality industry. As he described it, "Service at the W is unmatched. There is no margin of error, and we were building loyalty and also maintaining the W's reputation."

The W Austin takes up a whole city block in the trendy downtown Second Street District. Opened in December of 2010, the W Austin sits inside a $300 million property made up of a thirty-seven-story tower and 251 hotel rooms topped by 159 luxury condominiums. Also called "Block 21," the W complex houses the Moody Theater, where the PBS series *Austin City Limits* tapes its shows, as well as multiple restaurants, a spa, retail businesses, and a recently built "luxury" Starbucks—with design inspired by a mix of music and recycling.

The W Austin positions itself as *the* place to stay when visiting the "Live Music Capital of the World," promising on its website to "unleash your inner soul man, rock god, or indie hipster." As one of the trendiest luxury hotels in town, the W touts itself as the destination

for the young, rich, and famous. Ethan's work there involved catering to the needs of people paying upward of $400 a night. During Austin's many festivals and events—from the Formula One races to the South by Southwest music festival—rooms at the W start at $999 a night, and the hotel requires a five-night minimum stay.

Ethan spoke for hours about the W, and I noticed while transcribing our interviews that he frequently used the present tense. If I hadn't known he didn't work there anymore, I would have been convinced he was still managing the front desk.

Ethan bragged about his former workplace, telling me about its impressive statistics. The W in Austin, I came to find out, is the second highest performing location in the W brand. It also has the highest average occupancy rate of any hotel in the United States. "Sitting at a 90 percent occupancy all year long, your clientele is completely different," Ethan told me. People want to stay there. "There are not kids running around your hotel; there's actually just dogs with their owners."

Living on the Edge of His Life

Service work is often distinguished from other types of jobs based on the degree of interaction with the customer. When the customer is king, service workers navigate a triangle of relations, having to respond not only to their bosses' demands but also to those of their customers. To Ethan, however, working in service is about much more than the customers. It is also about a lifestyle: "Most waiters and bartenders and service industry people live for excitement, fun, spontaneity. They live on the edge of their lives, really. We like the instant gratification. We like being in the spotlight. We're narcissists. We are into punishing ourselves as well. We live in that high-stress life—that high-reward life too."

Ethan has strong views about work in the service industry, often making broad claims about why people choose that work and what kind of life it entails. Despite these generalizations, Ethan knows that he has worked at the top of the industry. Not all service workers make impressive tips, work in luxury facilities, or even choose to do service at all. Yet at the highest end of the service sector, Ethan continually emphasizes the lifestyle: "People stay in it [service] because . . . they are in that lifestyle. They still drink a lot. They still party a lot. Or, that's the lifestyle that they prefer. And then there are other people that stay in it . . . because they still need that quick money; no savings—living, you know, night to night. It's like, 'Well, I'm going to work tonight so I can pay my bill, my phone bill, and then I work tomorrow so I can pay electric.'"

Ethan is reflective about his life experiences. He is good at waiting tables and providing services, but he didn't start working in service because he wanted to "be of service to people." He did it for the lifestyle that enabled him to do what he wanted in a way that was "more forgiving than a nine-to-five job." Luxury service work allowed Ethan to "work, party, [and] make fast cash."

From "Server" to "Talent"

Ethan has worked in the service industry since high school. His first job as a teenager was at Wal-Mart, although he laughs when he assures me that he wouldn't be caught dead there now. He also did an internship at Disney World and worked in clubs, restaurants, and hotels in Las Vegas—and the list goes on. But it was at the W that he says he learned how to provide real luxury service.

Through connections he had made in the hospitality industry, Ethan went to a "casting call" at the W (the hotel doesn't hold "job fairs," and prefers the Hollywood term "casting call") and quickly got a job. "I went in there with my head so big, thinking, 'Oh, I'm gonna go run this shit.'" But the W was a different story:

"I'm like, 'Oh, okay. I'll start off as a front desk agent, but you just watch.' You know? That's what [was] happening in my head. And so I get there, and I'm quickly humbled. I realize that what's happening at the W is a whole other level of service, knowledge, expectation, performance—just service overall. It's just a whole different ballgame."

This "whole different ballgame" is part of a global brand that concentrates on design and luxury at the highest end of the hospitality industry. In 2013 there were forty-five W hotels around the globe, each intended to have its own "personality" by incorporating local influences and cultures into high-design spaces. In the company's words, W hotels mingle "vibes and elements" to create a sense of comfort, style, and technology.

The lobby at all W hotels—the "Living Room"—is made up of multiple lounge areas styled according to different themes. As the W's press materials insist, this represents "the transformation of the traditional, transactional hotel lobby into the W Living Room centered around cocktail culture."

In Austin, the Living Room consists of variously sized spaces with different aesthetics. One long sunny room has tall windows and low couches accentuated by boldly colored walls and a small but well-stocked bar. If you walk through a doorway, you enter the "Records Room," which features midcentury modern furniture and a crackling fireplace. Not surprisingly, one full wall is covered in shelves filled with records. A couple evenings a month, the W hosts an event called "Off the Wall," where DJs play records on expensive vintage turntables; guests can select the music from the hotel's collection of vinyl or, as the online invitation suggests, "bring your fav record from home."

The lights dim as you step through heavy curtains and into the "Secret Bar," an interior room with tall ceilings and a long bar backlit in watery blue lights. Red velvet couches wrap the sides of the lounge, and couples drink fourteen-dollar cocktails and eat truffle popcorn or pork belly sliders while listening to music over a powerful sound system. Although local musicians sometimes play, the W brand also has a global music director, charged with curating around-the-clock soundtracks for W hotels.

At four o'clock on any given day one could lose track of time in this inner lounge. One Saturday afternoon I sat on the velvet couch, watching people walk to and from the bar. A man dressed in a tuxedo and a

woman in a full-length, backless gown ordered glasses of champagne while a group of women celebrated someone's thirtieth birthday. Hotel guests wandered through the lounge, and I counted at least six different dogs—a standard poodle, an italian greyhound, a golden retriever—that were paraded through over the course of an hour.

The W also sets out to reinterpret the "traditional hotel lexicon." Employees at the W are called the "talent," and other services also have shortened names, often starting with the letter *w*. The room service menu for dogs is called "woof" ("You know these dogs wouldn't be caught dead with kibble!"), part of the "P.A.W." program that reminds guests that their "pets are welcome." Housekeepers are "stylists," charged with the task of "designing" (a.k.a. cleaning) the rooms. The gym is called "sweat." The happy hour is called "S.I.P." ("social interactive playtime"). The valet, "wheels"; the swimming pool, "wet"; the laundry bag, "wash"; the concierge, "whatever/whenever."

All the Dads Were Gone

"Let's start at the beginning," Ethan suggested during our second meeting. Ethan was born in North Dakota and raised in a military family. He described a happy childhood that was marked by frequent relocations as his family hopped from air force bases in Nevada, Washington, California, the Netherlands, and then Florida. "My dad was in Desert Storm, Desert Shield. I remember the holidays with my dad being gone. He was—or is—a middle-class worker. He has worked for everything he's ever had."

Ethan grew up with his sister, just eighteen months his senior. "We never needed anything," he remembered. "We weren't spoiled, [but] we usually got most of what we wanted. We weren't the kind of family that, when turned sixteen, we both got cars. That wasn't the story. But we had everything we needed."

Through the many stories about his family, I got the sense that his parents acted as a unit, even during his dad's long absences. In one of his many uses of business analogies, Ethan compared his family to a corporation, likening his mom to the general manager and his dad to the CEO. With his charming smile, Ethan explained, "Mom is the one that is in the daily operations of the family, but dad's really the one in charge."

With his dad on duty, Ethan and his sister spent their days with their mother. "Mom was always there, always poker faced, very stoic. We never knew when things were rough or hard, you know?" Although he never remembers going without, Ethan is now aware that his parents struggled during his youth. "It's funny, because when I look back on it now, she [Mom] started working, like overnight sometimes, which I just couldn't understand. What I didn't realize was that she was sleeping while we were at school. It never occurred to me or crossed my mind what my parents were doing so that we would have what we needed."

"I hope you marry rich"

After living for four years on an air force base in the Netherlands, Ethan and his family moved back to the United States. "Can you imagine? Being fifteen years old, going to the spring break capital of the world?" Ethan asked me. This "spring break capital" was a scenic beach town in Florida: "white sand like flour and emerald water."

A tall and gregarious teenager, Ethan described himself as a star of his high school football team and an all-around achiever. "Good morning, Rams!" Ethan would announce over the PA system every morning at school. "This is Ethan, your student body president. Please stand for the Pledge of Allegiance and the playing of our national anthem."

In high school, Ethan explained, he developed "all these alter egos": he would play hard at the football game on Friday night, and then after, "I was completely wasted, tripping on acid with other jocks and cool kids. But then Monday morning would come around, and I would be somebody else again: student body president!"

"I have these old scripts that tell me, 'You have to be the best.'" Ethan's many stories of trying to be the best were frequent during our meetings. He had to be the best waiter at the best restaurant with the best chef or get promoted the fastest. As Ethan explained, "I have these expectations of people that are very high, and of myself and the things that are around me, and I don't know where that comes from. I'm just a prima donna, I guess!"

"My mom always tells me, 'I hope you marry rich, because your tastes came from some other family—it wasn't ours.'" Ethan laughed out loud and continued, "We always joke about that, you know, because I see it now. I'm like, 'What happened to me?'"

Different from his family and balancing his "alter egos," Ethan was also coming out of the closet, experimenting with his sexuality away from the gaze of his parents. "I felt a lot like I was overcompensating for something that I didn't know about," Ethan told me. "I was just in the closet and unaware of what was happening, but I knew that something was different."

"Sex, drugs, and rock and roll"

By the time Ethan finished high school, he had been offered a football scholarship, had earned decent grades, and had become fully educated in the art of hard-core partying.

"I remember the first time I did cocaine [in high school] was in my friend's Camaro—the newer Camaro, like right when they first came out. She was the coolest girl in school, who had the new Camaro, and I remember doing a bump of cocaine in her car before we went into [the club]. I'll never forget it."

The summer of "firsts" continued when Ethan met his first boyfriend before he went away to college. "He was thirty-five, I was eighteen," he told me. "And, um, I experienced a lot of stuff I probably shouldn't have at eighteen." After a pause he second-guessed himself. "Not shouldn't have . . . but I experienced a lot of stuff before most people would probably have thought about it. You know, sex, drugs, and rock and roll, and having a really good time, and partying and nightclubs and music and dancing and sex."

Throughout our conversations over the course of many months, Ethan offered different explanations for his rocky transition into adulthood. He was slowly coming out of the closet and used to adapting quickly to new places, given his family's frequent moves. "I always had to find out who I was going to be or who I was, you know? And so, then I was also compensating for who I was and trying to be liked and validated." Another day, he explained it again: "I don't know what it was but there was a lot of that validation and that emptiness and loneliness."

The Lookbook

Just over a decade after he graduated from high school, Ethan was living in Austin and had been recently promoted to front desk manager at the W Hotel. As a manager, his number one goal was to maximize the "guest experience index." This index, Ethan explained, was a way to measure service beyond a single transaction. He gave me an example: "If I asked you to rate this latte, you could tell me it was good. But if I ask you about your experience at this coffee shop, you would evaluate the ambiance, the people here, the music, and the barista." At the W, Ethan insisted, everyone is ranked and judged just like this.

To fit in as "talent" at the W, you also have to look the part, but this was never a problem for Ethan. As a self-described prima donna, Ethan is also fastidious about his appearance. He exercises regularly, grooms himself professionally, and likes designer clothes. He often arrived to our meetings five minutes late, rushing from a workout class and wearing gym clothes: a black tank top, athletic shorts, and tennis shoes. Upon arrival one day, he gave me a tight hug as he took off his Ray-Ban sunglasses and said, "I just came from Spinning!" Another day, he watched the clock as we spoke to make sure he wasn't late for an appointment to get his eyebrows waxed. Yet another, he had shaved off his beard, explaining that he was trying to get a new "look."

When employees are required to change their appearance according to corporate standards, they are doing aesthetic work. Some see this as a particularly demeaning and intrusive form of management, crossing a line in terms of what should reasonably be required for a job. Yet Ethan talked about getting "the look" with pride.

The look starts before you are even hired: the W has a certain style they want. Everyone hired is then "fully outfitted" with three uniforms designed by Michael Kors. After each shift, the talent turn in their uniforms to be dry-cleaned by the W, so you, according to Ethan, "never have an excuse not to look good."

"But how do you know how to look?" I asked.

"Oh, it's an actual *book*!" he explained. "For each position in the hotel." It's updated regularly according to what is in style, and it also varies city by city. Ethan could tell I was interested. "Do you know that Skrillex haircut that some girls had a while back? Where they shaved the sides of their head but kept their hair long?"

"Sure," I responded.

"Well, girls at the W here [in Austin] had that haircut. If you can rock it, you can have it. But if it's a mess, you can't."

The talent at the W conform their attitudes and outfits in an effort to provide the highest level of customer service in the trendiest environment. In addition to guidelines laid out in the lookbook, the talent also police each other, making sure individual fashion statements meet luxury standards. Ethan remembers a time when a female manager confronted another woman about her makeup. "She looked like a mess," Ethan explained. "It's all kind of under the table and unspoken," he said, "But you have to look a certain way and be confident with your style."

During a Saturday afternoon months later that I spent at the W in Austin, the cocktail waitress who kept my drink filled was wearing a long skirt and low-cut shirt, both of which were black, accented by a long gold necklace. Many of the waitresses, I noticed, had similar outfits, matched with heavy black eye makeup and long, straight dark hair. "They all look like Stevie Nicks!" my partner observed. "Or a witch!"

"The happiest place on Earth"

The W wasn't the first place that Ethan had been required to do aesthetic labor by changing his appearance for his job. He also learned how to brand his body in the quintessential service environment: Disney World.

After a brief stint on a football scholarship in Illinois ("I was a fish out of water, living in the cornfields. Oh my god, ugh! It was terrible!"), Ethan moved to Orlando, Florida, at age nineteen to participate in the six-month Disney College Program, located at the Disney World resort and amusement park.

"When I went to Disney, I was learning a lot about the 'smiling fascism,' as I call it—"

I interrupted him as he was about to change the topic. "So, wait! What does 'smiling fascism' mean?"

He explained, "It's kinda like, you're gonna do it our way. There's no other way but our way, our way or the highway . . . with a smile." Ethan was learning the art of customer service at the "happiest place on Earth."

Designed as an internship program and offered at a variety of Disney properties, the Disney College Program is marketed as an educational opportunity to get hands-on work experience in addition to opportunities to network with staff, take professional development classes, and, as the website explains, "build transferable skills such as problem-solving, teamwork, guest service, and effective communication."

Ethan said that the Disney College Program was framed as both a learning opportunity and a place where college students could get first-hand experience with both business and the attractions. But, as he described, "I never once saw any office." As an intern, he worked exclusively in the parks and was paid $5.15 an hour, less than the minimum wage. He was also charged sixty dollars per week to live in the Disney apartments, where he shared a three-room apartment with nine other employees. "It was a racket," he said. He remembers having to regularly ask his parents for money, even though he was working full-time.

Every morning Ethan was shuttled from his apartment to a massive parking lot ("filled with Mickeys and Cinderellas smoking cigarettes"), and from there he entered the underground tunnels and changed into his uniform in a "ginormous" locker room. After getting dressed, he would find his way to the particular staircase he was required to use to enter the park.

"You have to find the right one," he explained. "If I'm wearing a costume for 'It's a Small World,' I can't go into another exhibit—I'm not branded for it."

Ethan would climb the stairs, take a deep breath, and "open the door and just smile, even though I was miserable." On multiple occasions, he called his time at Disney "internship enslavement," but he also acknowledged the path it had set him on. "I hated it, but it was very beneficial for me and a big learning lesson and an experience that was unmatched."

"Parent rehab"

When Ethan finished the Disney College Program, he dropped out of college to stay in Orlando, working as a waiter and partying harder than

ever. "I was working in a couple restaurants . . . and it was just the lifestyle that I was living was very go, go, go, go, go. But that's how the industry is. It's . . . you'll find the next job that's gonna make me more
money. Next job, more money. Better opportunity, more money." He
eventually started working at Planet Hollywood and Pleasure Island,
"making more money than I probably needed to be making at twenty."

As Ethan's drug use ramped up and his social life deteriorated, his
parents—who now lived across the country—became increasingly concerned. After a particularly scattered phone call, Ethan remembers his
dad coming into town: "I picked my dad up at the airport. We went to
my apartment. Immediately, not even like the next day or that night, but
like immediately, [we] got out, packed up my shit, put it in the back of
the truck. Like, mattresses, everything I had. I owed money for drugs
or something, and my dad said, 'Get in the car. We're leaving.'"

Ethan and his dad spent the next three days in the car, driving from
Orlando to Mobile, Alabama, then on through El Paso, Texas, and finally to his parents' new home in Las Vegas.

This was the first of a handful of times that Ethan went to "parent rehab," moving from wherever he was to live with his parents. He referred
to his moves, first from Orlando to Las Vegas, then Las Vegas to Dallas,
and finally Dallas to Austin, as "geographics." He explained, "We call it
a 'geographic' when you move somewhere to get clean."

Server to the (B-List) Stars

At twenty-one years old, Ethan was now living with his parents near
an air force base in Las Vegas, Nevada, and it wasn't long before he was
back on his feet and back to work. Although his dad was reassigned to
work in Texas a couple months later, Ethan stayed and started working
in service: first at Applebee's ("For like a week!"), then House of Blues,
Mandalay Bay, and eventually the super-trendy sushi restaurant Nobu,
inside the Hard Rock Hotel.

Ethan remembers earning between $400 and $500 dollars a night in
tips. "I was making so much money that I could afford everything. I
could afford my [drug] habit. I could afford the bills. I could afford the
fun. I could afford everything."

The money was critical, but working in service wasn't just about the
pay. For Ethan, it was also about the status. It was about his association
with a chef, or a brand, or even with his affluent customers: "There's a
difference from working at Applebee's and then working at House of

Blues, which is a level up, and then working at Nobu. You know? At Applebee's you're waiting on Joe and Jane Smith. She's wearing Keds. And then going to Nobu, where the ladies are wearing Louis Vuittons with a Prada purse and [have] money to throw at you [while they are] sitting next to a celebrity."

Ethan's stories were peppered with celebrity names. At Nobu, he told me, he waited on stars like Howard Stern (and his "whole gang"), Heidi Klum, and Brooke Burke.

"Who is that?" I would ask.

"She used to do a lot of the *E! News* and her kids were the only kids that were allowed in the restaurant, and that would be at like 5:00 p.m."

Of all the places he has lived, Ethan remembers more celebrities in Austin—more than he had expected. "I thought I had seen it all in Las Vegas!" When he worked at the W, Ethan often coordinated the complicated needs of the celebrity guests. He remembers scheduling Lady Gaga's clandestine entrance into the hotel by way of the service elevator in the underground parking garage, making sure she arrived at her penthouse unseen by the "talent" or other guests.

He remembered one day, during South by Southwest, when he helped Usher into his car, made sure P. Diddy got to his room, and attended to Fergie, who was pregnant in her suite. "We are on a need-to-know basis at the W," Ethan said. "Unless you were styling their rooms or serving them, the talent wouldn't know that Britney Spears was a guest." He talked about these stars with an air of professionalism, but it seemed clear to me that he loved the proximity to the rich and famous.

Service as a Craft

For every jab he takes at his past workplaces, Ethan is adamant about one thing: service work is a craft, and to do it well, you have to love it. "After a while it's also about being good, because the reality is you can't just go into Nobu thinking that you can just go be a waiter at Nobu. There is a craft, there is a skill, and there is a love for it. After a while, it does become a profession."

It was at the trendy Nobu sushi restaurant that Ethan was first exposed to "that upper echelon of service," and his manager took him under his wing. "He was amazing," Ethan remembered. "I mean, he could see a Sweet'N Low wrapper empty on a table across the room. He was *that* on it."

"What other skills did you need to be the best?" I asked.

"Memory is part of it," he said. "But I also think that it's a natural kind of thing. Some people can do it, and some people can't. I believe that [my manager] used to call it a well-oiled machine." The craft of luxury service also required "a certain desire to live and work at those standards." Skills and training were essential. But according to Ethan, those who excelled in service were attracted to the work for other reasons.

Service work is different from manual or professional jobs because it requires more emotional labor. Not only do waiters and hotel workers have to be physically and mentally engaged, they also have to manage their feelings according to workplace rules. For example, Ethan couldn't yell at the angry bride who had reserved a room in the hotel he managed ("She was a *bridezilla*, I'm telling you!") or chastise restaurant patrons who gave stingy tips. For this reason, some scholars consider service work to be even more exploiting and alienating than other forms of paid labor. Service work, however, is not all bad. At times, Ethan described his work as enjoyable and even fulfilling.

For Ethan, his career in the service industry has been hectic and exciting, stressful and invigorating, unstable and flexible. When he worked as the manager of a three-star hotel in a Dallas suburb, Ethan explained, "It's my responsibility to buffer between the hotel and the guest." Guests yelled at him, patrons threw things at him, and a client at the W even insulted his mother after a particularly raucous weekend. "It was the worst day of my life. I went home exhausted."

Yet Ethan also speaks fondly, evenly lovingly, about "being the best" and about the thrill of waiting tables in a busy restaurant: "I know the love that you have to have for it because I have that love. I have that appreciation. And it's a certain skill set—not everybody can do it. You know, I love waiting tables, and I love that atmosphere, and that high intensity, and the talking to people, and the engaging people, and then the chase of the tip. That's part of it. The service, the love of service, the execution of service—it's all part of that, and I am really good at it."

"What happens in Vegas, stays in Vegas"

Describing the five years he spent in Las Vegas, Ethan said, "I was going from one restaurant to the other, getting better jobs, making more money, spending more money, partying harder, living a harder, faster life." While climbing the career ladder in the restaurant industry, Ethan also worked as a cocktail boy at Krave, the first gay bar on the strip. On the nights he worked at Krave, "I would walk out with $700, $800, $1000 dollars, you know? And it's just, just flirting, just being a hooker, you know what I mean? Because after a while it becomes about the chase of money. Because that's what it's about. It's not about being happy in your job as a waiter. It's about, 'Where am I making the most money?'"

Ethan talked about his life like it was totally enmeshed in service work, often blending stories of partying in his free time with those of providing customer "experiences." He described himself as part of the crowd that "produced experiences" for tourists who came to have a good time. "[Have] you heard that little saying, 'What happens in Vegas, stays in Vegas'? Well, you would meet somebody like me, and we would supply you with that good time."

I followed up: "What does a 'good time' include?"

Ethan paused for a moment and then explained himself. "It included drugs, club entrances, you know? We knew the people at the doors. The locals' tour, which is a lot different than the tourist tour. That's where the real parties are, where the drugs are, the great DJs are, those who are in the know, beautiful people—the fun, exciting, glamorous life that looks glamorous on the outside until noon the next day comes around and everybody is, like, still fucked up and awake. I've been to every penthouse in every hotel on the strip. And the flip side—I've also been to crack houses on the strip."

Ethan was living the "service lifestyle" in Las Vegas. He worked hard, partied harder, and showed people a good time—both inside and out-side of the workplace. Throughout our meetings, Ethan talked fondly about the fun he had but was also quick to reflect on his experiences. "Let me also just clarify, too, that towards the end it wasn't glamorous, it wasn't fun, I wasn't social. I . . . went from staying in the penthouses with men . . ." He paused, looking down at his cappuccino and pushing around a sugar cube. "Or women, whatever, mostly men then, to ending up in some hotel room across the highway from the strip that was not clean or safe. So, that's where it ended me up."

"Those ladies will shut you down in a second"

Twenty-seven years old and struggling with addiction, Ethan did an-other "geographic" and moved in with his parents in North Texas. Once he was back on his feet, he started working in a midrange hotel in a Dal-las suburb, learning the ropes of a different kind of service environment.

"I used to work at Mandalay Bay, which was a really nice hotel," Ethan reminded me, "[and now] I was just working at a kind of a cheap hotel!" Although slightly embarrassed by its location (close to an amusement park) and the three-star clientele (kids and families), Ethan was quickly promoted to the position of front desk manager. "I was a good man-ager," he remembered. He was friendly and direct, but sometimes his approach came off as too harsh. "That's something I've had to learn," he said. "How to communicate with different people and different styles, and that was one of the biggest challenges that I had to learn—and I still have to learn sometimes."

"Most of the time I was living in Dallas, I was pretty sober," Ethan insisted as we talked about why he had moved to Austin. Working in the hotel had become too time-consuming ("I was always on call"), so he decided to go back to waiting tables while he took classes at a commu-nity college. Ethan was working again in five-star restaurants, or, as he called them, "fine dining restaurant[s], serving lobster and shaved truf-fles on top of, like, bone-in filets, and $1,000 bottles of wine, and cham-pagne, and celebrities everywhere."

Ethan was back in his element: "working with a bunch of really good waiters who know food and wine just like the chef does, and I felt at home again." He loved working in Dallas. As he explained, "Dallas is all about society, and who you know, and where you're at, and who you're with, and all of that. I eat that stuff up."

As in Las Vegas, Ethan's personal life in Dallas was inextricably tied to his workplace. His friends were his coworkers. He worried over his restaurant's rating ("Those ladies there, once they start talking, will shut your restaurant down in a second!"), and he knew the food reviewers and competitor chefs by name. "It is about status and ego," Ethan explained. "I'm working for this chef now, and I [am] making this much money, you know? And it's just like, it's a whole 'nother underworld, the service industry."

Nine Hours to Austin

Ethan was working as a waiter and had gone back to community college in Dallas when he relapsed on drugs. But this time he didn't go to "parent rehab." His family wanted to send him to a residential treatment facility, and they decided it would be in Austin.

"I ended up falling off the wagon," Ethan told me. "I got really stressed out and said, 'You know what? I'm just going to smoke some weed. I deserve it. Weed is harmless, right?' From one hit of weed, all of a sudden I'm in rehab in Austin."

His friends agreed to pack up his apartment in Dallas while Ethan made the drive to Austin. It was a straight shot down Interstate 35. As Ethan remembered, his friends in Dallas called other friends in Austin: "Catch him on the other side!"

"I barely made it," Ethan told me as he described what should have been a three-hour trip. After nine hours and a brief stint in a small town jail after being pulled over, Ethan arrived in Austin, and the next day he checked himself into rehab.

Three months later Ethan was clean and ready to stay sober. "When I moved to Austin, I decided, 'Okay, it's time to grow.'" Just out of rehab, he moved into transitional housing and regularly attended the gay AA meetings in town while looking for a job.

Ethan immediately fell in love with Austin. During that first summer he would ride his bike around town for exercise and go swimming at Barton Springs, a spring-fed pool and one of the city's most popular destinations on a hot day.

Austin offered everything he had been looking for: "green space, jobs, $10 million houses, and the gentrified bungalow." For Ethan, Austin was a mix of trendiness, which he had come to love in Vegas and Dallas ("Look around Austin during ACL, F1, and SXSW! You see it's really a happening place."), and down-to-earth flair ("You can wear sandals to the steak house.").

Living Paycheck to Paycheck

When Ethan got a job at the W, he started off as an hourly attendant at the front desk. He checked guests in and out, while learning the ropes of luxury service with Austin flair.

The W in Austin is unique in many ways. The hotel, its design, and its events all center on Austin's music history. For example, a life-sized statue of Willie Nelson sits close to the front entrance, as if the iconic country music singer himself, famous for his support for the legalization of marijuana and his signature braids, greets you as you approach. In the guest rooms, bathroom mirrors are etched with a guitar strap design, and the weekly events in the Living Room regularly feature musical performances.

The W Austin is also concerned with sourcing local food. The in-house restaurant, TRACE, offers a menu filled with local items, and it is the only W property to employ a "local forager" charged with building relationships with Austin-area farmers. According to one local weekly paper, TRACE serves "food so local it could run for city council." In another initiative, the hotel installed an apiary on its rooftop, where boxes of bees are rotated to produce four thousand pounds of local honey each year, which is then used in meals at the restaurant, cocktails at the bar, and even treatments at the spa.

Ethan thinks that because of all these Austin influences, people assume that W employees are well paid. But in his experience, they actually make comparatively low wages. Ethan started off earning $11.25 per hour doing check-ins, what he described as "Sheraton-level" wages, and living paycheck to paycheck. Once he started working full-time, he had access to benefits, but he warned me that it wasn't as good as it sounded: "It was bad insurance, and they take money for your 401(k) directly out of your paycheck."

Although he wasn't making much money, "people were kissing my ass," and he soon became well connected around town.

He said he regularly worked sixty hours a week and didn't have time to do much else. However, he credited this high-pressure environment with attracting high-quality staff: "Everyone who works in the W is really smart. It's so high pressure that you can't not be."

According to Ethan, the "bridge" between the W's high performance standards and low pay is the way the company builds morale and "takes care" of its workers. I asked if this meant incentives or bonuses, but Ethan corrected me: "It's all about the perks of the job." These include membership in a corporate softball league, a massive employee holiday party (with a budget of $15,000 to $20,000 per year), and projects that support the tripartite mission of the hotel: fashion, music, and design.

Ethan offered an example: "The W is a LEED-certified facility, so the employees put on a 'trashion show' to make people 'eco-ware' of the hotel's green certifications." These perks, combined with free food, prepared meals during shifts, and local discounts, made working at the W a coveted position for Ethan, despite the low hourly wage.

"A product of the industry"

Ethan had been working at the W for almost two years by mid-March of 2013, when South by Southwest, a ten-day whirlwind of music, art, and film festivals, began again. Ethan relapsed one night after work and stopped going in. "I get stoned, and all of the sudden I want to get higher. But you know, it all is so impulsive, and so that whole service industry is like, 'I want what I want, when I want it, how I want it. And do it now.'"

After three weeks of trying to go to work and falling down on his responsibilities at the hotel, Ethan checked himself into another three-month rehab program.

Ethan explains his addiction as "a product of the [service] industry." He later tells me that he's sure he would have been an addict anyway, but the industry enabled his addiction to grow. According to him, people who work in luxury service like instant gratification, fast-paced environments, living on the edge, and being involved and included. They are the "it" people who know what is cool before it is cool. When you are working at a high level, meeting people and being exposed to those lifestyles, Ethan explained, you get used to it.

"It's kind of a way of life that gets very comfortable—and very instant gratification, you know? That life was very attractive to me because I was able to compensate for not being able to take care of myself."

Ethan calls the lifestyle of service work "very, very, very addictive." He was surrounded by outgoing, personable people who loved to compete with each other. "We are the genuine junkies," he insisted. "Waiting tables and working in hospitality is very, very stressful and demanding, you know? And so all that fuels the fire. Money, the stress, the environment, the competition, the status, the quick money."

The $30,000 Millionaire

For Ethan, working at the W was all about the people he knew, and once he worked there, he had all sorts of access. "And you can get a job anywhere else," he reminded me. "People see the W on your résumé and hire you like that," he said with a snap of his fingers.

Businesses also offer what Ethan calls "bribes" in order to "build relationships" with people who work at the hotel. In turn, those people recommend the businesses to the guests.

At the front desk, Ethan would give recommendations to guests based on where he himself liked to go. "For example," he said, "I would book a five-top table at a Mexican restaurant downtown, and in return I would get [a] fifty-dollar credit—ten dollars a head—from the restaurant." He also got 25 percent off his purchases in the shops in the Second Street District, 10 percent off at nearby coffee shops like Halcyon and Jo's, free movies on Monday nights at the Violet Crown Cinema, free dinners at restaurants, free bottle service at clubs, and free entrance to live music shows.

As a manager, Ethan could also stay at other W hotels at a discounted rate. Ethan told me that one weekend he and some coworker friends caught a flight to Miami, where they stayed at the W Miami for next to nothing. "We were $30,000 millionaires," Ethan told me. "Me and my friends acted like we were rich on service industry perks, but [we] were actually living paycheck to paycheck."

To Ethan, paying for a $400 hotel room or a $100 meal is not the same thing as receiving those services comped or at a discounted rate. "I couldn't afford that stuff," he observed. "But I lived like I could." When I asked him why he did this, he explained:

"That's what I am used to. I'm buying whatever clothes I want and eating at these restaurants that I work in—living these lives and staying in these hotel rooms with these people who can afford it and living in these really nice places because I can afford it . . . but [I] have nothing to show for it. Nothing to show for it—except for some really nice clothes, a bunch of shoes, a really nice apartment, and some things. Heaven forbid my car breaks down. I have to empty my 401(k)."

Working in service was a demanding line of work, and Ethan spoke candidly about its pitfalls. Aging is one of them. "I'm still young," he said, smiling as he looked across the table at me. "At a certain age, if you haven't prepared, there's no social security check coming. I mean there might be a social security check coming, but most people don't have pensions, and 401(k)s, and insurance for medical, and all this stuff."

As Ethan told me about his experiences working in hotels and restaurants in cities around the country, he was almost painfully aware of the disjuncture between his lifestyle and his income. "I act like I'm entitled to this kind of lifestyle, but I'm not part of it—I just work in it."

Wanting Something More

During the months that Ethan and I met regularly, he described himself as at a turning point in his life. "I'm at that crossroads right now where I have an opportunity, and I know that I'm capable, and I have good experience and knowledge and a different idea of where I'm at in my life." He repeatedly told me that he was tired of "always chasing" the next best thing and working in the intense service industry—and lifestyle—that has repeatedly landed him in rehab.

"What I realized," he explained one day, "is the pursuit of all of the other stuff is no longer gratifying to me. Not like there's anything wrong with waiting tables, but there are other things that I want to do that are more fulfilling." He speculated about becoming a teacher, or maybe a counselor, but he planned to finish his degree first.

But Ethan missed his first day of classes and is still in jail awaiting trial for multiple drug-related charges. We continue to exchange letters through an automated system, www.4inmates.com. "Prison is not for me!" Ethan wrote after explaining his most recent relapse and arrest. "Don't they know who I am?" He drew a small smiley face on the paper, knowing that I would understand his joke. "The universe always has a funny way of bringing me back to center. I just hope this one sticks."

Recommended Readings

Hochschild, A. R. 2012. *The Managed Heart: Commercialization of Human Feeling*. Berkeley: University of California Press. The classic study on the commodification of feelings examines how "public-contact workers"—namely flight attendants and bill collectors—are required to do emotional labor in order to provide services.

Leidner, R. 1993. *Fast Food, Fast Talk: Service Work and the Routinization of Everyday Life*. Berkeley: University of California Press. A comparative study that examines the methods and consequences of regulating service work at McDonald's and at a life insurance agency.

Lopez, S. H. 2010. "Workers, Managers, and Customers: Triangles of Power in Work Communities." *Work and Occupations* 37:251–271. An article chronicling new debates in the sociology of service work, reviewing developments around emotional labor; the service triangle of worker, manager, and customer; and the role of race and gender in these processes.

Sherman, R. 2007. *Class Acts: Service and Inequality in Luxury Hotels*. Berkeley: University of California Press. This ethnography of two urban hotels in the United States examines how luxury service is organized and how inequality is resisted and reproduced through interactive service work.

Weinberg, D. 2011. "Sociological Perspectives on Addiction." *Sociology Compass* 5 (4): 298–310. A critical survey of how sociologists have framed and analyzed addiction since the 1950s, emphasizing the ongoing slippage between questions of social approval and considerations of whether or not substance abuse is voluntary or involuntary.

Wharton, A. S. 2009. "The Sociology of Emotional Labor." *Annual Review of Sociology* 35 (1): 147–165. This update on the theory and research on emotional labor since Hochschild's classic book reviews studies that use interactive service work to better understand organizations and individual efforts to manage emotions.

CHAPTER 9

Keith: A Musician at the Margins

AMIAS MALDONADO

It was fitting that the first time I saw Keith he was onstage. This stage happened to be at Gumbo's North, a Cajun bar and restaurant located in Georgetown, a town of fifty thousand about a half hour's drive north of Austin. Gumbo's used to be downtown—which caused me some confusion at first—but has since relocated to this booming exurb. Keith was working as the musical accompaniment for happy hour there on a particularly brutal wintery night, and I remember hoping that the icy conditions outside were the reason for the sparse crowd. But the crowd—or lack thereof—didn't seem to be affecting Keith as he sat confidently on a wooden stool playing a song from his upcoming solo album on a humble acoustic guitar.

Keith was the embodiment that night of what we might think a modern country musician should look like: the tight-but-not-too-tight jeans, a green-and-white plaid long-sleeved button-down shirt, and worn-in boots. The only things missing were a cowboy hat and an oversized belt buckle. Keith has short sandy-blond hair, which that night was styled a little spiky but which appeared more as a mop top in some of the promotional pictures I saw online. His eyes are a piercing grayish blue, and his boyish good looks seemed to be aging well, with only the slightest of wrinkles around his eyes and mouth.

"Hey man, good to meet ya!" Keith exclaimed when I introduced myself after his set. He appeared to me content yet weary, like someone who had just finished a satisfying but busy day of labor. He shook my hand securely, and I could feel calluses on his fingertips, something I would learn is a characteristic of career guitarists. This was the first of many conversations we would have over the following months. And as I would come to find out, our meeting outside of Austin, amongst the

suburban sprawl, was emblematic of Keith's existence. Like Gumbo's, Keith's social world of country rock and Americana music has been pushed to the urban margins of Austin. This process has many names—redevelopment, gentrification, and a focus on younger, hipper musical styles—but for Keith it ultimately means more driving, less sleep, and a deep disconnection between his current musical career and the downtown streets on which it began.

"It meant freedom, it meant connection"

Born into a musical family, Keith knew from a very early age that music was something that he loved. He has fond memories of learning to play the guitar through old blues standards, eventually working up to informal jam sessions in the family living room, with his father on the piano and his brother playing the drums. But music was never something that Keith saw as a career, at least not at first.

"I never thought I would make a living from music," he told me one chilly January day over a cup of coffee. When Keith graduated high school he came to the University of Texas, paying his tuition and board from a college fund his grandparents had slowly saved. As Keith told me, "I was planning on being responsible. I enrolled in the business school and just sort of plugged away at the class work. I can't say I was really excited about it, but I was kind of resigned to it."

All that changed when a high school friend decided to rush for a fraternity and urged Keith to join him. In a show of solidarity and "just to try it out since I was doing the whole college thing," Keith agreed. Once in, Keith found several other fraternity members who also played instruments, and within a few weeks some informal noodling had gradually transformed into something resembling a band. "It's probably a phase lots of college kids go through—starting a band, I mean—but for me it meant freedom, it meant connection," Keith told me. The practical piece of the music-as-career puzzle fell into place when the president of the fraternity happened to hear them practice. "He told us he was a booker and that he could get us gigs at fraternity parties. We thought that was awesome, so we started out on the party circuit, but in those days it was relatively easy to transition from there to getting some paying gigs down on Sixth Street."

According to Keith, those were the halcyon days of playing live music in Austin. "It was awesome, man," he slyly said, a nostalgic grin illuminating his face. "Just a bunch of bands and a bunch of good music. The whole town was flush with oil and gas money, and you would go downtown and you'd hear country, but you'd also hear rock, you'd hear jazz, R & B." Bars were desperate for live music to draw in crowds, sometimes paying bands up to $1000 for a single gig. "You had a place like Steamboat, which was king of the street," Keith told me. "They had touring acts, they had cover bands. Our band played every Thursday and Friday night. Kept the lights on in that place for awhile. You had Baxter's, a jazz club. Every other bar had bands in it."

In 1987 Keith and his friends graduated from UT, and his friends moved on from the musical dream. Keith "did some interviews coming out of UT—Procter & Gamble and stuff like that. I had the suit and the haircut and everything. Because, you know, you've got career counselors and by the end of it they've turned you inside out telling you that you need to get a career."

During this liminal period, Keith continued to play music. No longer in a college band, he joined up with "the sickest cover band in the world, man! All black guys: the drummer from Rick James; the keyboardist went on to be Prince's musical director; the saxophonist hooked up with Kenny Loggins after. Everybody really did good from that band and during that time. You could find three or four funk bands playing at one time. That was something I loved that's totally gone, man: the diversity of music."

This was the first time I experienced something that would be a common occurrence in our talks: Keith had a vivid, almost photographic sense of his social network, past and present. Conversations about a band or a time would quickly transition into a genealogy of relationships, with Keith mentioning how this band member eventually toured with Cher; how he knew somebody who got him on a session as a studio musician with Brad Paisley; how he got to jam before a gig with the guitarist from Mr. Mister. At first I was eager to cast a cynical eye on all this name-dropping: Was this the way Keith made meaning of a ho-hum musical career? Were these grasps at people more famous than he a way to link his own career with their success? Perhaps. But as I would come to find out, perhaps not.

Due to some mixture of musical success and "suit-and-haircut" failure, Keith decided to seriously embark on the path of being a career musician. "But if I was going to play music," he said, "I was going to study: specific, intensive music and guitar theory. And that's when I went to Los Angeles." Keith enrolled at the Guitar Institute of Technology in 1990, where he got to "play with some kick-ass musicians, like Jeff 'Skunk' Baxter from the Doobie Brothers and Steely Dan." Keith graduated in 1992 and subsequently returned to Austin. "L.A. was great for me," Keith said in between sips of his latte. "It was where I learned what I needed to do to make a living in music." I asked him what that entailed. "You've got to approach it seriously, brother! And above all, you've got to hustle. That time in L.A., that's where I learned how to hustle."

"Like we were all in this together"

On a sunny and breezy spring day I visited Keith at his apartment on the south side of Austin. My drive took me past the emerging retail centers, condominiums, and mixed-use developments that dot the sides of

William Cannon—the nearest main street to Keith's home. I took a right and drove down a sleepy street for ten minutes, passing grassy vacant lots and increasingly humble homes. Finally I turned at an old gas station and then into Keith's complex. Keith greeted me warmly at the door, wearing a plain white T-shirt along with the customary blue jeans, his dog yapping noisily as I entered his place. He had left the front door open to catch some of the breeze, and it felt like we were outside.

"So," I began as I sat down in his living room, our previous conversation still ringing in my ears, "what is the 'hustle'?"

Keith thought for a bit before answering. "Hustling is all the little things you have to do to make it in this business. You've got to give favors to get favors. You've got to spend time working people, massaging venues, bothering radio managers. It's a constant, never-ending thing. When I'm working in a studio or on a touring act, I make sure to get to know people, know faces, maybe something about people's family or likes that I can bring up later."

When Keith returned to Austin in 1992, "the place was pretty much in the same place as I had left it." The musical tastes had changed, or as Keith put it, "There was less crazy hairstyles, more Doc Martens and motorcycle jackets." But Sixth Street was still musically diverse, and it still paid well. Austin had just declared itself the "Live Music Capital of the World" in 1991. The tech boom was nascent, and the music scene eagerly looked to grab a piece of the massive disposable-income pie the creative class was beginning to bake.

This doesn't mean things were easy for Keith. He described long practice sessions and grueling nighttime drives. He told me about a time in 1996 when the band's trailer had a flat tire "out in the middle of nowhere." Keith had to drive back to Austin, rent a U-Haul, drive back to the trailer, load up the gear, and then get to the show. "And then to top it off, when we're done playin' the owner stiffs us. That was probably my worst night ever as a musician." Keith laughed bitterly. But when Keith spoke about this time period, what stuck out most in his mind wasn't the tough days on the road or in the practice room—and it definitely wasn't the amount gigs were paying. No, what Keith remembered most was the musical camaraderie. "Even though there was a bunch of different kinds of music, there was still a sense of community, you know? Like we were all in this together."

Keith attributed a large degree of this unity to the Austin Rehearsal Complex (ARC), a communal space for Austin musicians where people from various genres could go to jam, record, and generally just hang out. "It was awesome, man," Keith said wistfully. "It probably was the last time I felt any kind of real, open Austin music community." For Keith, ARC was what kept a sense of community going through the early days of the nineties boom, what provided a social network and a place to cheaply record. I sensed in Keith an acute feeling of loss over the privatization of the complex. I didn't know if Austin's musical scene and ARC actually functioned as the diverse musical and social utopia Keith described. But what I did know was that Keith's experience of a unified musical community was something he cherished. And its disso-lution was something he mourned.

"That, my friend, is addictive"

The next time I saw Keith play was at a medium-sized venue located near Cedar Park. Like Georgetown, Cedar Park is a once sleepy town north of Austin. A decade ago, the only thing most travelers would no-tice about Cedar Park would be the "Now Entering" and "Now Exit-ing" signs alongside the highway; a few miles of road and a convenience store or two would have been your experience. As Austin's population has swelled, however, its surrounding satellite communities have taken on the spillover. In south Austin this has meant that working-class com-munities and communities of color are being pushed out farther from the city as rents rise in the urban core.

According to Keith, however, north Austin is "full of the transplants, the people who came to Austin with money in their pockets, looking to stretch their bucks with Texas's cost of living. They just gradually moved here, and while some spend the money for a location in the city, a lot of them decide to live a little farther out so they can have the Mc-Mansion and the whole white-picket-fence thing while still getting the Austin experience."

"How do you know they're transplants?" I wondered aloud.

Keith pondered the question, his eyes wandering toward the ceiling. "Well, I can't say for sure, I suppose, but after a lot of shows up there I get people coming up to me and saying, 'That was so cool! This is the kind of show I was hoping to see when I came to Texas.' Others, I can just tell from the accents."

The particular venue in Cedar Park where I saw Keith was located in a strip mall next to a road whose sides were dotted with evidence of the community's growth: construction sites in various stages of completion, bright-white freshly laid concrete, and stoplights at newly busy intersections, installed but not yet turned on. As I entered the concert hall I heard the owner excitedly talking to two uniformed police officers. Apparently the club itself had been open only a few weeks, and this was the owner's first chance to hobnob with the police as a proud manager. "Ya'll are welcome here whenever you want, guys!" he said to them with all the bluster of a new father. "But let me know if you need to go to the backstage area, because you guys know you never know what musicians are up to, and I don't want to get anybody in trouble." The police officers and the owner shared a laugh over the idea, and I sensed that the owner had some degree of excitement at the prospect of musicians drinking, or smoking, or doing who knows what else in the back of *his* club.

But Keith was not drinking, or smoking, or doing who knows what else in the back of the club. He was quietly sipping water, and he was worrying about a drummer who was running late because his car wouldn't start. "Well, suppose I'd better go out there and do some hustling," he said with an air of resignation. He stood up from the metal folding chair, set down his water, and smoothed out his red-and-white plaid button-down shirt, making sure it was still tucked into his jeans. Then he pushed through the double doors separating the backstage from the seating area and walked into the darkly lit room, his boots rhythmically thudding against the wooden floor.

He first went to the gregarious owner, now finished conversing with the police, and they exchanged pleasantries and firm handshakes. After that I watched Keith meet and greet with a steady stream of fans, contacts, and staff: the longtime friend who came out to the show; the new fan who had just caught him at a gig last week; the buxom blonde who asked for a picture; the old bearded fellow in a motorized scooter who seemed to be a frequent presence at Keith's performances; the concert promoter who just happened to be there; the five-year-old boy who wanted to meet the musician but then hid nervously behind his father's leg.

By the time the show began there were close to one hundred people in the building. Overhearing their informal conversations, I could tell that many of them worked down the street and just happened to be there because it was the closest happy hour. "Did you get a chance to look at that new batch of code?" a tall bearded young man asked a shorter red-haired fellow. At that moment I realized Keith was performing for the "creative class" of the new north Austin.

But the show was also about people coming specifically to see Keith. "You're going to like him. I saw him at Cedar Street last year," one woman said to her girlfriend. "I saw him with his cover band, and they were incredible," a tall man mentioned to his waitress as he leaned back in his chair. But whatever the reason for being there, all eyes turned to the stage when Keith introduced himself and said the words I imagined he had been waiting to say for a while: "This is from my new album."

As I heard Keith play in a bigger venue and with a backing band, I began to appreciate his showmanship. This was a man who had devoted his life to being not just a musician but an entertainer, and it showed. He deployed classic concert tropes, from the exciting—standing back-to-back with his lead guitarist during a blistering guitar solo, taking giant windmill strums on his instrument—to the mundane, as when he gave shout-outs to his band members (Dave on the bass, everybody!), or when he mentioned multiple times that "if you like the show, come see me by the merchandise table after! I've got a bunch of freshly pressed CDs and T-Shirts and lots of other goodies!"

There was an energy in the building throughout the show. My sociological mind quickly recognized this as an instance of collective effervescence, the time when a community comes together and participates in the same action, creating a sense of excitement and unity that produces social cohesion between those who might have previously been strangers. Keith put it more succinctly than I when he told me one night over a beer, "The spark that you get when you're performing on a stage, and you're causing people to act a certain way, and that reaction comes back and causes you to reciprocate, and you've got that energy? That, my friend, is addictive."

Like all good things, Keith's show eventually came to a close, finishing in a cacophony of sound, a flurry of lights, and a roar of applause. People began to file out or talk amongst themselves as Keith exited the stage to man the merchandise table and begin the postshow hustle. Merchandise, I learned, is another key revenue stream for struggling musicians. While I wouldn't say things flew off the table, there was definitely some commerce going on. According to Keith, the profit margin on merchandise is extremely lucrative, so even selling a handful of things at each gig can add up substantially when it comes to monthly budgeting.

"I see music; it's a language I can understand"

Keith lives alone. He was married once, for a few years, and then divorced. He has no children. I got the sense from our conversations that he doesn't see a family fitting into his lifestyle. His stories of forming and dissolving bands were peppered not only with people moving on to better things associated with bigger names but also with band members dropping out of music altogether—after college, after marriage, after the birth of a child.

Keith, however, "never wanted to go practically—you know, for the nuclear family. Go here, get my degree, get a job in this so I can get my retirement, my insurance, take care of a family. I didn't want to live a practical life, and so I took a risk doing what I love. I'm not opposed to having a family, but at this point I feel like I've kind of missed the boat on that one." For Keith, family is a luxury that his music career has not afforded him.

Apologizing for not asking the question sooner, I queried Keith as to exactly why he likes music. "Some people are just born with it, man. It's like race car drivers. You're predisposed genetically to be good at something. I see music. It's a language I can understand." Keith seemed a bit pained to explain something that to him was akin to asking why fish swim. "I dunno, man, this stuff's in my blood. So it's easy for me to write a song that doesn't suck. Whether or not it's going to be a hit, who knows? You can never know. But I can tell you that it's not going to suck."

While writing a song that "doesn't suck" may be easy for Keith, he still carries with him a very workmanlike approach to his craft. "To be a songwriter, you have to write," he told me. "You can't have just written some songs. You've gotta set goals like anything else, and you have to write songs to be a songwriter." Every weekday morning, Keith wakes up early, makes himself some breakfast—usually oatmeal and coffee or orange juice—and gets to work. Mondays are "business" days, when he books gigs or gets caught up on his e-mails. Wednesdays and Fridays are rehearsal days, when he gets together with his fellow musicians to hone a song. I listened to Keith giddily describe the ability to share versions of songs with fellow musicians via e-mail or file storage sites. "When I started out, man, you had work tapes. And if you changed something, you had to give everyone new cassettes. Now I just drag and drop it, share the folder, and BOOM, we're all on the same page." Tuesdays and Thursdays are writing days. I asked him about his writing process: "It all starts with a spark. Then you have a focus: In my live set, I need some upbeat songs that define me—not about love, but who am I? Who's this country singer, what am I about? Then I also write for a publishing catalog, and so people might be singing my songs out there, and I get a cut from that."

I scribbled on a piece of paper "song publishing," adding it to a quickly growing list of small ways Keith makes money. I could see it beginning to add up to a livable life as a professional musician in Austin. It was not death by a hundred cuts; it was life by a hundred revenue streams. It was a collection of bits and pieces that, strung together, allowed Keith to precariously live in Austin on the basis of music alone. Keith continued:

"Sometimes you can make it doing what you love. I don't think a lot of people work as hard as I have. A lot of people just hang out and think, 'Okay, I'm good.' But you've got to market yourself. You've got to hustle, to establish relations. And you've got to seek out those opportunities—the merch, the song publishing—that will let you make it."

Keith does not take being a professional musician for granted. If he did, he would have lost the title long ago. The daily practices of work—the ritual of the mornings, the hours of sitting with a guitar, the feeling of obligation toward producing songs—ground Keith's existence as a musician and are how he justifies his modest success. Add these habits together with a sometimes grueling schedule of live gigs, and a livable life can be made playing music in Austin. According to Keith, this life dictates constant uncertainty, periodic economic vulnerability, never-ending effort, and habitual sleep deprivation. On the day of a gig, Keith is often looking at a ten- to twelve-hour workday. A steep cost, to be sure. The benefits, Keith told me, are measured not in dollars or in autographs but in respect. "Did you ever want to be famous?" I asked Keith one day before a gig. Keith looked up at the ceiling and rolled his tongue around in his mouth for a second before answering. "I don't want to be famous. I want to be respected. Writing songs, publishing songs, playing songs—I want people to respect me as a songwriter."

As Keith tried to position himself as a solo artist, he had to learn a new skill: the digital hustle. For an "old guy" like Keith this was a process filled with both opportunity and trepidation. "On one hand," he said, gesturing with his left arm, "it's great because it's easier for me to connect with fans. I don't need to depend on a PR department or some record label for my success. I can depend on myself. On the other hand, this was all new to me, man. I didn't have a Facebook or know what tweets were five years ago. So there was a big learning curve, but it was fun. I knew that in today's music industry, I have to sell myself. I have to kind of make a brand out of me and then market it. So yeah, it's a hustle, but it's a digital hustle."

Keith's experience of having to brand and market himself as an individual product is characteristic of today's neoliberal economy. This is both a revolutionary opportunity borne through technology that allows people such as Keith to have a much stronger say in their careers and a symptom of an individualizing trend in modern society that puts occupational success or failure squarely on the shoulders of the individual. In a prior era Keith could have pointed to the label's PR department or bad bookings if an album didn't sell as well as expected. Now, for better or worse, Keith has no one to depend on but himself.

"Before you go, let me show you a new song I'm working on," Keith said as he motioned toward the spare bedroom. Inside was a dense web of musical and electronic equipment: a computer connected to various components, some identifiable—amps, effects boards, speakers—and some I had no clue about. A few guitars were lined up against the wall. On one side of the room, Keith's high school and college diplomas were proudly framed and hung. On the other side were pictures, a few from gigs but mostly old pictures of family and childhood. Keith told me this music setup was made up of various pieces he had slowly and steadily collected over the years, with a large investment made in software when he decided to embark on a solo career.

Keith went to work pulling up a recent song. As he cued it up, I recalled Keith telling me about his experience of recording. "When you get to recording," he said, "you're an artist trying to put it on the canvas. And when you get that ultimate stroke, it's forever. You can go back twenty years from now and go, 'Damn!'" The opening piano notes came out, and I looked at Keith. He was doing a bit of air drumming and humming, trying his best to cover his enthusiasm with professionalism for the sociologist in the room. Keith may not have any children, but I think Keith sees these songs as his legacy.

"'Live Music Capital of the World'? Not here"

Since 2000, Keith has witnessed profound changes in the Austin music scene. These days, playing gigs doesn't make as much as it used to. Whereas Keith might have made $200 by himself doing a gig in the eighties, now bands are lucky to get $300 as a group. "And then when you factor in promotion, gas, and paying everyone, I'm either even or out of pocket for playing a gig!" he explained to me incredulously. In these instances, Keith always makes sure to pay his band before he pays himself. "Chances are they're doing worse than me," he told me.

The dwindling economic prospects of being a musician in Austin caused Keith to look elsewhere. At first Keith took up real estate to survive. Unfortunately, Keith's entry into real estate happened at precisely the time the Austin market experienced a downturn. Thus in 2002 Keith weighed his options and decided to move to Nashville, where he stayed until 2007, working as a studio musician and touring with big acts as part of a backup band. "I had played with this guy in a band back in the nineties, and he told me about this opportunity in Nashville. Some of the people there were already familiar with some of my stuff, so I was able to go up there and get pretty steady work. It always helps to know people who know people, especially in this business."

And here is where I had an epiphany about the many long and winding strands of Keith's social network. They are not about showing off. They are not about trying to create some narrative of inflated success. Rather, these connections are social capital. This network is an essential part of Keith's survival strategy. It's an integral part of his hustle; those names and connections can at any point become key entry points to new opportunities. I was reminded of a famous sociological concept: the strength of weak ties.

When it comes to certain tasks—such as job finding—weak social ties allow people to reach populations and audiences with whom they might not have been able to connect through strong ties. Keith may not be lifelong friends with the guy who helped him get into the Nashville music scene, but the simple act of forming and then maintaining a tie through infrequent interactions turned out to be incredibly essential for Keith in terms of surviving through this period of economic scarcity. This is why Keith's web of friends, contacts, and ex-bandmates was so essential to the way he described his life to me.

When Keith returned from Nashville, "that's when the changes really stuck out. Don't get me wrong, they were likely happening before, but leaving and coming back? Before, all the places downtown had bands. Now it's not so much a live music scene as it is a drinkin' scene. It really is." I asked Keith how he feels about this.

"All these developments—the W, Austin City Lofts, all those other condos—those places went up in the center of the 'Live Music Capital of the World,' and . . . it's no secret, but they cut corners on those things. They could have done soundproof glass on the windows. But, you know, it's all about money down there. All about development. So they didn't finish out those places with adequate insulation, and the people who stay there complain about the noise. Now you've got a UT professor living downtown. Now you've got a surgeon. So when you've got money and power, the power just squeezes out the live music. I've been watching that for the last decade or so."

In downtown clubs with outside venues all live music must be finished by 10:00 p.m. because of a city ordinance that limits noise after 10:30 p.m. to eighty-five decibels. For comparison, your average dishwasher or garbage disposal operates at eighty decibels. The express purpose of this ordinance is to allow new full-time downtown residents—professors, surgeons—some peace and quiet. This is notable for two reasons. One, enforcement of the ordinance is classed: bars and clubs east of Interstate 35 are not monitored, presumably because the city cares less about producing peace and quiet for the residents there, or, to use Keith's terminology, because there's no money and thus no power. And two, this has indeed muzzled the mingling of music that used to emerge from every doorway on Sixth Street and that Keith recalled so fondly from his playing days in the eighties and nineties. Keith, however, showed a remarkable degree of sanguinity toward these large-scale urban trends:

"If I spent a million on a place, I don't necessarily want a band coming through my window at midnight, you know? But I make my living in music. And it's hard to keep a straight face when they call Austin the

'Live Music Capital of the World,' and all they're trying to do is stamp it out! 'Live Music Capital of the World'? Not here. Not in this zip code. Not downtown. Everything's moving out to the perimeters, [and] you lose the unity. There was a scene. It was the same people. Now there's no scene. You've got urban growth—these places that pop up on the fringes of the city. People don't like going downtown. It's just a hassle. And so that's where it's headed now."

Like Gumbo's, Keith, his blue-collar fans, and apparently live music itself have been displaced from the heart of the city. Where there was once "a rockin' scene," there are now shot bars, luxury condos, and corporate interests.

In a bit of irony, however, it is precisely those corporate interests that play a large part in Keith's extremely modest financial success. When Keith returned to Austin full-time in 2007, he "pulled a few strings, made a few calls, and rustled up a cover band," again showing the very essential role weak social ties have played in Keith's hustling career. In cover bands, Keith told me, "it's a different art. We play our instruments at a very high level. Our job is to make people feel something, to make them go, 'Oh, wow, that's my favorite song!'"

Over the intervening seven years, through a combination of grit, sweat, and determination Keith's cover band has developed a reputation. The band is often booked in the handful of downtown venues that still promote live music. For example, they played Cedar Street Courtyard on Fourth Street for New Year's Eve in 2013 and then again on St. Patrick's Day. But more importantly, the band is a popular booking for corporate events and private parties.

"We play a lot of weddings. There, you never know what they want, so you've got to come prepared—some of the new pop stuff for the girls and some of the classic rock for the guys and then a bunch of country standards, jazz standards. Al Green, 'Let's Stay Together'—that kind of thing," Keith told me.

"But the best money is corporate parties—Dell meetings, Apple corporate conferences, whatever. At those gigs you have to have a dinner set, where you're playing, but you're docile—Harry Connick Jr., Frank Sinatra, George Strait, Michael Bublé, that kind of stuff. It's kind of routine, but I find fun in the execution of the material. Just to play together and deliver those songs better than the artist that recorded them? That makes it worth it. So yeah, you can make money on the corporate circuit if you can get in and do it well."

For Keith, the cover band and the corporate bookings are what have enabled him to live the simple but hard-won life he has today.

"I'm just tired, man"

When I talked to Keith, he was juggling the steady paychecks of his cover band with his attempt to begin a solo career. Because his "voice is best suited for country," Keith has branded himself as a country rock solo artist; "with country, it's all about a good feel, a good story." But how do you start a solo career, I wondered aloud. "My plan is to go after the college kids. That's my demographic," Keith told me. "Those kids listen to a lot of country, and you've got the Texas music scene—Kevin Fowler, Pat Green, Randy Rogers, Josh Abbott—they make that same circuit, and I hear they do quite well. So that would be my ideal future. But those are college kids, so it's a bit of a crapshoot."

"How does that circuit work?" I asked him. "Can you rely on contacts you already have?"

Keith looked down and spoke a bit more quietly. "It's a different scene, so on some level I'm starting from scratch. I've got some hustle there. But, you know, College Station—nobody's heard of me. I'll have to break in on radio and then piggyback on someone else, opening up for them. That's part of the hustle too. 'Hey, can I open up that show?' That's the thing; it's all shaking hands, doing favors, asking people for favors."

"Do you ever dream of getting past hustling?" I asked, pressing the issue further. "Seems like a lot of uncertainty and elbow grease."

Keith was quick to respond. "Well, what's the alternative? If you don't do it, you're not going to make it. There are plenty of musicians who would love to have what I have right now, so I'm not going to complain."

In our conversations, Keith spoke to me about the difficulties of juggling self-promotion, self-booking, and self-merchandising with writing, playing, and recording songs. He recognized the mental and emotional anxiety this produced in himself, but at the time he was short on solutions to escape the cycle of book, play, repeat that comprises the majority of his income.

Some may see Keith's embracement of daily uncertainty, individualism, and fatalism as masculine bravado. And indeed, a central part of what it means to be a man in society is to be sturdy and unemotional. Working-class masculinities often embrace the physical daily grind of labor as hypermasculine, distinguishing themselves and their work from the feminized worlds of white-collar occupations. Additionally, men are expected to be independent, relying on themselves and their own abilities to "make it." This feeling is even more acute in a place like Texas, where the myth of the self-made man and a history steeped in frontier masculinities continue to inform the concept of how to be a man in modern Texan culture. From this perspective, Keith's bravado is a normative way for him to understand his own vulnerabilities while still appearing manly.

However, I often felt that Keith was also trying to be humble. His so-called weak ties bring him into daily contact with other musicians who likely do envy Keith's life—musicians who, from Keith's perspective, work less, write less, and don't work the phones. It is the hustle, and his dedication to it, that distinguishes Keith and allows him to understand his ability to fashion a career in a difficult industry. The hustle may be never ending, but that also means it's dependable.

In one of our final conversations, however, I learned that Keith had a strategy to get himself out of the cycle, or at least to take a break from it. He told me he had recently taken on a second job, drawing on his short foray into real estate in the early two-thousands: working at a title company as a marketing rep. Concerned, I asked if everything was alright.

"I'm just tired, man."

He had indeed seemed tired on that day, his eyes drooping slightly and his usually animated personality muted. The problem was not money; it was time. While music was continuing to pay the bills, Keith was putting in sixty- to seventy-hour weeks—with workdays not ending until the bars closed at 2:00 a.m. Keith's modest life was coming at the price of his social life, his free time, and even his sleep. "If I can pull in some money with this title job," he said, "then I can cut back on some of the weekday gigs—maybe get some actual time off." I nodded. Keith yawned sleepily.

"It's too late to turn back now"

The last time I see Keith play is at a place called Shooters, this time about a half-hour drive southwest of downtown Austin. As I sit in traffic, anxious about making it in time to see the band take the stage, I am re-minded of Keith telling me about his own traffic strategy. "Nothin' left to do but leave early, man," he said. "If the gig's at seven, and I've got to drive through Austin—which I usually do—I'm on the road by four at the latest. It's gotten worse over the years, but what are you gonna do?" Keith told me with a sigh.

This night Keith is with his cover band, and you can tell by the

packed house that the band's reputation is as Keith advertised. I get there just as they take the stage. Keith, who has dropped his country-tinged outfit, is sporting a rock-and-roll vintage T-shirt and torn blue jeans. He looks as comfortable being the silent lead guitarist as he did being front and center during his solo gigs.

The amount of energy and excitement in the show is cranked to eleven. Or at least that's how I experience it. I am squished between people, I hear songs I know, and I even get a beer spilled on me. If this isn't a rocking rock concert, I don't know what is. And indeed, a night like this night may be as close as Keith ever gets to playing out a rock star dream. But if there's one thing I've learned from Keith, it's that working in reality is more important than playing out dreams. Keith may never get rich, but that was never the point.

And what about his newly minted solo career? While I certainly en-joyed his album, I have no idea whether it will drastically change Keith's life. What is success for a musician now? The days of pining for a record label to sign you so you can release a major album and hopefully sell millions of copies are gone. In its place is an atomized musical world, a world made possible by the Internet's unique ability to democratize con-tent by eliminating the major record label middlemen in the relation-ships between musicians and their fans. This means that there's a less clear path to the richness of stardom, but many more roads that can lead to a semifunctional life as a musician.

In this way, while the "Live Music Capital of the World" has changed drastically, Keith is just as emblematic of a working Austin musician now as he was three decades ago. For Keith, success is not a mansion and fast cars; success is doing what you love and being respected for it. Sure, Keith might prefer making his money from his solo work, but if playing pop songs for white-collar Dell workers is what it takes, if driving for hours to get to a gig is what it takes, if the hustle of pushing burned CDs, T-shirts, and other "merch" is what it takes to live a musician's life in 2014 in Austin, then that's a small price to pay in Keith's eyes. Even then, you may need to get a side job if you'd like to enjoy amenities like weekends and forty-hour workweeks.

Of course, one free perk of the job is the elation of an appreciative crowd, whose wave of applause and shouts startle me back into the present. The show is over; the crowd is appreciative and buzzing as I meet up with Keith backstage. "I just want to keep doin' what I'm doin'," he tells me in between sips of bottled water after the show. "It's too late to turn back now."

Recommended Readings

Durkheim, E. 1995. *The Elementary Forms of Religious Life*. New York: Free Press. In this foundational piece of sociology, Emile Durkheim analyzes the collective behaviors of religious worship and develops his notion of "collective effervescence."

Horfsfall, S., J. Meij, and M. Probstfield, eds. 2013. *Music Sociology: Examining the Role of Music in Social Life*. Boulder, CO: Paradigm. This edited volume provides diverse sociological analyses of music, offering basic concepts of musical sociology and providing a historical overview of the role of music in society.

Mellard, J. 2013. *Progressive Country: How the 1970s Transformed the Texan in Popular Culture*. Austin: University of Texas Press. Historian Jason Mellard traces the role of country music in transforming notions of what being a Texan means in U.S. culture, paying particular attention to the development of Anglo-Texan masculinity and the cultural construction of Austin as a progressive city in Texas.

Shank, B. 1994. *Dissonant Identities: The Rock'n'Roll Scene in Austin, Texas*. Hanover, CT: University of Wesleyan Press. Barry Shank, himself a musician who played and lived in the Texas capital, studies the history of its popular music, the cultural and economic context, and the broader ramifications of that music as a signifying practice capable of transforming identities.

CHAPTER 10

Xiomara: Working toward Home

JENNIFER SCOTT

I ran into Xiomara recently at the worker center in Austin. We embraced warmly with the customary kiss on the cheek and exchanged pleasantries. I asked her what good fortune had brought her out to the meeting that evening. She was an infrequent visitor these days to the weekly meetings where we had first met while serving as volunteers years before.

She said that she was there to recruit new members for her housecleaning cooperative. "We have so much work now, we are having to turn away jobs!" she said and laughed. "Imagine it. Before, we were worried that we didn't have enough work. Now we need more workers."

A warm woman with a cherubic face, Xiomara has light brown skin and naturally curly hair. While always well-groomed, she is nononsense about her appearance—the exact opposite of her oldest daughter, Annabel, whom she describes as having "alta paciencia para pintarse [so much patience for making herself up]." Xiomara always pulls her hair back in a ponytail and generally wears some combination of jeans and a T-shirt or pullover. Though I have seen her dressed up with full makeup (usually her daughter's doing), she "doesn't see the point" of going to all the trouble.

Whether due to the absence of makeup or the determined positivity with which she approaches life, Xiomara looks much younger than her thirty-eight years. The second of six children, she assumed charge of most of the household responsibilities at twelve years old, when her father passed away, so that her mother and older sister could work. She followed her husband from Mexico to Austin twelve years ago, and, despite early isolation and hardship, she has started her own cooperative business, making a life for her family in the city she now calls home.

"Thank God we didn't suffer"

The first thing Xiomara said when I asked her about crossing the border from Mexico was "thank God it wasn't sad. We didn't suffer, thank God. . . . So many stories I've heard where people had a really hard time. Thankfully, we were just fine." In the nonchalant and unassuming tone that I've come to realize is not just her customary way of speaking, but rather indicative of the humility with which she speaks about her life— as though it were somehow unremarkable—Xiomara continued. She described a journey that included spending four freezing November nights in the Sonoran desert. Though saved from the cold by discarded blankets that they had found during the day, they barely slept for fear of the rattlesnakes whose lethal music cut through the night air.

"I remember we came by Arizona," she said. "They told us we would walk for about five hours and when we arrived at . . . I can't remember what mile, a truck would pick us up. Well, we arrived there at 11:00 p.m., but they didn't pick us up." It was rumored that someone had been killed by immigration officials, resulting in extra vigilance that had made it difficult for the truck to arrive. So they had to wait, which meant sleeping in the desert. They had come with very little. Xiomara, her then nine-year-old daughter, Annabel, and the oldest of her younger brothers had joined a group of fourteen others destined to try their luck in El Norte. It was 2002, just a year after the World Trade Center towers had fallen in New York, an event with ripple effects that would reshape not only border life and border passages in the name of national security but also the daily lives of those who crossed the border clandestinely.

Luckily they were on an American Indian reservation, she said, and the seventeen-year-old boy who was guiding them on their journey knew Indians who would sell them food. During the day they waited, and in the afternoon they had to move. Recalling the landscape, Xiomara exclaimed to me, "There were too many clothes!" Picturing the Arizona desert as a closet floor with clothes strewn about, I listened to her describe how the blankets and bedspreads—discarded by the migrants in whose footsteps they followed—saved them during the freezing nights. On the fourth night the van finally arrived and carried them to Tucson.

As I listened to Xiomara tell this story I glanced over at a nearby table, overhearing a seemingly heated discussion. A young white woman with large glasses and a full sleeve tattoo was telling her companions about her participation in a recent rally for equality in women's health care at the state capitol building. We were seated at a picnic table under the live oak trees at a hip new café in the part of town that realty ads now describe as Austin's "hot East Side." This rapidly gentrifying neighborhood, located north of the Colorado River and east of Interstate 35, is where Latino families have historically lived, due in part to the intentional and then de facto segregation of the city. We chose this place for a number of our meetings because it was near a house Xiomara cleaned at that time and midway between our homes.

Turning back to Xiomara, I listened as she told me how they stayed for a week with the man in Tucson who was originally supposed to drive them to Austin. He had been picked up by police the week before their arrival, though, and his papers had been taken from him. This meant they had to wait. After a week he found them a spot in a car that would drop them off in Austin on its way to North Carolina. Though a potentially unnerving scenario, Xiomara told me she felt instantly at ease once she found out that she and the driver were actually "conocidos [acquaintances]." The man's wife was from her hometown and had gone to school with her brother, though they hadn't known each other back home. Next thing they knew, they were on her husband's doorstep in Austin.

Risking It All for Love

Xiomara decided to come to the United States by accident—or, more accurately, by way of an accident. When I asked her about the decision, she said, "I *never* even thought about coming here to this country." Even when her husband immigrated, it seemed natural for her to stay behind; she had been uninterested in moving and confident that he would return to live with her in her hometown. An accident happened though, and all of a sudden she was faced with the realization that her love and companion of almost nine years was "here [in the United States] alone, by himself."

She had been fifteen years old and living on a military base with her family when a young man from the military school began paying attention to her as she walked her younger brother to and from school. Their courtship moved swiftly from walks in the neighborhood park and rejections of his advances, to her becoming his girlfriend, to a marriage proposal. As she remembered, "We had been boyfriend/girlfriend no more than six months. It was only a little time, but I was very much in love with him. So I told him yes." After dating for a total of nine months they were married in her hometown. She had just turned sixteen, and he was eighteen.

The first years of her marriage were perhaps unsurprisingly tumultuous, considering not only the couple's youth but also the fact that they became parents within the year. Her eyes flashed as she told me how she felt disrespected by the doctor who attended her during the birth of Annabel, because she was just sixteen and, in her words, "just a little girl [*bien chamaca*]." She said she yelled at him, saying, "Hey, I'm married, and my husband is outside waiting for me," and then she called for her husband, who was waiting outside the door, so that he would answer back and prove her point.

Their young relationship also weathered a number of early separations (his family lived in another town), several bouts of unemployment and underemployment, and multiple moves between three cities. They finally settled down in her hometown, where her husband, Eduardo, eventually got a job as a police officer. His job not only provided steady work but also contacts for plumbing jobs that allowed him to continue working in the career he had begun in Mexico City. He made enough money to support them, but Xiomara would sometimes supplement their income by helping her mother clean at the hacienda where the latter worked. They were doing all right, as she told me: "We didn't have a lot of luxury, but we lived well. We weren't lacking for anything. We lived with the necessary." Her husband, however, in his constant search for different opportunities and better work, had developed a penchant for adventure. And so, when he was offered the opportunity to travel to the United States to work in construction, he took it.

When Eduardo first came to the United States he worked for about a year and a half in roofing, keeping steady communication with Xiomara and sending her money for herself and their daughter. Then all of a sudden there was nothing. She didn't hear from him for over a week. Terrified and completely unsure of how to find out what happened, she finally got a call from him. He was at a hospital in Austin. He had been working on the roof of a two-story house without a harness while it was raining and had fallen. He told her that his back was broken, but his spinal cord was intact, and that he was scheduled to have an operation in two days' time.

The only state in the country that doesn't mandate that employers carry workers' compensation insurance, Texas—and its construction industry in particular—is notorious for its poor and often dangerous working conditions. The state ranks highest in the number of construction-related deaths, twice that of the state with the next highest number, California, which has a bigger industry. Following a too familiar pattern of construction employers, her husband's boss (and his principal connection in the United States) told him that when he entered the hospital he had to use a different name, and that if he told them who he was he would be deported. Terrified that he was going to be paralyzed and feeling like he was in no position to argue, he obliged. "Had I called and asked for him," she said, "they wouldn't have told me anything, because he was there under another name."

Thankfully he didn't end up paralyzed, nor did he need an operation. He wanted to return home—and his employer was all too eager to finance his trip back to Mexico—but the doctors warned him that travel with his twisted spine would leave him paralyzed. "And so I came here," she said. "He didn't want this. He didn't want me to come, but I told him I was coming. And within about a week I had everything arranged."

Learning to Drive

"I like my work," Xiomara said one day as we sat at the café that we had taken up as our semi-usual meeting spot. "Even though I get really tired, I like when people like it—when they see that [my work] is good. I take a lot of pride in it." When I asked her how she got started cleaning, she began by first telling me how she learned to drive.

For the first year or so, Xiomara managed fine using Austin's public transportation, but after her second daughter, Alex, was born (within a year of her arrival in the United States) things got more complicated. One day Alex fell ill, and Xiomara was stranded trying to get back from the clinic. It was then that she decided it was time to learn to drive. She had mentioned this to her husband, and although she had practiced driving a few times with her neighbor, it was the night he came home and declared "I'm going to teach you to drive" that set her on a new course. They got in the car and started out in her neighborhood. There weren't many cars on the road, and she felt okay until they came to the entrance ramp of a highway near their home. Not understanding what he was asking her to do, she followed his instructions to get onto the highway. She then immediately realized where they were and started trembling with fear—the cars were going by fast. She managed to get them to the next exit and off the highway, but the experience stayed with her. "It was the first and last time I let my husband teach me," she said.

After mastering driving, she began to look for reasons to get out of the house. Initially, "it didn't really get to a point where I had to go to work," she said, "but as I got really bored I began to do catalogs and sell things to the neighbors. I would sell them for a period of time." Work at first wasn't about the money, but rather more about the distraction. When Alex finally entered elementary school Xiomara had had enough of feeling confined within her house and told her husband she was getting a job. Ignoring his lack of enthusiasm for the idea, she spent the next six months filling out applications for restaurants, hotels, cleaning companies—anywhere she thought might give her a job—only to receive the dismissive response of "we'll call you back." ("Never, never did they talk to me.") Getting nowhere, she and Annabel, then fifteen, decided to take matters into their own hands.

They printed over one thousand business cards advertising their cleaning services, and, with the help of her brother and one of Annabel's friends, they distributed them all throughout the nearby neighborhoods where they thought they might find work. No one called them.

Then their break came at H-E-B, a local grocery store. Xiomara noticed a cleaning van and, with little to lose, decided to talk to the driver. She asked the woman for work and was told that she was too late—they had just hired someone. The woman took her number and promised to call if something opened up, and though she smiled and nodded, Xiomara said she remembers thinking, "Okay, that's never happening." Yet two weeks later the woman called. She asked her to go that day for an "interview" and gave her directions to a house in one of the wealthiest Austin neighborhoods on the western edge of town.

Xiomara arrived at the house, which she described, wide-eyed, as "enormous," and was instructed to clean all of the wood trim throughout the five-thousand-square-foot home. The woman was impressed with her work and offered her a job on the spot. She would earn ten dollars an hour to clean the house three times a week for five hours each time. Going from nothing to $150 a week felt to Xiomara like a windfall, especially coupled with the stories she had heard from others about earning only seven dollars an hour or thirty dollars a house. Additionally, it turned out that, despite the detailed instructions about how carefully the upkeep should be handled, her new *patrona* wasn't overly demanding. Setting the tone for the loyalty that would characterize her relationships with employers, she continued cleaning this home until it was sold by the owners over a year later.

It wasn't until after she began this job that she received the only two phone calls that would result from the distribution of the thousand business cards. Those two calls would, however, lay the foundation for her cleaning career. The first call was from a man who requested a price estimate for cleaning his house. As she recounted this first experience of providing an estimate for a cleaning job, Xiomara interrupted herself to tell me that she was sad because this same man was now moving to California. Indeed, she had seen him at his home just the day before, as he had hired her to help him pack for the move. That first estimate had turned into a six-year employment relationship, over the course of which she cleaned four different houses as her boss (a real estate enthusiast) moved from home to home. The second call was from a man whose house she continues to clean as a side contract separate from the houses she services for her cleaning cooperative. Although she was in fact already working for the *patrona* before receiving these calls, it is these two men whom she refers to as her first employers.

Cleaning as Service Work

Once, in the winter of 2013, when we were at Xiomara's home, I noticed a child's rocking chair that, though it fit Alex perfectly, had the name

Franklin written on it. When I inquired as to who owned the chair with the unfamiliar name, she said it was a gift from her boss. She then pointed to a large picture (still in its box on the floor) and several other things in the living room that she had received as gifts from employers who were moving, downsizing, or simply redecorating. Such patronage is effective in encouraging employees to continue working, even without improvements in wages. Xiomara said it was not altogether uncommon that she would receive "gifts" from employers for whom she had worked for awhile. Indeed, it was one of her favorite aspects of the job. "What I like is that my bosses, the owners, treat me well and have always been nice to me. It [the work] makes me tired, but they always like it."

The benevolent *patrón* that Xiomara describes is a common archetype of the domestic service sector and reflective of the intimate nature of the work. While certainly better than outright abuse, and often well-intended and even sincerely nice, benevolence on the part of the employer does little to change the existing income inequality that places one person in the service of another. According to a national survey of domestic workers, the median wage for housecleaners is still $10 an hour (though $12 hourly for whites), a rate that, while above the federal minimum wage of $7.25, is below the city living wage rate of $11 an hour and far below the $16.04 hourly rate considered to be a living wage for a family in Austin (based on 2013 fair market rent). At $20,800 annually (if the work is consistent and full-time) a $10 an hour wage is still below the $23,850 annual income threshold that defines a family of four as living in poverty according to the 2014 federal poverty guidelines.

The expectation of often unquestioned subservience, occurring even under the best of working conditions marked by real kindness, is reflected in what Xiomara described as her worst experience with an employer. While Xiomara situates the episode as relatively benign in comparison to the experiences of many of her colleagues in domestic work, in its subtlety it illustrates the centrality of the power hierarchy in the lives of domestic laborers.

Xiomara had been cleaning the house of a woman for about a year. Her boss, a little eccentric, had been exponentially increasing the collection of knickknacks and ornamental pieces that Xiomara was required to remove and replace while dusting. As a result, the hours required to do the job began increasing, yet there was no simultaneous increase in pay. Deciding that it was only reasonable to receive more money for more work, Xiomara asked for a raise. A little put out, her

boss agreed. But the next week when Xiomara showed up for work, the woman fired her, claiming that she had found someone who would do the job and even more for the same rate. "Me dió coraje [I was angry]," said Xiomara, "because it was such little extra money, and it was just because I had asked her to give me a raise." When Xiomara complained to one of her boss's other employees, the woman explained it plainly to her: "La patrona has to be the one to decide to give you a raise, Xiomara. It has to be her idea. You can't ask her for one. You can't make demands."

Unlike most jobs in the United States, domestic work is almost universally excluded from the protection of most federal labor laws. Characterized by low pay (often even less than the state minimum wage), mostly nonexistent employment benefits, the high likelihood of work-related injury, and little to no control over working conditions because contracts are almost nonexistent, domestic work falls in the category of what some scholars have referred to as "precarious employment." At the same time, domestic work is also intimate and, by nature, intensely personal. Workers labor in close contact with the most private aspects of families' personal lives—they have keys to their homes and often know their relatives and children, if not in person then by photograph.

While this leads to almost familial interactions—like the friendly reprimand Xiomara received once for showing up to work on Christmas Eve—being treated as a member of the family can be far from being treated as an equal.

Better to Not Work at All

When she first came to the United States Xiomara didn't work, because she didn't have to. As she recalls, the family was able to make ends meet on just the income her husband brought home from construction. "When we arrived here my husband had a stable job, and we did well," she said. "Every fifteen days he would get paid, earning around $1,000 or $1,200, so we had enough to pay all the bills and to go out." The good life was hard earned: ten-hour workdays, Monday through Saturday, initially for just $55 a day. When he became an independent contractor, though, things changed.

Though the money was better and the work was the same, the nature of his responsibilities changed in ways for which the family was unprepared. Things began to go wrong the first time he did a job and his employer refused to pay him. He was out over $5,000. Though not receiving his own salary was hard enough, what was even more devastating to the family was the fact that he employed other workers and had to come up with their wages.

The first time it happened the family lost his truck, which he used for work. Having already paid off nearly $14,000, he owed just under $3,000. They had to use all of their money and savings to pay his workers, leaving nothing to cover their own bills, including the payments on the truck. There was little they could do. The truck was repossessed, and they lost all the money they had put into it. This, she said, became a pattern.

"He would get one [a truck] and be paying for a year, and then after a year a boss would refuse to pay him. We would have to get money to pay the workers and the bills, and then they would repossess the car." It happened twice more, each time leaving them worse off. "I tell him, 'Don't work for people you don't know,'" said Xiomara. "'You know it's better you don't work than let this happen to you.'"

This practice is so rampant in industries like construction and domestic service that employ a large contingent (and immigrant) workforce that it follows a seemingly textbook pattern. As Xiomara explained, "You begin to work, and they begin to pay you. It's fine initially, but then after that they don't pay."

Known as "wage theft," the practice is completely illegal; all people who work in the United States are entitled to be paid the promised wage (and in most cases at least the minimum wage) for any work performed, regardless of their eligibility to work or the quality of the work performed. Legal action against employers, however, is rare and requires the initiation of processes through the state bureaucracy that are largely unknown and difficult to access for even the most highly educated English-speaking citizens. Pressures to meet impossible bottom lines in order to secure the highest profit, working in tandem with an easy mechanism of ensuring employee subjugation—threatening them with deportation should they complain or report—provide employers with both the incentives and the tools that enable worker exploitation.

With the truck gone and no means to pay the bills, Xiomara turned to a resource used almost exclusively by individuals denied access to more mainstream financial services like credit cards and bank loans: the cash store or pawn shop. "I had acquired a number of pieces of gold jewelry," said Xiomara, "and what I had to do was sell all of it so that we could pay the bills, like the rent, and go on paying the bills of the house." Emotional, Xiomara went on to tell me that she pawned all of her jewelry at a rate that required her to pay $600 in interest monthly if she intended to keep it. Not wanting to let it go, she paid for three months. Then, realizing that she could pay every month and would still never have enough to pay it off, she gave it all up.

Ironically, it was a claim against her husband for wage theft that set her on the path to establishing her cleaning cooperative. The claim was the result of the second time her husband's wages had been stolen—he had negotiated and completed a construction job, but once it was complete his employer refused to pay him. He was owed a total of $4,000. While it was bad enough that he did not receive his own wages or the money to cover the cost of the materials, what further complicated the situation was the fact that the amount he was owed included money he needed to pay the wages of the workers he had hired to complete the job. Obligated to pay them, regardless of whether or not he himself was paid, the family was left scrambling to come up with the money. Then there was a knock on their door.

Xiomara answered to find herself confronted by one of her husband's workers. The man, irate, told her that if he wasn't paid what he was owed, he was going to bring a bunch of people from his organization to picket on their lawn to show their neighbors that her husband was the kind of man who didn't pay his workers. Determined to avoid such a scandal at her home and convinced that she just needed to explain to someone that her husband was also a victim in this situation, Xiomara did some investigating to find the organization that the worker had mentioned.

Recalling a Univision commercial advertising a meeting for people who hadn't been paid for their work, she found the organization's contact information and called. To her dismay they were not wholly welcoming. When she explained the situation and admitted that her husband had not yet paid his workers, she was told that they could not help, despite the fact that the reason her husband hadn't paid was because he himself had not yet been paid. If they wanted help recovering what her husband was owed, he would have to pay his workers first. Explaining this to her husband, Xiomara declared, "Vamanos [we're going], and we're going to pay him in front of them so they know we pay. Then we're getting them to help us." They pieced the money together and paid his workers. Then, with the organization's support and advocacy, they eventually recovered the $4,000 her husband was owed.

After the case was closed, Xiomara continued to participate in the organization, attending meetings where she assisted other unpaid workers in filling out wage claim paperwork. She and her husband ended up using the organization's services again, this time recovering $1,500 in back wages. After participating on and off for a few years, she was presented with an opportunity to become a business owner. Some of the organization's advocates had been working with a partner organization that supports workers in organizing worker cooperatives. They thought Xiomara and some of the other women might be interested in the idea. More than a little skeptical that the idea would go anywhere but intrigued by the possibility of steady clients and a more stable income, Xiomara said, "Okay, we'll see," and agreed to attend a meeting.

Cooperative Accounts

"Now that I am in the cooperative, I can tell you that it is much better than having a standard job, and, at the very least, I have learned many things" Xiomara said. "One of the things is about working in a team, which at the beginning was really, really difficult, and we had many conflicts, but now we are more or less going and adapting ourselves." After about eight years of cleaning houses on her own or with her daughter Annabel, Xiomara took an opportunity to establish a cooperative cleaning business.

The cooperative business model is unique in that it allows each worker to become an equal owner of the business, each earning an equal share of the profit in addition to their wages. For Xiomara, however, the cooperative was not just an opportunity to move forward and grow in her work by becoming an official business owner; it was also a response to the real insecurity of her work. When clients moved or their needs for cleaning services changed, she was left without income, often for significant periods of time. Talking about her decision to participate in forming the cooperative, she said, "I had lost two clients, and my monthly income changed a lot. This was about six months before the project of the cooperative. And so when the idea about a co-op came up I needed work, and through it I thought I would get more work; so it seemed like a good idea."

Establishing the cooperative took just under a year. She and her colleagues took a six-month course from a local organization, during which they learned about running a cooperative business. They attended the two-hour class twice a week and discussed everything from administration to the business model and cleaning practices. It was hard, this period, she recalls. The class time was unpaid, and she completed it in addition to her existing cleaning job and family responsibilities.

What was promised in the long run, though, was stability. As Xiomara said, "The thing is, you know how much you are going to earn. It's what you work, and if you work more, you get more, and if you work less, less." Each participant is a business owner instead of an employee, and decisions that impact the business, and in turn the owners' lives, are made by consensus. This leaves them with few surprises. Houses are scheduled out weeks in advance for fixed rates paid to the cooperative, and they pay themselves an hourly wage of fifteen dollars for all the hours they work. The earnings beyond their wages fund first their business expenses (from cleaning products to the business taxes and gasoline) and then become profits that they distribute evenly at the end of the year.

This stability is important. However, while she appreciates the knowledge she has acquired about cooperative businesses, what really excites her, career-wise, is accounting. In one of our last meetings at her favorite restaurant, a taquería near her home, she arrived animated, excited to tell me about a new system she had devised for managing the cooperative's earnings.

She was trying to find a way to direct more of their earnings into the collective account so that they would have more profit to distribute at the end of the year. She had come up with two ideas that she was going to present to the others in their meeting the next day. I asked her how she had come up with them, and she said, "Since I was little, I have always liked doing the accounts. I would always keep lists of everything I earned and everything I spent." She has tried her best to instill this in

Annabel as well and proudly told me how, by being disciplined, Annabel would pay off the car she had bought the previous year in half the expected time frame, saving a lot of money in the long term.

The women in the cooperative have established a structure that, now that their client base is large enough, provides them all with full-time work if they want it. That means they each now earn just under $600 a week (before taxes) at their set wage rate of fifteen dollars an hour. One of the members acts as part-time administrator and handles all of the client communication and scheduling, dedicating her other hours to cleaning. The houses are set up ahead of time and distributed amongst the members according to the hours estimated to be needed for each home. The business has grown to the point that it is now over capacity; each member is working full-time, and they are having to turn away houses. The hardest part, however, has been figuring out how to work together and deal with internal conflicts in a way that supports their business. As Xiomara puts it, they have developed a "system of communication" to encourage direct communication among members. "So that's what we're doing, knowing that we can get along better, and [we're] always trying to get along and support each other."

Querido México

While Xiomara takes pride in the cooperative and in doing her work well, to hear her tell stories of her life in Mexico, you'd think it was heaven on earth. As she explains, she had never wanted to leave, and the desire to come to the United States had never entered her mind. She came because she had to, and, having done so, she misses home.

Her hometown in southern Mexico, it seems, always had perfect weather. Though Xiomara's father was very strict and didn't permit the children to play outside, she has fond memories of playing volleyball in the streets when he was at work or away. Indeed, the family had chosen to settle there even after living for a short time in Mexico City after her father died. Though Xiomara and her husband met and began their life together in Mexico City, before moving to the United States they had returned to live in her hometown. They moved into a house next door to her mother, and her whole family lived nearby. In stark contrast to her early years in the United States, when she often found herself stuck in her house, in Mexico she would often go on her own to the city center or to Mexico City to visit her siblings.

Xiomara's nostalgia for her homeland is interwoven with a deep longing for her extended family. Generally positive and forward looking about both her past and her future, Xiomara has cried only twice in my presence, both times for the same reason. The first time she was telling me a story about her youth. Her eyes were wet, yet she skillfully managed to hold back tears as she interrupted herself, saying, "Can you believe it, Jen? It's been twelve years since I have hugged my mother."

For Xiomara, the sense of loss and separation from her family is both indefinite and insurmountable. For many immigrants, family separation is an inevitable reality as temporary stays turn into permanent relocations. The maintenance of ties through visits is often highly dependent on disposable income. For undocumented families, the separation is like the border wall; while migration between the United States and Mexico without legal immigration status was once more fluid, increases in border security have made it more expensive and dangerous to cross, making temporary visits a less than viable option. Families that would once have come to the United States to work and then eventually returned back home (to Mexico or further south) now choose to stay because of the difficulty of returning.

When she was younger, Xiomara was always "glued to her [mother's] side." They did everything together. Indeed, her mother was a major source of support to her as she became a young adult. She was there during her pregnancy when her husband could not be, she lived with them to take care of Annabel during her first years while they worked in the city, and it was on her land in Xiomara's hometown that they had been building a house before the family left to come to Austin. And so she says, "It's hard to spend so many years here. . . . I have my daughters, who are studying and maybe will get better work, but it is hard to stay so far from the family. Each year, it seems as though it's been fine, but to have passed twelve years without seeing my mom—in November it will be twelve years . . . twelve years without seeing her or being able to hug her, it's something sad."

"We Skype now," Xiomara said, again approaching tears, "but it's not the same."

The Craft of Cleaning

Though Xiomara was once an active participant and volunteer at the community worker center, assisting other families who had experienced problems like wage theft, since she and her colleagues launched the cooperative, she has found that she no longer has the time to volunteer. Though she had several steady clients before, now she has enough to fill more than a full forty-hour workweek. Not only is each day consistently too full to fit in more meetings, the work itself is exhausting. The physicality of the tasks required—climbing up and down stairs, bending to scrub bathrooms, and pushing vacuums and heavy furniture—means that after over eight hours of work, and sometimes meetings of the cooperative, Xiomara arrives home with rarely enough energy left to cook an evening meal.

Xiomara begins her day around 6:00 a.m., when ten-year-old Alex wakes up and makes her way to her parents' room—turning on all the lights along the way—before curling up in their bed to catch a few last minutes of sleep. After turning all the lights back off and getting herself ready, Xiomara makes breakfast for the two of them and then helps Alex finish getting ready for school. Her husband gets up as they are finishing, and the two of them walk Alex to school around seven fifteen. Some mornings she and her husband enjoy a brief cup of coffee together when they return home, before they each head off to work. At around eight Xiomara leaves for the first house on her schedule.

She cleans three to four houses a day, sometimes substituting an office space for a house. The schedule of houses is predetermined by the co-op member who handles the administration and depends upon whether Xiomara will be working with a partner, as well as on the size of the home to be cleaned, the frequency of the home's cleaning, and the provision of special services like a deep clean or move out. Xiomara works until around 6:00 p.m., and on some days as late as 8:00 or 9:00 p.m. Most days this means that Annabel (or sometimes Xiomara's husband) is charged with picking up Alex from school. Because the days are long, each of them figures out the evening meal on his or her own. After Xiomara returns home in the evening the family spends a little time together, often watching TV, before they each retire to begin the day's routine again the next morning.

Xiomara has cleaned homes all over the city. Most often, the homes the cooperative cleans are located in west Austin, in the areas most associated with affluence. But she also regularly cleans homes on the East Side and in south Austin. The homes differ in size and style—the homes in the west typically fall into the category that she describes, wide eyed, as "enormous," while homes on the East Side are typically smaller.

However, Xiomara noted no explicit differences based on area with regard to patterns of upkeep or cleanliness of the homes—the main difference between the various houses, she said, was really whether the co-operative had cleaned the home before or whether it was a special circumstance, like a move in or move out, or if the owners had pets.

I joined Xiomara and Annabel one morning to assist them with a job cleaning a home in West Lake Hills, one of the wealthiest neighborhoods in the Austin area. As we pulled up the drive, it was hard not to be impressed. The front yard, large enough to fit both of our own homes, was shaded by several large live oak trees and home to a large gazebo that looked like it must be used for a band stage. We pulled up to the side of the three-story home and began unloading supplies.

Though the houses vary, the practice of cleaning follows a standard script. Upon arrival, Xiomara selects the tools of her trade—bucket, mop, vacuum, bag of rags of assorted colors, and the crate of cleaning products (all certified environmentally friendly)—unloads them from the trunk of her car, and brings them into the house. This chore is particularly cumbersome when one works alone, as it requires carrying all the equipment not just inside but often up one, and sometimes two, flights of stairs. Tasks are then divided. Xiomara typically assigns herself the bathrooms and the kitchen, as, she explained, "These are the rooms the owners always pay the most attention to." She prefers to clean them to ensure that the job is done to her satisfaction.

If Xiomara is working in a pair, her partner will take on the tasks of dusting and changing the bedding and then will begin to clean the floors. Whoever finishes first then joins the other to complete the rest of the tasks. In closing, Xiomara returns the tools to the mobile office that the trunk of her car has become, makes a final inspection to ensure that all is in order, pauses to retrieve the check from the table, and locks up.

After dusting the top floor of the house with Annabel, I paused at the window. From our vantage point the entire skyline of Austin was visible over the trees. As I stood there I could hear Xiomara coughing downstairs while she cleaned the bathroom. Finished with my first job, I joined her and began to clean the sinks. "Use the yellow or white rags," she said, adding, "The white are the best for doing the mirror." She explained that they have a strict color-coding system for the rags, to keep things sanitary—white and yellow rags are reserved for all the bathroom tasks, while blue rags are used to dust everywhere else. As I worked, I began coughing too, all of a sudden realizing that it was the odor of the products causing my reaction.

Taking cues from Austin's long history of environmental activism

and its internationally recognized programs like the green building program, Xiomara and her colleagues had decided to "go green" and distinguish their cooperative by exclusively using green cleaning products. I
was thus surprised by my reaction to the products—in my mind, envi-
ronment-friendly also meant people-friendly. Initially, the women had
tried to make their own products, combining a secret recipe of non-
toxic household products every week. But they discovered that not only
were the products marginally effective (it would take nearly twice as
long to get the bathroom sufficiently clean), they were also impossible
to produce in a way that consistently provided enough product. So they
switched to an eco-friendly corporate brand. Though the new products
are effective, Xiomara still wishes they could use standard products for
the deep cleans—the green products just aren't as powerful, and so using them means extra physical effort.

While it probably can't be said that green cleaning products are worse
for individual health than conventional cleaning products, the physical
reaction that our bodies have to their use is just another reminder of
the risky nature of cleaning and domestic service work. In line with the
trends of the sector, Xiomara does not have health insurance. Should
she fall sick from any illness resulting from exposure to the chemicals or
other work-related hazards, not to mention illness from any other cause,
the burden is on her to cover the cost. While the cooperative is commit-

ted to purchasing and providing health insurance for all members and is researching a way to do so, at this point the members have not yet found a plan that is within their means.

Professional cleaning contains an element of art. Though my childhood chores had included cleaning my family's home, working with Xiomara taught me that I missed the details—cleaning the water spots under the faucets and neatly folding the top sheet of paper on the toilet paper roll. Patiently, Xiomara pointed them out, waiting for me to redo the mirrors before we moved on to the bottom floor. She explained to me how these were key elements of the craft, the details that presented the home not only as clean, but as professionally clean. Though the owners were obviously most concerned about the overall cleanliness she said, confident in the cooperative's skills, simple cleanliness was not a question. It was these details that she knew helped convince them that it was her business that should keep coming back.

"Hasta aquí no más"

When Xiomara came to the United States she found her relationship with her husband changed. Her husband had become accustomed to the bachelor life, going out with friends, often drinking, and Xiomara was accustomed to nothing that she found here. On top of that, she had to care for Annabel, who was then approaching ten years of age, and she became pregnant with Alex within a couple months of arrival. Not only unaccustomed to the new place and patterns of life here, as she tells it, she was also a bit afraid.

She couldn't drive, she didn't speak the language, she had no work or even the hope of obtaining any, and her brother—the only family she had here other than her husband and her daughter—soon left. She remembers feeling torn at this time:

"I missed my family, Mexico. I wanted to go back. I wanted to be here to take care of my husband, but I wanted to go back. It took me more than a year to adapt to here. My brother was here, but I was about eight months pregnant when he decided to go back to Mexico. And I stayed here alone. Alone with my little girl . . ."

What became increasingly apparent too was her near complete dependence upon her husband. When he went out after work or on the weekends and stayed away too long, she found herself constantly tracking him down, begging him to come home, imploring him to think of her and the girls. More than just concerned about their relationship or his behavior per se, she was terrified of the consequences—that he would hurt himself or get arrested for driving drunk. "I would tell him, 'You can't do this, you'll end up in the hospital or in jail,'" she told me. "'They'll pick you up and deport you.'"

While they might seem overprotective or reactive, Xiomara's fears were not ill founded. Though sometimes described as a sanctuary city, Austin is far from a sanctuary for undocumented families. Thanks to a program called Secure Communities, the federal Immigration and Customs Enforcement agency (ICE) has an information sharing partnership with the Travis County Sheriff's Office. This allows the office to check the immigration status of anyone it detains, even if just for a minor offense, like a traffic violation or public intoxication. Despite the fact that the stated emphasis of the program is to target serious felons for deportation, according to a recent analysis of Travis County Jail and ICE data conducted by the *Austin American-Statesman*, almost twice as many people have been deported from Travis County after a misdemeanor arrest as have been deported after a felony arrest. Secure Communities has led to the current situation in which, on average, nineteen Travis County residents are deported and separated from their families each week.

This pattern of checking up on him, Xiomara told me, endured for the first few years she was living in Austin. Then, about five years ago, things changed. As I listened to her explanation, I thought back to what she had told me about her life at that time. Five years ago she was beginning to establish relationships with several loyal clients, to work with a community organization engaging other workers in learning about their rights, and to help her husband recover lost income. She remembers the moment when she let go. They were arguing, and she was again imploring him to see the grave consequences that could result from his behavior, and he told her to stop acting like his mother. And just like that she was done. "Okay," she told him. "Hasta aquí no más. I am not going to worry about you anymore." And she stopped following him.

She reflected on this, saying, "You know, I realized I was so scared about what he was doing because I didn't know what would happen to me, to my girls. If something happened to him, we would have nothing and no way of surviving. I guess that stopped being a problem."

Refocusing then on her goals and on taking care of her daughters appeared to shift everything. Her husband also began to refocus on the family, spending more time at home and going out less. "Of course he still goes out some," she said, but after several cycles of watching his friends disappear when things went awry, she suspected that he had begun to appreciate her support. Approaching their twenty-second year of marriage, she reflected on their journey, noting, "Now my husband and I take Alex to school every morning together. Before, it was never like this. But now, we go together everyday." He has even become explicit in his recognition of the vital contribution her work has made to the family. Just that morning, she said that he had thanked her, saying, "Thanks to you, we're gonna be okay." She gave me a slight smile and said, "We'll see."

A Home of Our Own

The story of Xiomara's life can be constructed around houses—the houses where she has lived, the houses in which she works, the houses built, owned, and lost by her family. As such, she thinks of her hopes for the future in terms of homes.

"Lo que quiero yo es volver a tener una casa mía [what I want is to have my own house again]," Xiomara explained. "I always think about something so that when we are older we don't have to depend on our children." She described her mother's current situation of dependence. Sick and unable to continue working, Xiomara's mother was now reliant on Xiomara's siblings in Mexico and on money that Xiomara and Annabel sent her from the United States. "I just want us to have something so that we can be content when we are old."

Xiomara spent her childhood with her family in a single-family home that her parents owned. In that home she and all of her brothers and sisters were born. When she and her family moved back to her hometown after living and working in Mexico City, they returned to live in that home. Shortly thereafter, she and her husband began to build their own home next door. It was a small home—two bedrooms and one bathroom, with an open kitchen-dining-living room. All they had had left to do before she left for the United States was install the doors and windows. She was sending money from the United States to finish it so that she could rent it out for income while they were gone.

Then the family lost it all. Her younger brother, the one who had originally accompanied her to the United States, had fallen in love with a woman who was being pursued by another man. Problems ensued, and he ended up on the wrong side of the law. Bailing him out and clearing his name took all of the family's assets. They lost everything. Both homes. Xiomara said that afterward she kept thinking about her childhood home and trying to figure out how to recover it. Though she tried to get some money together to buy the home back, the person who bought it would not sell.

Her mom had prepared for her future by planning to live on rent she earned from homes. Though she lost the house and thus her retirement plan, her plan to use real estate to support herself when she became too old to work has had a deep impact on Xiomara, whose major plans now revolve around trying to buy a home here in Austin. While she would like to return to Mexico, she and her family have made a life here. Generalizing about both her family and culture, she says, "We are accustomed to the idea that one makes their life in a place, and there they stay." But in order to stay, she needs a place to call home.

Lacking access to conventional bank loans because she lacks a social security number, Xiomara knows the process will be difficult—and maybe impossible. Even if it does work, they couldn't rent out and live in the same home, so she needs another source of income for when they can no longer work. She traces three squares on the table to indicate three land parcels as she tells me about her retirement plan. Over the years she has been paying toward three pieces of land in her hometown in Mexico. On these three plots she will construct three small homes to rent out, and the income will support them. That way, they will have both a place to go in Mexico and a way to live if they stay here. Most importantly, she says, they are leaving something for the girls.

Recommended Readings

Bunham, L., and N. Theodore. 2012. *Home Economics: The Invisible and Unregulated World of Domestic Work.* New York: National Domestic Workers Alliance. The first national survey of domestic workers in the United States, this report describes the working conditions and wages of workers in the domestic service industry disaggregated by occupational type, race, and gender.

Edin, K., and L. Lein. 1997. *Making Ends Meet: How Single Mothers Survive Welfare and Low-Wage Work.* New York: Russell Sage Foundation. In their classic study of the economic practices of low-income women in the United States, Edin and Lein document the budgeting and spending practices of women who receive income support from the government and of women who work low-wage jobs.

Hondagneu-Sotelo, P. 2007. *Doméstica: Immigrant Workers Cleaning and Caring in the Shadows of Affluence.* Berkeley: University of California Press.

Hondagneu-Sotelo deconstructs the nature of domestic service and caring work in the United States, focusing on the race- and class-based dynamics of the relationships between domestic workers and their employers.

Massey, D. S., J. Durand, and N. J. Malone. 2003. *Beyond Smoke and Mirrors: Mexican Immigration in an Era of Economic Integration.* New York: Russell Sage Foundation. Tracing the history of U.S.-Mexico migration, Massey, Durand, and Malone examine migration patterns via shifts in economic/trade and immigration policy and provide recommendations for policy reforms.

Ngai, M. 2004. *Impossible Subjects: Illegal Aliens and the Making of Modern America.* Princeton, NJ: Princeton University Press. Ngai reorients the debate on "illegal" (im)migration, repositioning the illegal alien as a necessary product of immigration law and policy rather than a criminal agent actively seeking to violate the law. This work shows how policies of immigration restriction served to produce contemporary American ideas about citizenship, race, and the nation-state.

Price, A., E. Timm, and C. Tzintzun. 2013. *Build a Better Texas: Construction Working Conditions in the Lone Star State.* Austin, TX: Workers Defense Project. A comprehensive statewide survey of construction workers in five major cities in Texas, this report documents the working conditions of Texas construction workers, finding that 22 percent of workers surveyed report wage theft and one in five report a workplace injury requiring medical attention.

Ella: Fighting to Save a Few

PAMELA NEUMANN

"All of it had to be"

Any life spanning seven decades is bound to have its share of twists, turns, and dreams deferred—maybe some that are never realized at all. After I had been meeting for months with Ella, a petite and loquacious seventy-two-year-old woman, she told me, "You know, I didn't really want all this stuff to be like this. I wanted that brick house, two-car garage, and a husband and all that respectability. I always wanted that stuff." Instead, Ella raised her two children alone and took on a career she hated, plumbing, to provide for her family.

Yet if you listen to her for long, you begin to realize that Ella has a different dream now, one forged in large part by her neighborhood's seemingly endless struggle for resources and recognition over the last sixty years. A quick walk through Ella's neighborhood, known as St. John's, nestled in a small corner of northeast Austin, tells part of the story. Its narrow streets have few sidewalks, and many blocks contain overgrown vacant lots. A few newer brick homes with freshly planted flowers sit side by side with more dilapidated houses enveloped in chain-link fences sporting "no trespassing" signs. Less-than-friendly dogs roam the streets freely, often startling me on my periodic jogs through the neighborhood. Rusty old cars, tires, and discarded furniture are common fixtures in many front yards.

Statistics tell another part of the story. According to the U.S. Census, the neighborhood's median annual household income in 2010 was $29,237, compared to a citywide median of $52,453. Of the children in St. John's, 43 percent currently live in poverty, and 26 percent of sixteen-to nineteen-year-olds are out of school or unemployed. Although Ella's

neighborhood now occupies less than two square miles, today it is inhabited by almost ten thousand people.

Ella, who wears her white hair closely cropped and is perpetually searching for her eyeglasses, is now retired. Every once in a while, a small hint of the inevitable fatigue that comes with age reveals itself in what Ella describes as her memory "glitches." Most days, though, her energy still seems nearly boundless—in fact, each time we met she had another new idea to share with me, often related to her efforts to mentor a small group of black and Latino teenage boys in her neighborhood, whom she feels everyone else has given up on. "Every time they come over to my house, I try to give them a new dream," she told me as we sat together on her maroon plaid couch, where most of our conversations over the last year took place. It was Ella's reputation as an active community member in this historically neglected neighborhood that initially led me to contact her—and from the very beginning, she was eager to share her experiences.

Ella's stories are punctuated by infectious, boisterous laughter, often provoked by her own incredulity about what she has lived through. "I've had so many 'firsts' in my life," she observed one balmy October afternoon. The walls of her home—one hallway of which she proudly calls her "gallery"—are covered with family photos and carefully preserved newspaper clippings of historic events, marking the passage of time. "It's all about honor," she told me as she showed me a photo of her now deceased mother—honoring her family's past and the potential of her community's future.

For Ella, the past and the present, her journey and her community, are inseparable. Every memory is a launching pad to twenty more. As she weaves them together, she often jumps backward and forward in time as recollections of different people and places come flooding back to her. "As I look back," Ella said, "I feel like all of it had to be."

"I was a sponge"

The youngest of six children, Ella is the self-described "baby of the family." Although she got picked on regularly, being the youngest child did sometimes work to her advantage. With her signature twinkle in her eyes, she told me, "I did all kinds of crazy stuff, but then when they went to spank me, I just cried. Crying worked for me. Helped me get out of stuff."

As a child, Ella wasn't close to either of her parents. "The thing I remember most about my mother is silence. She just went along to get along. And my dad, he was the overpossessive, controlling bonehead guy. He was the man in charge, period." Because her parents worked long hours (her mother as a domestic and her father as a carpenter), Ella spent much of her childhood with her grandparents, watching soap operas or listening to their stories.

"My grandfather was my hero," Ella told me. "He's the only one who ever validated me. He loved history, too—and I was a sponge." Through her grandfather, Ella became keenly interested in the history of the black experience in the United States. His example also served as her moral compass in dealing with adversity. Ella proudly described how her grandfather took care of his twelve children—and how he later adopted three more when another family member died. Years later, when Ella began feeding the hungry teenage boys on her street, she recalled her grandfather's words. "He always said, 'If you can make enough beans for twelve, you can feed fifteen.'"

"Not knowing is pain"

Ella's grandfather encouraged her to pursue her education. For a long time, he was the only one. "Out of everyone in my family, I was the dumb one. I was laughed at," Ella told me. She recalled a particularly traumatic experience in her third-grade spelling bee. As Ella stood in front of the class, the teacher pronounced a word and waited for her to respond. "It was a two-letter word," Ella said, "and I thought, 'If I just keep saying my letters, I know I'll get it.'" Soon her teacher began laughing and called other teachers into the room to watch her. "They call the word again, and I just start spelling. Tears are running down my face, snot coming out of my nose." She tried over and over again to get it right. "It almost totally destroyed my trust for learning and my faith in grown-ups," she admitted sadly. "But it gave me compassion for others who are slow to learn. Not knowing is pain."

Ella read voraciously while growing up and developed an extensive vocabulary, but she was always frustrated by her troubles with spelling. "I was a C student, but I should have been an A student," she told me. Over time she grew increasingly discouraged, and in ninth grade she dropped out altogether. But this didn't turn out to be much better, she soon realized. "I didn't have no friends to talk to, didn't have anyone to play with. I just stayed in the house every day and looked at soap operas." Angry with her parents for not disciplining her, she decided she had to take matters into her own hands. "Sitting at home, I ain't gonna be nothing. I have to be the parent of me."

"Kids learn what their parents live"

One of the things that caught my attention when I first visited Ella's house on a sunny spring day in May was a large map of the United States painted on a small patch of concrete in her spacious front yard. When I inquired about it, she told me, "The whole concept here is that whenever kids come onto the property, I want them to be learning something. I want them to know the possibilities of all the different places they can live."

Ella explained to me that she wants to show the kids who visit her things that she believes they aren't seeing at home. "Kids learn what their parents live. Nobody is teaching anything else, so they have no way of knowing that there's something better for them." Ella described the St. John's neighborhood today as moms who have "given up," dads who are "gone, or controlling, or in prison," and kids who drop out of school by eighth or ninth grade. "But all of those [parents] have had kids, and then those kids have had kids. We're dealing with the third generation of dysfunction. Those are the kids I'm dealing with," Ella ex-

claimed. Before I could ask her what she meant by dysfunction, she elaborated. "None of the routine things that happen in an ordinary family happen: washing the clothes on time, fixing more than one meal a day."

While at first it might sound like Ella believes that poverty persists in the St. John's neighborhood solely because of some families' unhealthy behaviors, her own experiences have taught her that the issues in her neighborhood are a product of generations of official neglect. "We've had absolutely no respect from the city of Austin. They never put any money into our community," Ella observed matter-of-factly.

But there are only so many battles that one person can fight alone.

"Let's give it to the black folk"

Ella was just seven years old when her family moved to the St. John's neighborhood, at that time the northeastern edge of Austin. Although the entire neighborhood today can be walked in less than an hour, St. John's used to be a sprawling rural area that was home to hundreds of black families, many of whom were former sharecroppers. Back then, Ella told me, there was nothing there. "It was a great dairy farm, and the cows had tromped the land down to where it was land of no use, and who would want land when you can't grow anything on it? So let's give it to the black folk."

The city eventually installed one water fountain in St. John's. For many years, though, there was no electricity, paved roads, or sewage disposal—only outhouses. Men and women walked two miles to the nearest bus stop to go to work in the city. Like everything else in Austin in those days, schools were segregated. Children from the neighborhood were bused to an all-black school in the more urbanized central East Side near Rosewood and Chicon. As Ella recalled, "We were the St. John's kids—we were like the country kids' bus."

Although black families owned land in St. John's, for decades discriminatory practices like redlining (marking maps of certain areas populated by people of color as "off-limits" for bank loans) made it virtually impossible for them to access credit to build or improve their homes. "We couldn't do upkeep," Ella explained, "so they could say, 'Blacks are trifling—they won't fix up their property,' but everyone else could go and get a loan and then pay it off over time." Moreover, the companies that did come in and offer to finance home building often did so in predatory ways. "If you missed one payment, they'd come and try to foreclose on you."

When Ella moved back to St. John's in her early forties, one of the first things she did was buy a home. "My parents sold this lot [adjacent to theirs] to me for ten dollars. I was always taught that the only way to be secure was to own something." A few years later, she missed a payment on the house, and the building company tried to foreclose on her, "but I was educated by then, so they couldn't touch me." Her parents, though, "were shaking and scared, and they said, we have to leave. . . . But if you leave, you can't fight." When the company came to tell her parents to get their things and leave, Ella stood her ground. "I said, 'What you need to do is you need to *get the hell off my property*,'" she told me, emphasizing each word as she spoke.

Similar attempts at foreclosure disproportionately affect communities of color to this day, as a 2010 report by the Center for Responsible Lending indicates.[1] According to this report, the foreclosure rate from 2007 to 2009 among African American and Latino homeowners was approximately 20 percent higher than the rate among non-Hispanic whites. Moreover, among recent borrowers, 8 percent of both African Americans and Latinos lost their homes, compared to 4.5 percent of whites.

Ultimately, Ella was able to keep her home, but her frustration with housing companies and city government only grew. "You've got a community that's been out here for [decades], and you put no money in—not a penny. That's where my anger came."

"I never intended to come back to Texas"

Ella returned to high school, but as a tenth grader rather than a ninth grader. It wasn't until two years later, just when she thought she was about to graduate, that the school counselor discovered the mistake. Rather than going back to ninth grade, Ella enrolled at a community college in San Antonio (there were no community colleges in Austin yet). "I went to college before I graduated from high school," Ella joked. But the lack of support from her family took a heavy toll on her body as well as her spirit. "My dad was running with women, and my mom was the only one working—a little maid job, like twenty dollars per week. She was the only financial support I had." While living in San Antonio, Ella scraped by eating only her mother's homemade peach preserves and bread she took from the kitchen of the house where she rented a small room. "I ate more peach preserve sandwiches than I ever want to remember." "Staring at starvation," she thought to herself, "I need to find a way out of this." After one semester, she decided to return to Austin to get her diploma so she could join the military. Like many other people from similar socioeconomic backgrounds, Ella saw the military as both a way up and a way out.

At twenty-one, Ella joined the air force. "I said, 'I'm getting the hell out of Dodge.' I called my mother that night, when I had already arrived at basic, and she was like, 'Where *is* you?' And I told her, 'I'm in the air force.'" Ella was first stationed in Massachusetts and later in Hawaii, where her love for books continued. "I'd be reading all night long—people thought I was nuts, a radical. Before I got out of the military, I probably read every slavery book there ever was, because I really wanted to understand where I came from." It was the middle of the tumultuous 1960s, the height of the civil rights movement and the Vietnam War, and Ella was immersing herself in the writings of Malcom X and Martin Luther King Jr.

Working in the airport reservations terminal at a military base in Hawaii was a "good assignment" for Ella, one that gave her a chance to "watch everything that was going on" and take advantage of empty seats to fly places she'd always wanted to visit. "We rode on a C-130, which is like the raggediest plane you'd ever want to be on. You just hold your breath till you get there." Ella also loved spending time near the ocean. "I had a little crew, and every weekend we went to the beach." Ella would barbecue spareribs, and everyone would get drunk together, first on "good liquor," and later on "rotgut" wine. "That junk made us sick as a dog," Ella said, laughing.

It was such a good, "magic" life that Ella never intended to come back to Texas. "I had lived; I just had a taste of the hate and the prejudice and the limitations for a black person [in Texas], and then to get into the military, it was a lot different. They just wasn't allowed to arbitrarily mistreat people."

But then she fell in love with a man she met in the military and got pregnant. Because of military rules at the time, Ella's pregnancy meant she had to leave her job—though she still received full medical care until her daughter was born. Losing a job she found so fulfilling was bad enough, but what was truly devastating was losing the love of her life. Ella had little to say about the man who had captured her heart, other than this: "He was supposed to come back and get me. You know, you make all these plans—you think you're in love and all that stuff—but it just didn't happen."

"You gotta keep your insides free"

Ella returned to Austin, gave birth to her daughter, Janice, and then a few months later left again. "I couldn't stand to be here anymore," she told me. With her daughter in tow, she traveled with her sister to Kansas and later to North Dakota, where she got certified and worked briefly as a nurse's aide, a profession she mostly enjoyed. "But there was this one old white lady," Ella said, shaking her head. "Every time I came in to take care of her, [she] would beat me up as hard as she could hit me." Even as she recalled the offensive names she was called, Ella laughed as she imitated the gestures and the thin, high-pitched voice of the elderly woman.

When Ella talked about incidents of everyday racism she had experienced, she often did so in a lighthearted, matter-of-fact way—like her story of the girl from Mississippi who had shared a dorm room with her during basic training. Ella laughed hysterically as she imitated the girl's southern drawl: "George Wallace, he was just a won-der-ful man." Ella retaliated by whispering threats to the girl once the lights went out. "I had her so afraid, she'd wake up an hour early and get dressed. She was just terrified," Ella recalled.

But Ella saw the hate growing in herself, and it made her increasingly uncomfortable. "It hit me that this would destroy the essence of me," she said, staring at the television humming quietly in the background. She was reminded again of her grandfather. "My grandfather taught me to love." Ultimately, Ella decided, "It doesn't matter what anyone else is doing. You gotta keep your insides free." Ella's resolve to do this has been continually tested, perhaps no more so than when she later became the only black woman plumber working for a prominent company in Austin.

"I was so over my head"

After a year in North Dakota's extreme weather, Ella had had enough. "Our town was in a valley, and when the snow melted, the city flooded. People were riding down the streets in rowboats and stuff. And I said, 'Oh no.'" Ella returned to Austin with Janice, now two years old, and found a job at a local hospital. Because her military service had earned her four years of education benefits, Ella decided to take advantage of them. She enrolled again at a community college in San Antonio, where she majored in psychology and sociology. Ella tried several times to transfer to four-year schools, but she struggled to pass the required math courses. "I was so over my head," she remembered ruefully. One bright spot during this otherwise tough time was Ella's relationship with a literature professor, whom she still remembers fondly—someone who recognized her verbal talent and made accommodations for her spelling challenges by giving her oral exams.

When Janice was four years old, Ella got pregnant again. This time, the father, a professor at the community college in San Antonio, "ran away." When I asked her why, Ella told me, "He found out I was seven years older than him. That was kind of awkward." In order to stay in school and provide for Janice and her newborn son, Kyle, Ella needed extra income (and a babysitter), so she found a part-time job working the night shift as a nurse's aide at St. David's Hospital in Austin. "Every Friday, I got out of school [in San Antonio] and caught the Greyhound bus [to Austin], and my mother kept the baby overnight. It was horrible. I had no life." It was during this period that Ella began to write poetry, something she did more and more of as she grew older. One of her very first poems begins, "I am a single black mother with a black boy child. A crying mother, trying to be wise."

Juggling two children alone, Ella found that even simple tasks like laundry had become time-consuming and complicated. "I remember we had a wagon—I went to the washateria with this red wagon, and I put my clothes in there and my son on top of the clothes. I wore those tires out to rims." She eventually upgraded to a bicycle, which became her sole means of transportation. "I was known as the bike lady," she chuckled.

Because Ella worked so much, the firemen down the street became her backup babysitters. "They knew my kids were latchkey kids, and they looked out for them." One time, when she was in elementary school, Janice got into a pretty serious accident—"she had a big ol' gash on her leg"—and someone took her to the fire department. By the time Ella got there, Janice was all patched up. "I didn't have any money. If my kids weren't dying, they weren't going to the doctor."

Ella and her children (then aged six and two) moved into an old house in east San Antonio, where she belatedly discovered that the pipes were completely corroded. Lacking the money to get them fixed, she enrolled in a plumbing class, at the end of which all the students came over to help replace her pipes for free. To Ella's surprise, the military took notice of her good grades and extended her VA benefits so she could complete a plumbing degree. But there was just one problem. "I hate plumbing!" Ella exclaimed. "I was so miserable," she remembered, "but I couldn't just give away free money." So she took it.

"All that stuff unraveled"

Between taking classes, working part-time, and raising two small children alone, Ella felt increasingly exhausted and lonely. One night, she told me, "I came home [to Austin] and got involved with this guy—a one-night stand." Afterward, to her dismay, she discovered she was pregnant again. The guy wanted her to have the baby, but Ella refused. "I can't do this. I don't love him," she admitted thinking. It was 1973, just a few months after the Supreme Court had handed down its decision legalizing abortion in *Roe v. Wade*. Ella made some calls and discovered there was a doctor who was performing abortions out of his office. Ella borrowed money from her sister and made an appointment. "I got on the table, and I talked through the whole abortion," Ella remembered. "It was very, very easy—minor cramps, nothing traumatic."

What was harder for Ella to reconcile, though, was what she had always thought about other women in her same situation. "So many things was happening that I didn't believe in. I was religious and self-righteous, and I talked at girls real bad for being weak, and here I am with two kids, and I'm not married." Ella always dreamed that she would meet "the guy on the big white horse," someone who was "very academically intelligent," who would carry her away, and they would live together in a brick house with a two-car garage. But "all that stuff unraveled."

Following her abortion, Ella was offered a part-time job at the abortion clinic as a counselor. She worked thirty hours a week there, in addition to taking her plumbing classes. "I was so dynamic," Ella remembered proudly, "that they sent me out to do their PR work," which involved speaking to community groups and churches about issues like single parenthood and birth control. Ella felt very comfortable as an impromptu speaker, even when confronted with less than friendly audiences. When she spoke at black churches, for example, she would ask the people sitting in the pews, "How many black babies are you adopting? How many are you taking care of?" Ella's personal experience had given her a different perspective. "It wasn't even about abortion," she concluded. "It was about people. People in trouble."

"A short black woman in a white man's trade"

Ella continued to work for the clinic until she graduated with her plumbing degree and found a job with a local gas company. Then, one day, a representative of a major telecommunications company unexpectedly approached her. "He told me, 'We'd like to offer you a package.' I didn't even know what a package was." Ella wasn't too keen on the idea of working full-time as a plumber—what she really wanted was to do motivational speaking and work as a nurse's aide—but the financial package was tough to turn down. "It was more than I ever thought I would earn in a month," Ella told me.

Ella took the job, becoming the only black woman plumber in the entire company. From the very first day, she faced an uphill battle. "Everybody hated me—the supervisor, the manager, everybody." Ella soon discovered that it was company practice to hire temporary workers and then give the temp with the most seniority the next open position. Unbeknownst to her, Ella had been given the spot of the man who thought he was next in line. "I wanted to be accepted, just to work, and do my best," Ella wrote in a poem about the experience, "but it was so hard to pass the white man's test." She later found out that the company had hired her in order to fill four different "minority" employee classifications—black, female, veteran, and older (40+ years)—in one fell swoop. "I was four minorities in one body!" she exclaimed. Hiring Ella allowed the company to meet its legal requirements, but that did not stop them from treating her as incompetent for her position.

Given these dynamics, Ella struggled to find some way to connect with her male coworkers. Ultimately, she said, "I won over all the boys with sex. I was like their professional sex counselor." When work was slow, she would sit around with the men and break it down for them. "No one in their whole life had ever talked to them about relationships, about sex, about how to treat a woman." Ella chuckled as she recalled the lighthearted banter she exchanged with the men over these sensitive and taboo topics—but the truth is, this was a critical survival strategy for Ella in an openly hostile environment where she never felt like she could fully be herself.

Over time, Ella managed to develop some sense of camaraderie with most of her coworkers, but less qualified men were repeatedly promoted over her. Like many women and minorities, Ella was held to a higher standard in the workplace than her white male counterparts, and her supervisor was actively looking for some grounds to get rid of her. This proved to be a challenge, though, because "the guys protected me," Ella told me. "They would go to these meetings and come back and tell me exactly what went on." Then a new supervisor came in—"a real redneck manager"—who reassigned her to a separate area, where she worked alone organizing parts. "They had to isolate me, because they found one redneck that wanted to persecute me; his only job was to walk behind me and watch me and see if I made any mistakes." Sure enough, one day a huge load of parts came in, and Ella was in charge of sorting the "nineties" (right angles) from the "forty-fives" (curves). "Of all the parts I put out that morning, I put one forty-five in the ninety-degree bin, and so here they come to write me up because I didn't know my parts. And that was the straw hat, you know."

Around this time, Ella started going to a therapist. "They [her supervisors] were breaking me," she confessed to me. Yet Ella was stubborn—she didn't want to give in. "I knew they didn't want me, and I said,

'You can't tell me where I can be,' because I came from the Malcolm X place—you know, black and proud, and that whole thing."

Finally, though, after "seven years and eight months," Ella put in her resignation. "I quit because I was dying inside. You can only work so long in one place where you're not good enough."

"A place nobody wanted to be"

When Ella returned to Austin with her children in 1980, her neighborhood bore little resemblance to the one she had left some twenty years earlier. Drugs and prostitution were now rampant, and many black families had left. Taking their place was a growing Latino population, which today makes up about 70 percent of St. John's, according to the 2010 U.S. Census. When I asked Ella why she thought the neighborhood had changed, she explained: "You couldn't get any loans, you couldn't improve your house, you couldn't live with any kind of dignity, so people gonna leave. All the blacks who wanted something left."

Ella had left too—and had never wanted to come back. But by this point, something inside her had changed. "Working at [the telecommunications company] changed me. Everything that I had studied, it just kind of faded away. Somebody gotta fight back, you know?"

There was no shortage of battles to fight in the St. John's neighborhood in the 1980s. As the city of Austin was growing, the land on which St. John's had been built was becoming increasingly valuable given its strategic location just north of the University of Texas, the state's flagship public university, and its proximity to a major highway. Much of the western portion of the historic neighborhood had already disappeared, bought out and replaced with a sprawling new mall and other commercial developments. "They wanted us out of here," Ella told me matter-of-factly. The city made a concerted effort to get the remaining black families to sell their land, and when that didn't work it implemented certain zoning changes, like permitting apartments and duplexes in addition to single-family homes, a move designed to encourage new in-migration to the neighborhood. The result? Today, 86 percent of St. John's residents are renters.

To Ella, the city's policies seemed increasingly arbitrary. "The code inspector seem to watch everything we do, but they overlook the yards all junked out. They gonna find someone building something that looks good because you must not be paying your taxes," Ella observed wryly.

Once, when an inspector came to her property, she remembers telling him, "It seems like every time a black person makes a move, you guys [the city of Austin] are right there. Where were you guys when we didn't have but one faucet of water?"

Access to credit was another recurring problem. When Ella tried to get a loan to build her house, she found it almost impossible. "As a single parent I had no credibility," she said. But, she added, laughing incredulously, "If I had a husband to put on the note, he didn't have to work or bring in any money, but they would approve my loan." At the time, there was really only one company that would finance homes for families living in St. John's. "So I went to [Jim Walters], and for $22,000 they would do the home for me." It sounded like a good deal, until they told her she had to have another $5,000 for the hookups to city services. "I had no cash money, so they said, 'We'll refinance the $22K and lend you enough money so you can get a hookup.'" With the refinancing, though, her note soared from $22,000 to $38,000. She knew it was a rip-off, but she signed off on it anyway. She shrugged as she told me, "I didn't have any power."

Ella attended a number of city council meetings to advocate for greater investment in St. John's but grew tired of watching her efforts— such as the fight for a new neighborhood recreational center—be continually stymied or misinterpreted. "They [the city] gave us this house, where you give out groceries and you could have meetings. But they were just trying to shut us up. They hired a bunch of black people to be over this program, and none of them was from Austin, so they had absolutely no information about the culture." Years later, a larger multipurpose community center was eventually built in St. John's alongside a new elementary school. Once again, though, as Ella pointed out, the neighborhood's black history was erased in the process. The new school was named after a prominent white male politician (J. J. Pickle) rather than one of St. John's well-known founders, Rev. A. K. Black.

Ella paused and laughed, as she usually did, and watched for my reaction. When she spoke next, though, her voice contained both resignation and frustration. "Like [former Texas governor] Ann Richards used to say, these good ol' boys are too rough for me."

"The token"

It was a balmy Tuesday evening in September, and the monthly neighborhood association meeting was about to begin.[2] I looked casually

around the room—of the eight women and four men gathered, Ella was the only black person in attendance. (Afterward, she told me that normally there are a few others, but the meeting date had been changed at the last minute.) The big agenda item at this meeting was a vote on the community's development priorities, which would then be sent to the city council for consideration in the next budget cycle.

Plastered on the back wall was a laundry list of possible projects, ranging from park space to bike lanes to sidewalk improvements. We were each given ten red dots, which we were instructed to distribute among the projects based on our preferences. Dots in hand, we stood up and moved toward the wall to examine our options. A few of the men present were newer to the neighborhood, and they occasionally turned to Ella to ask her where different places were located. A discussion ensued about the relative merits of a kids' splash pad versus expanded green space. Ella and I finished placing our dots on the wall and took our seats, waiting for everyone else to finish. One of the neighborhood association leaders began taking pictures and suddenly called out to Ella from across the room. "Ella, can you come back over here and pretend to vote again? I need some color in this photo." Without a word, Ella stood up and walked back to the wall for the obligatory photo op.

"I'm the token black person," Ella told me once, when I asked her about her involvement with the neighborhood association. "Is that okay? Is that all right with me?" she asked semirhetorically, already anticipating my next question. Without skipping a beat, she answered her own query. "It's all right as it can be, because no one is trying to get that spot. And somebody needs to be there."

"Some of the kids can be saved"

When Ella first realized that her neighborhood association was no longer being run by black people, she was furious. "I said, 'What is this? This is a traditional all-black neighborhood, and now we have absolutely no control.'" Shortly after moving back to Austin, Ella ran against a white man for president of the neighborhood association but lost. "They [the other blacks] voted for him, and they should have." When I asked her why, somewhat surprised, she replied, "Because I came in as a troublemaker, but he was doing stuff."

Ella still shows up for association meetings and even holds an official (though to her, mostly symbolic) position, but she has no interest in dealing with "paperwork," as she calls it. What she most enjoys are "hands-on" activities, like hosting a block party on National Night Out (NNO), an annual event intended to help neighbors connect with each other. When I arrived at Ella's house for NNO in October 2013, a dozen Latino kids were already there, playing tetherball and volleyball in her backyard. Two large plastic tables were stacked with pizza, crackers, cookies, bottled water, and of course Ella's special homemade Kool-Aid—in red and purple varieties. Ella asked me to help serve the pizza while she went around asking each of the kids their names, ages, and the schools they attended. "I need to have all the info about these kids to know what their needs are and how to help them," Ella explained to me later.

Ella's passion is to help the teenage boys whom she feels most local organizations have been unable to reach—the ones who are dropping out of school. She sees a younger version of herself in their discouragement. "They stop learning by seventh or eighth grade," Ella said, "and then when they get to high school, they drop out." These kids, the ones who are slipping through the cracks left by a largely absent state, are the ones Ella is most concerned about.

With little access to government support services, many marginalized communities like St. John's are now primarily served by private sector nonprofit organizations, many of which operate on shoestring budgets and experience frequent staff turnover. Although Ella acknowledges that these nonprofits have worthy goals, in St. John's "all these organizations are working with the same kids—the lower- to middle-class people who are following the rules and trying to get their kids to college," Ella told me. "But that's not helping. There's a lot of hurting people, and I know some of the kids can be saved."

"The last real love"

One of the main sources of Ella's inspiration to work with struggling youth in her neighborhood came from her time working in transitional housing for people coming out of prison, one of the last jobs she held before retiring. "I wasn't really looking for work at that point," Ella told me. "But my friend said they needed me." Ella began working the night shift as a monitor at a small halfway house on Austin's East Side, from 11:00 p.m. to 7:00 a.m., three times a week. Her favorite part of the job, she told me proudly, was when the men woke up. "They got up real early, like 5:00 a.m., because they were going to look for jobs, and that's when they would talk to me."

Ella sat at a desk, and in the middle of the room was an empty chair. "The guys would come in, and they would say, 'Miss Ella, anyone in the chair?' And I said, 'No.' And then [they said], 'I need to get in there.' And they would just kind of spill their guts." Sometimes, Ella says, she didn't even look at them, but that didn't stop the men from talking. They needed an outlet. They told her, "You remind us of the last real love we remember, from our grandparents." Touched by the men's remarks, Ella decided to go by a new name: Grandma Wisdom.

"Fill a kid up, and they can listen"

It all began about two years ago with a twelve-year-old boy named Dennis. "At least once a week this kid was screaming and hollering, running up the street, and cursing everybody out," Ella told me. For months Ella and her now grown daughter, Janice, sat outside watching him and the other kids. "They were our entertainment," she said, laughing. Then one day Ella found out that Dennis's family was moving out, and she walked over "to be nosy." When she entered the house, she discovered that the family had hired someone to put down new stick-on tile, and the worker had done it all wrong yet still taken their money. Ella had plenty of experience with this sort of thing from her own home improvement projects, and she offered to help them fix up their floor. She went home, grabbed some tools and a big bucket, came back, and just started working. "I told them, 'I'm not going to charge you any money. This is something I know how to do.'"

Then, to Ella's surprise, Dennis suddenly came in and asked her, "What can I do?" So she set him to work scraping, and when he had finished that, he asked her what he could do next. "He didn't complain, he wasn't disruptive, he just worked and worked and worked." By the end of the project, Ella was so impressed with Dennis that she told him, "Dennis, I like the way you work, and I like your attitude." She offered to pay him to come over once a week and help her with different chores, like raking leaves. "That Thursday, he showed up, and he's been coming ever since."

Several times when Dennis came over to work, he told her, "I'm so hungry I feel like I'm gonna puke up my guts." So she invited him in, gave him a snack, and they sat at her kitchen counter and talked. Food makes a big difference, Ella discovered. "When you fill a kid up, they can listen. The things I teach, they remember." Later, Dennis began coming over to ask if Ella had any food she could give his family. "I found out over a period of time that six days before food stamp day, they had absolutely no food for anybody." So Ella started stocking up on extra pasta and sauce to give away, not only to Dennis but to other youth who started coming over to talk to her as well. "Food is a way of raising self-esteem," Ella said as she reflected on her work with the boys.

"What happens when the boys come over?" I asked Ella one afternoon.

"It's like a puzzle," she told me. "I gotta figure out each kid's strength, what they like, what they love, what they see themselves as; and then I have to find people to help them in that." Ella strives to teach them practical skills, like money management, by organizing events like garage sales, but she also tries to teach them emotional skills, like "how to take ownership of your own feelings." Ella has just one rule: no putting your family down. "I get on them about what their role in the family is. You know, when they ask you to take the trash out, did you sit around and wait? Or did you get up right then, real respectful?" Ella's long-term goal—one that her daughter has recently become involved in as well—is to turn what is now a home-based operation into an official neighborhood resource center that connects struggling youth to other local organizations and to services that can help them grow both educationally and vocationally.

Above all, though, Ella is trying to teach the boys to hope—to hope for a better future.

"A greater purpose"

It was an unusually warm December afternoon, and Ella and I were meeting for what would likely be the last time for several months. Ella's voice was raspy, but she ushered me in anyway. "It's not one of my better days," she admitted softly, but she was still eager to tell me about her visit with some new police cadets earlier that morning. As a widely recognized community figure, these days Ella often gets called upon to share her perspective in different forums.

The most important thing the police needed to do was not "walk in feeling like everybody's guilty," Ella said emphatically. The high-profile shooting of Trayvon Martin was still weighing heavily on her mind, and she couldn't help but worry that one day someone might also make the wrong assumptions about her son, Kyle, now a talented artist working at a community college in San Antonio.

"My son is a large black man, and if you didn't talk to him, then you wouldn't know that he's a gentle man. You wouldn't know that he's never been in any kind of trouble. You wouldn't know that he's never used any kind of illegal drug. You wouldn't know that he graduated from the University of Texas."

Ella may only have one biological son, but as Grandma Wisdom, she now has an extended family that includes all the neighborhood kids. Sometimes, she says, they come over just to tell her that they are doing okay. And it's rare, she adds, for them to leave without telling her that they love her. It's in these moments that Ella feels most strongly that all of the pain she went through happened for a reason.

"I think it was for a greater purpose than just me."

Notes

1. See Debbie Gruenstein, Wei Li Bociani, and Keith S. Ernst. 2010. "Foreclosures by Race and Ethnicity: The Demographics of a Crisis." Center for Responsible Lending. http://www.responsiblelending.org/mortgage-lending/research-analysis/foreclosures-by-race-and-ethnicity.pdf.

2. At the time of this project, I lived in the St. John's neighborhood.

Recommended Readings

Roscigno, V. J. 2007. *The Face of Discrimination: How Race and Gender Affect Work and Home Lives*. Lanham, MD: Rowman and Littlefield. Drawing on archived discrimination suits, this book documents the concrete ways that race and sex discrimination at work and in the housing market have impacted people's everyday lives.

Sánchez-Jankowski, M. 2008. *Cracks in the Pavement: Social Change and Resilience in Poor Neighborhoods.* Berkeley: University of California Press. An ethnographic study of how different local institutions such as barbershops, housing projects, gangs, high schools, and corner grocery stores foster stability and relational ties in neighborhoods that are often assumed to be isolated and disorganized.

Sharkey, P. 2013. *Stuck in Place: Urban Neighborhoods and the End of Progress toward Racial Equality.* Chicago: University of Chicago Press. The author shows how government policies over the last forty years have contributed to ongoing segregation, lack of economic opportunity, and increasing reliance on the criminal justice system (as opposed to social investment) to address the issues found in urban black communities. The lack of investment in black neighborhoods over the course of multiple generations has exacerbated long-standing racial inequalities in key areas such as employment and education.

CHAPTER 12

Manuel: The Luxury of Defending Yourself

MARCOS PÉREZ

One Student among Thousands

Manuel is an energetic young man with light brown skin and dark hair. He wears casual clothes most of the time, and it is rare to see him without his glasses or without a plastic water bottle in his hands. Like many people in this city, he moves around by bicycle and carries his belongings in a messenger bag. He is constantly on the move, because he leads a busy life. Every morning he wakes up around seven and has breakfast with other people in the student-run cooperative where he lives. Thirty minutes later he goes to campus and works out for about an hour. This semester he is taking five classes, all of them in the morning, so after leaving the gym he runs from one building to the other until lunchtime. Afterward, he bikes five miles to the nonprofit organization where he works. Around 7:00 p.m. he returns to his room, reads for the next day's classes, and does his share of housework (usually cooking dinner). He goes to bed well after midnight, only to wake up a few hours later.

At first glance, Manuel's routines do not differ much from those of other high-achieving students. However, one particular feature distinguishes Manuel from most of his classmates: he is one of the hundreds of undocumented students at the University of Texas at Austin. His lack of papers has left a profound mark on his life, in a double sense. First, it restricts his life choices and fills his future with uncertainty. Second, his immigration status was, until not long ago, a secret kept from most people, buried under a deep layer of fear and distrust that took many years to overcome.

"When I was eight," Manuel told me the first time we met, "I was assigned a student tutor in school. She was Chicana, they probably as-

signed her to me because she had a Hispanic-sounding last name, but she did not speak Spanish, and I hadn't learned English yet. I was good at math because it was just numbers, I didn't need to talk. One day she took my homework, erased my name, wrote her own, and got an awesome grade. I couldn't do anything about it, I did not know how to speak English."

A few years later, in middle school, Manuel got into a fight with a classmate who was picking on him. He was taken to the principal's office and placed on suspension. For some reason he does not understand, the police got involved, and his parents were called to the school. Later that day, they sat down with him and explained that he had to avoid fighting because he could get the family in trouble: "Don't fight back. You don't have that luxury," they told him. More painful than being called names was the inability to do much about it.

Manuel would repeat these stories several times over the course of our meetings. Yet despite this, it took me a while to realize why the two incidents were so important to him. After hours and hours of conversation, it dawned on me that Manuel's life is a constant search for efficacy—a relentless struggle to overcome arbitrary restrictions that prevent him from doing what most people around him take for granted. Manuel's dream is about more than just a college degree, a decent-paying job, or a driver's license. It is about being able to defend himself, to obtain that capacity that was denied to him as a child. He has pursued this dream since he learned of his undocumented status.

"We are going to El Norte"

Manuel was born in a city in central Mexico in the early 1990s. His parents worked as seasonal migrants who traveled to the United States every year to pick oranges and strawberries, venturing as far north as Tennessee. During their long absences, he and his sisters were raised by their grandparents. To this day, his mother regrets being away during her children's early years. She was the one who, convinced that the children needed to have a father around them, gave her husband an ultimatum: they would either settle in Mexico for good or the whole family would migrate. Economic opportunities and the prospect of jobs are magnets that attract millions of families like Manuel's to the United States. However, for Manuel's parents, the actual decision to risk their lives and cross the border with children was prompted by the desire to be together.

One afternoon, shortly after beginning elementary school, Manuel came home after classes and found his mother packing. She told him and his older sister, "Pack your stuff, we are going to El Norte." While the news was unexpected, Manuel was initially excited about the trip and did not understand at the time that once he crossed the border he would not come back. In his childish innocence, he asked if he could take the candy he was eating with him. His mother, full of secrecy, told him to just carry his backpack and wear comfortable shoes.

Crossing the border is a dangerous, scary, and strenuous process. Doing it with children is a nightmare. Manuel's mother left her two youngest daughters with her parents, took Manuel and his sister, who were both old enough to walk long distances, and boarded a bus to one of the largest cities on the U.S.-Mexico border. The family stayed in a hotel for two days, after which they took a taxi in the middle of the night. Following a short drive, they were dropped off on a deserted road, and they walked approximately forty minutes until they arrived at a spot along the river where a *coyote* was waiting for them, equipped with tire inner tubes and plastic bags. They inflated the inner tubes, took their clothes off, put them in the bags, and let themselves drift in the dark waters until they reached the other side. The first thing Manuel saw after setting foot on U.S. soil was a highway full of cars. To avoid detection in the impending dawn, they walked to a nearby neighborhood, where there was a house that served as a waiting place for unauthorized border crossers.

Although they had reached the United States, their journey was far from over. The biggest challenge ahead was to pass the checkpoints installed many miles from the border, where armed men in green uniforms ask for papers and inspect vehicles. "We stayed in the house for two weeks," Manuel recalled. "It looked like one of those buildings that are prepared for a hurricane, with plywood on the windows. They tried to make it seem as if it was abandoned, although there were twenty people staying there." Living conditions were bad: migrants slept on mattresses on the floor, and everyone shared one bathroom. After two weeks of anxious waiting with complete strangers, an eighteen-wheeler picked up the whole group and took them to San Antonio. Back then, trade agreements between the United States and Mexico made this kind of truck a relatively safe way of crossing checkpoints. However, soon after Manuel migrated, in the wake of the September 11 terrorist attacks, heightened controls increased the number of people who suffocated inside sealed containers while trucks waited hours to be inspected. Being a young child, Manuel was not worried about death. Yet during the weeks that the process of crossing took, he was very scared of getting caught: "I wanted to be safe with my mother and sister, so I stayed quiet."

Once the truck arrived in San Antonio, the driver left the migrants at a gas station and drove away. Ten of them squeezed into a car and continued to travel north, stopping in different towns. Eventually, Manuel, his mother, and his sister were dropped on the side of the road in a small town close to Austin, where his father was waiting for them. The family would not be fully reunited until months later, when Manuel's two younger sisters were taken to the United States by car, driven by an elderly couple who pretended to be their grandparents.

Manuel says he was lucky to make it alive. Statistics prove him right. Hundreds of human beings die attempting to enter the United States every year: they become dehydrated, they suffocate, or they drown. The increased militarization and surveillance of the border during the last decade has had the effect of channeling crossing attempts to more desolate and dangerous areas, away from urban centers. According to the U.S. Border Patrol, during the 2012 fiscal year, 477 people perished trying to cross the border, making it the deadliest year since 2005. A report by the ACLU calls for the recognition of a "humanitarian crisis" taking place at the U.S.-Mexico border, where from 1994 to 2009 between 3,861 and 5,607 individuals lost their lives. Moreover, official statistics may underestimate the severity of the situation, and the actual number of fatalities is likely to exceed even the highest body count, given that countless remains are never recovered.

Manuel's father worked as a handyman at a ranch, doing all types of maintenance jobs. The owner of the property offered him a house where he could stay with his family. While the offer was helpful, the house was small and in bad condition. Life was hard in the new environment, but Manuel remembers it fondly. The town where they settled had very few Latino households back then, and the social isolation imposed by racial and linguistic barriers forced Manuel's family to stick together. He tells stories of survival with a smile on his face: he recalls heating the house with nothing but wood and the whole family sleeping together on a mattress during the winter. Compared to the long absences and fragmented family of his early childhood, Manuel cherished the opportunity to be with his parents and siblings. He and his older sister developed a strong bond, since it took them some time to make new friends. They played together, helped each other learn English, and went to yard sales on the weekends to buy used toys.

Although by American standards they had low-paying jobs, Manuel's parents, through their hard work, gave the family a much higher standard of living than what they had had in Mexico. They bought a used car, clothes for the children, and household appliances. However, the family was largely estranged from the community that surrounded them. It took several months for Manuel's father to learn how to register his children in school, and he and his wife never trusted the authorities, even those who were supposed to help them. They instilled this caution in their children, who were told to stay inside while their parents were at work. One day, Manuel and his sister were playing with the family's most recent acquisition, a telephone, when they accidentally dialed 9-1-1. They hung up right away, but the damage was already done: the operator dispatched a police car to the location from where the call had originated. When a man in uniform knocked on the door, Manuel and his siblings were terrified and stayed quiet for a long time, even after the officer had left.

With time, Manuel and his sisters gained confidence and began to play outside the house, despite their parents' warnings. They would climb a tree in their front yard and wave to passing cars. Still, for many years Manuel remained scared of the police. He had learned that in order to protect his family, he had to avoid the authorities and be as invisible as possible. Only with the beginning of college would his views change. However, getting into higher education was not an easy task.

It's a Long Way to College

Obtaining good grades in school was not a serious challenge for a boy like Manuel, who graduated third in his high school class and has an A average in college despite a demanding workload. He attributes this capacity to the fact that he arrived in the United States at the beginning of elementary school, when he could simply relearn the basics. He soon understood that in order to continue his education after high school he would need to have the best grades. His mother contributed to this attitude by holding him to high standards: "A 90 was not enough. It had to be a 100." However, the road to college is not simple for students who lack papers. Manuel's high school counselor did not inform him about the options available to him, in particular that despite his immigration status he could still enroll in universities and even access reduced tuition.

His counselor's neglect did not deter Manuel from trying. Convinced that without papers he could not attend college, he developed a plan to marry his American girlfriend. She agreed, but shortly afterward the teenage couple split up, leaving him without an alternative plan to continue his studies. Despite his enthusiasm and capacity, he eventually gave up on his applications to many universities because he did not see the point in fighting for what seemed like a lost cause.

Then something happened. His former girlfriend's mother took matters into her own hands, putting him in contact with faculty at a major university and driving him to the campus to meet with professors and activists. There he learned about the opportunities open to him, in particular that many students in his situation attended college and organized to support each other. He came back home excited and resumed the process of applying. He would eventually get into three of the most prestigious schools in the state.

Getting into college was a life changer. For the first time in his life Manuel was able to overcome an obstacle caused by his immigration status. Furthermore, after many years of living in an overwhelmingly white town, he found himself in a much more diverse environment. He began participating in a campus organization that helped undocumented students. The start of his activist career helped him realize that the problems faced by people like his parents (not being paid on time, making little money, suffering accidents at work) were closely related to his own. In other words, for the first time he grasped the extent of the struggle for immigrant rights, and instead of feeling overwhelmed by the issue he became an enthusiastic activist.

More importantly, Manuel found a group of students who were also undocumented and who were open about their immigration status. After years of hiding his situation for fear of retribution or deportation, he found a safe space where he could be open about it. He also learned that most authorities could not question him about his status. One day during freshman year he ran a red light on his bicycle. A police officer stopped him and asked for some identification. Manuel only had his student card: "I do not carry the Mexican *matrícula* because it is almost like saying that I am undocumented. And the passport is too formal." The officer told him he needed something else, and requested to know his social security number. That is when Manuel did something he would never have done during high school. He read the name on the policeman's badge out loud and said, "Excuse me?" The officer hesitated for a moment and then let him go with a warning. "I think the policeman got the message: I could report him for asking that question. I know my rights, they cannot ask you that."

Eleven Million Dreams

In one way, Manuel's story is quite common. There are more than 11 million undocumented immigrants in the United States, 4.4 million of whom are under the age of thirty. Nevertheless, in another way his story is painfully atypical: it is estimated that only between 5 and 10 percent of undocumented high school graduates attend college. While paying for higher education is hard for most Americans, it is particularly difficult for undocumented youth. First, their families have fewer resources to help them; in 2007, before the recession, the median household income of unauthorized immigrants was $36,000, while it was $50,000 for U.S.-born residents. Second, they are ineligible for much of the financial aid that their classmates rely on; they cannot apply for federally funded scholarships, and only a few states grant them in-state tuition. Third, their employment options are limited to those jobs that do not ask for a social security number, where pay is often lower and working conditions worse. Furthermore, internships that would help them pay for their studies and give them valuable work experience are usually not available to them.

These difficulties are constantly present in Manuel's life. Although his academic achievements and work capacity would make him a good candidate for many scholarships, his options are very limited. He relies on a combination of personal savings, part-time jobs, state-level financial aid and loans, and small private grants. He is also very frugal and is incredibly capable of extracting resources from his environment, getting the most out of each dollar. He lives in a cooperatively run housing unit, where expenses and housework are shared by everyone. This allows him to spend about half of what other students spend on room and board. He also saves by not buying any books: he uses university resources and the city library to read his course materials without spending money. And he knows about almost every festival, concert, or activity going on in the city that is free of charge. When I asked him whether his parents helped him financially in any way, he candidly told me that "once in a while they give me twenty dollars to buy groceries." In order to make those twenty dollars, and any money he obtains, last longer, he has learned countless tricks. If a penny saved is a penny earned, Benjamin Franklin would be proud of Manuel.

A few months after meeting him, I tell Manuel that I am leaving town for a while. "You're leaving? We have to go out for dinner before you leave!" The next day he sends me a text message with the place: a wings bar close to the university. When we get there, five of us sit around a table, surrounded by television sets showing different sports games. We talk about sports while we wait for our food. When the waitress comes, she has mixed up our order, bringing a big plate of wings that no one asked for. She apologizes and begins to walk away, but before she can leave, Manuel jumps from his seat and tells her, "Wait, leave it here. You're gonna throw it away, aren't you?" The waitress nods in agreement; it is the policy of the establishment. Manuel replies that she can bring our whole order but she should leave the plate of wings. After all, it will cost the restaurant nothing, and it is bad to throw food away. We will eat it, he assures her. She agrees, probably happy to avoid a complaint from our table. Manuel smiles at the windfall of an extra plate of wings and tells me that he learned from others how restaurants deal with wrong orders and how you can use them to get more food for the same amount of money. This same resourcefulness emerged in other conversations. I was asking Manuel how he bought groceries, and he asked in turn if I ever went "dumpster diving." I said no, that sounds horrible. He laughed at my ignorance and explained. Restaurants usually throw away their unsold food at closing time. Many places separate food that is safe to eat from other trash. Hence, if you want some snacks and it is after midnight, you can go to the alley behind a bakery and get some good bagels. All it takes is for you to open the bags and check that the food is in good condition. Manuel insists, "It is fun! We definitely should do it one day."

Thus, from the beginning of his college years, Manuel rapidly learned of the different options available to him to make money (the scholarships he is eligible for, the state laws that support him, the different gigs he could do to earn an extra buck) and the countless ways with which he could make that money last longer. He had to do this because the people in charge of helping him obtain a college education (teachers, counselors, officials) had many times failed at their jobs.

Nevertheless, Manuel's resourcefulness has limits. The elimination of in-state tuition for undocumented students, a probable threat every time the Texas Legislature is in session, would most likely terminate his dreams of obtaining a degree. Budget cuts affect many of the programs on which he relies for financial support. Not even the implementation of Deferred Action for Childhood Arrivals (DACA) is a real relief. This policy, put in place by the Obama administration in 2012, gives undocumented youth the opportunity to apply for temporary work permits. Although it has allowed Manuel to obtain a part-time job that he loves and that helps him pay for college, the program only lasts for two years, its renewal is uncertain, and it is not backed by any law enacted by Congress. "If DACA is removed," he told me one day, "we would go back to square one. Back to being undocumented. My degree would be worthless."

A Horrible Student

Manuel faces other, more subtle barriers that may be even harder to overcome. The university environment can be very unwelcoming to minority and first-generation college students. People sometimes use words such as "illegal" that are deeply upsetting despite still being socially acceptable. There are racist incidents such as insensitively themed student parties (in 2012 a student organization held an event in downtown Austin in which some students dressed as "illegals" and others as "border patrol"). Even though they are not hostile, many university employees completely ignore the situation of students like Manuel. He frequently has to explain to them the different laws and regulations that allow him to attend college in order to get even the simplest administrative paperwork done.

Most students at the university level would agree that in order to do well in life they need to obtain a degree, but not many of them see education as the only option allowing them to live in this country. For Manuel, the stakes are too high, and this has proven to be a double-edged sword. On the one hand, it has been a strong incentive to do well in school, gain work experience, and develop a number of valuable skills. On the other hand, however, the pressure is sometimes too much.

"Do you consider yourself a good student?" I asked Manuel one morning over coffee. He replied right away: "No! I am a horrible student! My GPA is 3.7, it should be 4.0!" I told him that given that he is taking five classes, working part-time, and participating in a social movement, his grades are very high. There are many students who have much more time to study and yet get much lower grades. He was not convinced. "Anybody can do it. Everybody in the movement is doing the same thing."

Manuel is not only worried about his grades but also about his life in general: since he is working all day, he does not have the time to develop relationships with people. He sometimes feels lonely, and even though he is always surrounded by people, he says he has few close friends. "What is your biggest worry?" I asked him once. "My biggest worry? Never finding the love of my life."

Moreover, when faced with the pressures of university life, Manuel cannot rely on the main motivation that gets many students through college: the prospect of a decent job after graduation. Even though he is likely to graduate in less than four years, he might not be able to put his skills into practice. His lack of papers forces him to live in the present, hoping for a future that might never materialize. Hence, he is sometimes left without a clear motivation to sustain him when his coursework and workload become too demanding. Manuel simply does not have an easy answer to the questions "Why bother? What's the point?" The fact that he persists is an expression of his faith that better times will come and his belief that hard work eventually pays off, despite any evidence to the contrary.

"I know what the flag stands for"

Countless times since he arrived in the United States, Manuel has been reminded that he does not belong here. As a kid, when he did small pranks with his close friends, some of them would jokingly say, "What we did is against the law, but you're illegal anyway." He had to listen to hurtful terms: *mojado*, beaner, wetback. In high school he could not do many of the things other teenagers took for granted. Getting through college has been much harder for him than for many of his classmates. Even if he graduates, he might not be able to apply the skills he has worked so hard to achieve. Throughout it all, he has had to tolerate countless people who question his very presence in this country.

This constant exposure to rejection has left Manuel with a deep conflict. On the one hand, he is certain that he wants to stay in the United States and contribute to its society. In his own words, he does not want to become "a CEO, a rags-to-riches story," but instead he wants to use his degree to work as a union organizer. The main goal of his struggle is precisely to be allowed to live his life here. On the other hand, he is reluctant to openly embrace mainstream American culture and symbols and is very critical of immigrants who do so: "When we talk about America, I know the bad things too. I know what the flag stands for." During a May Day protest, some people in his group gave American flags to participants. He and others reacted harshly: "You embarrass yourself. You shouldn't have to appropriate another culture to have your rights respected." This conflict emerges most clearly in Manuel's idealization of his Mexican roots. His memories of Mexico are nostalgic: the big festivals—Christmas, Reyes—with large family gatherings, lots of food, and fireworks. He cherishes Mexican culture and symbols, from the eagle and the snake to music and movies. "What ties you to the United States, then?" I asked him. He responded in a self-evident tone, as if to suggest how foolish my question was: "My community. I have no community there [in Mexico]. I have no family."

Moreover, Manuel insists that he does not feel American because he does not *look* American. When I asked him if he considered himself part of this country, he pointed at his arm and responded that "America means light skin. I am a Mexican. That is how society sees me. I have dark skin. Americans have light skin. My sister has lighter skin; she could walk around campus and no one would tell her apart. I have darker skin, people tell me apart from a block away." In other words, Manuel feels that his skin color marks him as a perennial foreigner, even though he has lived most of his life in this country, excelled in school, knows more about U.S. history than most people, speaks perfect English, and wants to dedicate his life to helping others in this country.

Stand Up, Fight Back!

On a day of triple-digit temperatures, I join Manuel in a protest outside of Austin. A dozen construction workers at a new apartment complex have not been paid. Many of them are undocumented, and as Manuel tells me, "They could be my dad." We drive to the construction site in a caravan of cars, take out signs, and stand on the sidewalk chanting in Spanish and English. It is an awfully hot day in August, and there is no shade where our group of thirty people stands. The idea is simple: alert current workers that they might be cheated, let neighbors know about the situation, and deliver a letter to the site manager stating that if wages are not paid, legal actions might follow. After ten minutes a truck arrives, and a representative from the construction company approaches us. He is a tall and sturdy white man with an intimidating presence. He knows how to deal with these situations. He first points to some of the protesting workers and says, "I know you, and you too." He then says that his company is not responsible for the unpaid wages since a subcontractor hired the workers, and "the guy has already been paid." Manuel puts down the megaphone he was using, goes directly to the manager, and responds. There is tension as a brown boy addresses a big white man and respectfully, but with resolve, tells him he is wrong: If every party involved argues that it is not their problem, there will be no solution to the situation of the workers. Their families depend on their wages. Their kids may go hungry. The workers are just asking for their rights, and they might sue the company.

The manager repeats what he said before and ends with a warning: the construction site is private property, and trespassers will be treated accordingly. He then walks away and tells the current workers that they should not let anyone in, even though there is no fence separating the site from the sidewalk. Manuel takes up the megaphone, and the chanting begins again. We want justice, and we want it now! Watch out, workers! You might be next! They might not pay you! When we get back to the car, he is literally jumping with enthusiasm: "Did you see him? Did you see how nervous the guy was?" He drinks some water and says, "Too bad cops did not show up."

It will not take long for Manuel's wish to come true. We drive to the second location of the day's protests. We will do the same thing in front of the real estate agency that administers the new apartment complex. We get out of the cars, start chanting, and a few people head to the office to deliver the letter. However, the employees, supposedly fearing for their lives, lock the doors and call 9-1-1. A police car shows up in a few minutes. The driver is clearly not a rookie. He first checks that everything is fine at the office and then heads to the sidewalk, where our group is waving signs and asking the passing cars to honk for a good cause. He has a smile on his face as he asks what is going on. Once again, Manuel is the first to respond. He tells the officer about the situation and the plans for the protest. The policeman nods in agreement and kindly warns us that we cannot protest in the parking lot in front of the office, since that would be trespassing. We retreat a few feet and continue our protest for five minutes. At that point another police car comes, and two younger cops emerge from it. Probably not aware that an officer has already talked to us, they question Manuel and another activist, this time with a less friendly attitude. They ask the rest of the people to stand back while they run a background check on Manuel's colleague, who is talking to them in a relaxed manner. The situation goes from tense to ridiculous when a tire in the police car begins to lose air. The whistle is evident, and people try to advise the officers that they should check the tire or they might end up stranded in the parking lot. But they sustain their strict attitude and disregard the advice. Eventually, the results of the check come back clean; the officers warn us about not protesting in the parking lot and drive out with a flat tire. Everyone explodes with laughter.

A few days later I asked Manuel what he likes about confronting cops. I expected a display of bravado, or at least a few words about racial profiling and state violence. After all, he has been stopped by the police a few times, and he grew up being scared of them. Instead, he calmly replied that he has learned over time that policemen are there to help him and that since their mission is to serve and protect, he can use them for that purpose. Instead of viewing them as antagonists, Manuel describes the police as a potential resource and an audience for his message. He has found ways of using them for what they are supposed to do: protect law-abiding people. He even has a working relationship with members of his local police department, who help with cases of wage theft and infringement of labor regulations.

In other words, for Manuel, empowerment does not just mean confronting law enforcement; it also means finding ways of working with the police to defend his rights. He is careful in how he does it though. He never tells the police that he is undocumented—first and foremost because he might get in trouble, but also because he knows that the cops are supposed to help people regardless of whether they are citizens or not, and hence his immigration status should be irrelevant. The ambiguous nature of state institutions is ever present in his life. The same police force that talks nicely to the organizers of a protest might be the one that assists in the deportation of loved ones.

Families in Danger

Manuel's struggle reflects a national debate concerning the reform of an immigration system that imposes unnecessary suffering. His struggle also involves blocking state-level legislation aimed at removing the few policies that allow people like him to attend college. Yet this struggle is also experienced at a very personal level: Manuel has a particular problem that needs to be solved, which is how to obtain permanent legal residency for him and his loved ones. Going back to Mexico is hardly an option. The early age at which he migrated, coupled with the inability of his family to make visits and remain in contact, has severed his links to family networks that he could use to relocate there. In addition, he has lived more time in the United States than in his country of origin, and as a result he has developed his life here. The people he cares about the most are on this side of the border. When I asked him where he would like to live if he had the opportunity to travel, he replied Texas, without hesitation, because "that is where I am needed, where I can make a change."

Manuel is very much afraid of waking up one morning to a call informing him that a raid has taken his parents away. This event would not only destroy the family unity forged during his first years in the United States, something that he has come to cherish, but it would also leave him unable to do anything about it. His parents, hardworking people who have managed to educate their children and offer them opportunities that they themselves did not have, are among the most vulnerable immigrants to the United States. Manuel's fear makes sense: since 2008, almost 400,000 people have been deported each year from the United States, a significant increase from previous years (the average between 2003 and 2007 was slightly over 250,000). In the last five years approximately two million people were removed from the country. Cases of detained relatives and painful separations abound. In some instances grassroots organizations have provided skilled lawyers and mobilized enough support to stop deportation procedures, but in many other cases they have failed.

The growing number of deportations, as well as Congress's failure to pass the DREAM Act (which would have given undocumented youth a pathway to citizenship if they pursued higher education or joined the armed forces), has convinced Manuel that a bill to assist students is not enough. While it would solve his individual problem, it would leave his family in the same condition as before. "I am privileged because I am a student. What about the people who could not go to college? What about my parents? What about the people who don't want to go to college, who want to just work, or be a stay-at-home mom?"

The debate concerning immigration policy tends to hide many things, but among the most important consequences that have been overlooked are those affecting mixed-status families. Deportations not only hurt undocumented immigrants but also affect citizens and res-

idents. Due to the complexities of immigration laws, and the fact that children born in the United States are granted citizenship, it is not hard to find families with some members who are undocumented, some others who are awaiting application proceedings, and some others who are green card holders or citizens. In the case of Manuel, his youngest sibling is a citizen, he and two sisters have been granted deferred action under DACA, another sister is waiting to hear about her application to DACA, and his parents are undocumented. For a family like Manuel's, any policy change will affect each of its members differently. The idea that it is possible to expel some immigrants and leave the rest of the social body unaffected is a fiction. The record numbers of removals in the last few years have hurt not just immigrant families but also countless American citizens in whose name the deportations are carried out.

The City We Want

On a sunny spring afternoon, Manuel, a hundred people, and I protest around a rapidly developing area of town, where real estate companies have built more than a dozen luxury condo developments in the last few years. In the process of this development, companies have violated safety regulations, workers have been injured and died, and employers have skipped water breaks for workers laboring in the sun. We gather at a street corner, hold banners, and sing for half an hour. The atmosphere is jovial: it is a beautiful day, and everyone is in high spirits.

We walk around the neighborhood, stopping at several different buildings. Manuel holds a megaphone and leads the way. The first stop is a new high-end apartment complex. Three workers fell to their deaths during its construction. Religious leaders say a few words and lead a prayer, and then we sing a few songs, demanding the implementation of safety measures. We continue our march toward another construction site, where we yell to the workers that they should be careful, since they might not be paid. Our third stop is an almost complete building, where we remind the managers that water breaks are mandatory by law. The workers seem pleased by our presence, but other people are less supportive. A police officer on a motorcycle forces us to stand on the side of the road opposite the building, even though it is a very quiet street with almost no traffic. Manuel and a few others challenge the order and approach the fence to offer bottles of cold water to the workers, who laugh at the evident discomfort of the managers. After the policeman repeats his order a few more times, Manuel complies, crosses the street, and starts chanting again over the megaphone.

After an hour of walking, we return to the starting point, sing a few more lines, and end the demonstration. Manuel looks tired from shouting almost nonstop for an hour, but his voice is fine when he thanks me for showing up. He then goes with other organizers to collect banners, pack everything, and talk to the community leaders who supported the action. He has been smiling the whole time.

It would be easy to see Manuel as a hero, especially if you agree with his cause. However, focusing only on the features that make him a remarkable person would obscure the social forces that are beyond his individual control and that constantly threaten his future and that of his loved ones. These forces are the same ones that cause his parents to work in poorly paid and risky jobs, that exclude talented young people from higher education, and that tear families apart through deportation. Manuel's many achievements stem from his constant awareness of this vulnerability: he knows that he alone cannot do much to prevent the negative effects of growing social inequality and an increasingly punitive state. In other words, Manuel needs to fight for others today because he might need others to fight for him tomorrow. He and his siblings may not be able to continue studying. His father might be the next injured worker. His mother could be the next deportee. His efforts to overcome vulnerability are intrinsically tied to the struggles of other people.

"My favorite time of the day," Manuel told me once, "is when I bike five miles to my job after class. I love to be outside, see everything, explore the city." A few moments later, he said, "Every time I bike around town and I see those big, new, shiny apartment complexes, I see the poor houses around them, and I know that those people will have to move soon. That gets me angry." For some time, I believed that Manuel's love for Austin was due to the fact that he grew up in a small town in Texas, where there were fewer things for a young person to do and ethnic diversity was far lower. Compared to that, the state capital must look like a beacon of diversity and excitement. Nevertheless, as I got to know him I came to understand that the city is an arena where he can achieve some control over his life. Not only is it a relatively safe space where he can be open about his status, it is also a place where he can work with others to improve his community, having a small impact on the world rather than the other way around. Since he came to the United States, Austin is the only place where he has been able to overcome the profound barriers that stand between him and the dream of a higher education and a better life. However, he knows the city is changing fast. As a result, just as he fights for the luxury of defending himself, he also works hard to defend the kind of city he wants.

Recommended Readings

Department of Homeland Security. 2014. "Immigration Statistics." http://www
.dhs.gov/immigration-statistics. A significant number of statistics regarding the enforcement of immigration law, made available by the Department of Homeland Security. Includes data on deportations, apprehensions, and detentions.

Gonzales, R. 2009. "Young Lives on Hold: The College Dreams of Undocumented Students." College Board. http://professionals.collegeboard.com/
profdownload/young-lives-on-hold-college-board.pdf. A detailed report on the situation of undocumented students, particularly with regard to the limitations they face when trying to obtain higher education.

Jimenez, M. 2009. "Humanitarian Crisis: Migrant Deaths at the U.S.-Mexico Border." ACLU of San Diego & Imperial Counties and Mexico's National Commission of Human Rights. https://www.aclu.org/files/pdfs/immigrants
/humanitariancrisisreport.pdf. A report examining the increasing numbers of deaths that take place during attempted crossings and identifying the policies responsible for this situation. Based on the evidence presented, the author describes the situation as a "humanitarian crisis."

Nicholls, W. 2013. *The DREAMers: How the Undocumented Youth Movement Transformed the Immigrant Rights Debate.* Stanford, CA: Stanford University Press. One of the first books about the movement centered around undocumented students, also known as DREAMers. It explores the movement's emergence and development as well as its impact on the immigration debate in the United States.

Orner, P., ed. 2008. *Underground America: Narratives of Undocumented Lives.* San Francisco: McSweeney's. A collection of personal stories by undocumented immigrants to the United States. The book is part of a series by Voices of Witness, a nonprofit organization that uses personal narratives and oral history to raise awareness about human rights crises.

Passel, J., D. Cohn, and A. Gonzalez-Barrera. 2013. "Population Decline of Unauthorized Immigrants Stalls, May Have Reversed." Pew Hispanic Center. http://www.pewhispanic.org/2013/09/23/population-decline-of-un authorized -immigrants-stalls-may-have-reversed/.

Passel, J., and M. Lopez. 2012. "Up to 1.7 Million Unauthorized Immigrant Youth May Benefit from New Deportation Rules." Pew Hispanic Center. http://www.pewhispanic.org/files/2012/12/unauthroized_immigrant_youth _update.pdf. The Pew Hispanic Center has valuable information and statistics on the situation of undocumented immigrants in the United States. This and the previous report were used as sources for this chapter.

Portes, A., and R. Rumbaut. 2006. *Immigrant America: A Portrait*, 3rd ed. Berkeley: University of California Press. A detailed study of the experiences of immigrants in the United States, from information on their countries of origin to an exploration of the challenges faced by second-generation Americans.

Rubio-Goldsmith, R., M. M. McCormick, D. Martinez, and I. M. Duarte. 2007. "A Humanitarian Crisis at the Border: New Estimates of Deaths Among Unauthorized Immigrants." Immigration Policy Center. http://www .immigrationpolicy.org/sites/default/files/docs/Crisis%20at%20the%20Bor der.pdf. A policy brief that estimates the number of deaths of unauthorized migrants in the U.S.-Mexico border region. The Immigration Policy Center is a useful source of information on issues of migration to the United States.

United States Border Patrol. 2014. "Southwest Border Deaths by Fiscal Year." http://www.cbp.gov/sites/default/files/documents/U.S.%20Border%20Pa trol%20Fiscal%20Year%20Statistics%20SWB%20Sector%20Deaths%20 FY1998%20-%20FY2013.pdf. Official statistics provided by the U.S. Border Patrol on migrant deaths in the U.S.-Mexico border region.

AFTERWORD

Plumbing the Social Underbelly
of the Dual City

LOÏC WACQUANT

Invisible in Austin tracks the peregrinations of a dozen people dwelling in the nether regions of the city's class and spatial structure. Most of the characters who populate its chapters are constituents of, and contributors to, that irregular but steadily growing human stream that one may call the *urban precariat*—that is, the *precarious* fractions of the post-industrial *proletariat* (in the technical sense of sellers of raw labor power) struggling to make a home in the shadows, cracks, and ditches of the polarizing city after the dismantling of the Fordist-Keynesian social compact (Wacquant 2008).[1] Several distinctive features of the everyday horizon of the urban precariat emerge as one reads through the present volume, which amplify, complicate, and validate more macroscopic and statistical accounts of its predicament.

① The first feature is *rampant economic instability and abiding social insecurity*, rooted in the degrading parameters of employment in the lower tier (in terms of pay, hours, tasks, tenure, and prospects) and aggravated by the absence of unemployment coverage, sick leave, paid vacation, medical insurance, and retirement plans. These basic social rights are written into the wage-labor contract in nearly every advanced nation but continue to elude American workers, for whom they are "benefits" granted or, more commonly here, withheld at the behest of their employers (Kalleberg 2011; Freeman 2008). Next comes the paradoxi-
② cal and *crushing combination of underwork and overwork*, with successive bouts of employment scarcity and employment glut or gluttony, laced with chronic underemployment and fueled by famine earnings, dependency on despotic bosses or fickle demand, and gnawing uncertainty as to the future availability of accessible jobs.

A related third characteristic of the occupational life of the precariat

(3) is the *banality of periodic downward mobility,* commonly triggered or ac-
celerated not only by market vagaries, the externalization strategies of
firms, and the disruptive events of family life (childbirth, divorce, death,
etc.) but also, crucially, by accidents, injuries, and work-related issues of
health that spiral out of control because of the ruinous cost of medical
care in the American city. We glimpse how the working poor routinely
postpone or forgo essential care, with the result that they frequently live
with chronic pain and festering physical impairments that further constrict their employment possibilities as well as their social commerce,
not to mention their quality of life.

A fourth emergent reality, little studied even by scholars of urban
poverty and the working class because it contravenes their inclination to
valorize a disparaged segment of society, is the pervasiveness of *horizon-*
(4) *tal abuse and lateral animosity.* When the minimal social stability needed
to foster mutuality and to buttress solidarity among and across wage-
earning households evaporates, the poor cannot but prey on the poor;
they strive to avoid and distance themselves from their own kind; and
they come to openly despise and blame those like them, or those just a
notch below them but too close for comfort. Recall how old Santos gets
swindled out of his winning lottery ticket by the convenience store clerk
from whom he purchases his daily scratch tickets because his illiteracy makes him easy game. Note how "Chip's frustrations have been directed more and more toward his neighbors" in the informal settlement
where he resides due to the meager earnings he draws despite working for decades as a copying machine technician for a large corporation, rather than toward the city government that fails to deliver basic
public services to peripheral boroughs and refuses to enforce minimal
housing codes (see chap. 5, p. 103). Similarly, Raven divulges how the
"exotic dancers" who perform at her strip club loathe and shun working-
class clients like car mechanics and construction workers, not just because they tip less but because they are "sweaty and smelly" (see chap. 6,
p. 129), and effectively connect the dancers back to the world of physical toil they so ardently wish to extirpate themselves from, even as they
plunge further into its murky depths.

Precarity breeds misanthropy and erodes mutual identification and
reciprocity, which are the preconditions for solidarity. Instead, it feeds
(5) a suffusive *sentiment of indignity among the dispossessed.* In an era that has
witnessed both the dismantling of traditional institutions of working-
class defense, such as unions, and the universalization of the "school-
mediated mode of reproduction," resulting in the sacralization of "the

second capital" of educational credentials (Bourdieu [1994] 1998), today's lower-tier workers have no reliable sources of collective pride to draw upon. So they come to view their kind, if not themselves, as lacking in worthiness. They are not just politically expendable and culturally invisible, as argued by David Shipler in his portrait of *The Working Poor* in America; they are also socially dishonored: the *humiliores* of the contemporary city. (The *honestiores* and *humiliores* formed the two legally defined and rigidly separated classes of freemen at the bloom of ancient Rome circa the second century. The former possessed influence and prestige based upon titles, property, and office—much as managers, professionals, and owners do in today's advanced society. The latter, also called *plebeii*, formed a malleable and faceless mass of laborers and servants, subjected to harsh exploitation and degrading public punishment, whose condition was barely above that of slaves [Shipler 2008; Dunstan 2010].)

This feeling of social ignominy at the bottom is reinforced daily by *injurious and humiliating interactions with personal service customers,* represented in hyperbolic form by those "uncivilized" riders who vomit in Kumar's taxi at night and then holler at him that it is up to him to clean up the mess they leave behind. It feeds social and symbolic strategies designed to distance oneself from the lowly: "I want to be portrayed as a woman who fell on hard times, not someone who is disadvantaged," insists Clarissa, the injured waitress in her fifties who sleeps illegally in a storage unit but remains keen to "detach herself from 'the wrong crowd'" (see chap. 3, p. 74), including the homeless. This collective sentiment gives prima facie plausibility to individualist accounts of destitution that discount the decisive role of institutions in shaping both objective positions and subjective dispositions. Even community activist Ella, whom one might think would know better, adopts a moralistic explanation of poverty when she asserts that generations of dysfunction are spawned by "families' unhealthy behaviors" (see chap. 11, p. 229) and therefore account for their hardship.

The abiding sense of indignity of today's precarious workers is both cause and consequence of their striking absence of perspective for collective upgrading. By contradistinction to the industrial proletariat, consolidating over the long century opening circa 1870, which grew both more numerous and more cohesive by forging a collective identity as proud builders of the world (Hobsbawm 1985; Noiriel 2002; Lichtenstein 2002), the postindustrial precariat is a stillborn group, a dispersed collection of disparate categories riven by fissiparous impulses and centrifugal tendencies, as *everyone yearns to escape, not join, it.* No wonder this book finds that their efforts at betterment consistently concentrate on personal upgrading and individual flight across social and physical space, even at the cost of leaving behind one's loved ones (temporarily or permanently, as with those migrants from Mexico who can no longer bring their kin to America or visit them back home because of astringent border enforcement and monitoring). In the classic triad of "exit, voice, loyalty" identified by Albert Hirschman (1970) as tipping people toward protesting or leaving the institutions that fail them, depending on how attached they have grown to them, loyalty has vanished, voice is silenced, and the bias in favor of exit built into the architecture of core American institutions has never been stronger.

This is due not just to the debilitation of unions (which were strong only sectorally, regionally, and momentarily and were never a major force in the Texan economy in any case), but, more broadly, to the weakening of all manners of collectives endowed with the capacity to secure some degree of mastery over the future by sheltering individuals from the exigencies of the market and the rapacity of firms, first among them the state. At the heart of *Invisible in Austin* sits the glaring yet undiscerned *void left by the organized atrophy of the protective and supportive wings of the state*, as federal government absconds and local government turns away from sustaining low-income neighborhoods and populations toward attracting corporations and high-income households to the city turned playground for the beautiful people. The only domain in which municipal and county authorities spring forth to deliver forceful action in "invisible Austin" is the penal management of wayward children and their parents, who are slammed under the disciplinary tutelage of "zero-tolerance" programs in special schools that are educational only in name.[2] No wonder that what little collective action emerges across the book is concerned with minimizing the impact of extreme marginality and punitive containment on poor teenagers, finding cleaning work for maids, and opening a path to citizenship for the children of undocumented migrants, who find themselves doubly relegated by the market and the state.

For the struggling Austinites pictured in this tome, the hiatus between appearance and reality, aspirations and possibilities, the happy front stage of diligent service performance bleeding into seemingly contented servility and the brutal backstage of ruthless labor extraction stripped of social protection and economic sureties, can become existentially grating, even at times unbearable. This hiatus—which Ethan, the luxury hotel clerk, encapsulates with bittersweet irony in his oxy-moronic notion of the lifestyle of the "$30,000 millionaire"—gets filled by flights of social oneirism that take three recurrent forms. The first is to engage in excessive or conspicuous consumption; the second is to fall into chronic substance abuse punctuated by bouts of debilitating bing-ing; and the third is to play games of chance and (in what amounts to the same) to yearn to open a business as a gateway to independence. One wonders whether the excessive—even pathological—optimism and faith in the prospect of individual self-salvation exhibited by so many char-acters in *Invisible in Austin* who aspire to become "their own bosses" is not a cognitive coping strategy fashioned to relieve the emotional strain of facing a closed future. Imagine a ray of hope and concentrate on the glimmering of social darkness, for, as Clarissa puts it, "I don't have the time to be depressed for very long. It doesn't help" (see chap. 3, p. 75). The very harshness of the condition of the urban precariat combines with the long national tradition of vituperation against the undeserving poor, the weakness of instruments of collective redress, the malign ne-glect of government, and the "positive symmetry" of American culture that prods individuals to always "think positive" and overestimate favor-able outcomes (Cerulo 2006) to produce something akin to a *structurally mandated social escapism.* The spirit of resiliency can thus be interpreted indifferently either as an inspiring mark of human bravery or as the self-defeating delusion of a dispirited aggregate.

Located at the crossroads between urban studies, life story and life history, and the sociology of labor, this team inquiry into social suffer-ing in an American technopolis offers rich materials for probing the ex-istential contours of the contemporary precariat. Beyond its empirical object, *Invisible in Austin* is worth reading, pondering, and emulating on three counts. First, it demonstrates that sociology can provide full-color accounts of social life and indeed make the metropolis come to life on the page. Sociology is a multivocal discipline that harbors within it-self the full gamut of perspectives, methods, and empirical sensitivities of the specialized social sciences, including in-depth interviewing in-formed by the construction of social trajectories and propelled by inten-sive engagement with, and strong emotive ties to, subjects. As a result, it is well equipped to weave robust analytic constructs together with the shifting folk notions that animate ordinary reality and to plumb the id-iosyncrasies of individual lives while connecting them to impersonal forces and invisible social mechanisms. And it can mobilize the narra-tive techniques and tropes of the humanities, not only to put experiential flesh on structural bones but also to tap the spring of social structures inside situated social beings.

To produce this kind of vibrating sociological account that enables the reader to enter, as through a spiraling movement, into the mundane existence of its subjects to grasp how social necessity turns into human flesh and form requires three ingredients. The first is a map of the social world that recognizes its multidimensionality and enables us to locate people in a space of possibles defined by the distribution of resources efficient in the universe under investigation. The second is an attentiveness to the details of everyday life as it unfolds to capture the tacit cognitive categories, the embedded skills and the embodied desires—what Bourdieu ([1997] 2000) gathers under the notion of habitus—whose dynamic bundle makes up and moves concrete people in action. Last but not least, it takes a special concern for the craft of writing, so that the final text does not erase the lived reality it has strived to capture and illumine. "Know them well," as Javier Auyero admonishes in his introduction, finds its complement in "write them well."

The sociology of knowledge, art, and science teaches us that knowing and writing are quintessentially collective activities, and a second merit of this book is to document the virtues of team studies. Born of a research seminar and resulting from a joint endeavor to produce a coordinated kaleidoscope of the city's underbelly, *Invisible in Austin* shows how mutual support and crisscrossing control at multiple stages help each contributor to fashion a better research object than would have been possible on one's own and to craft a text that is seamlessly integrated into a collective book that is more than the mere sum of its individual chapters.

Finally, *Invisible in Austin* is pregnant with the promise of multiple extensions and replications. The first would take us across social space to encompass people occupying the middle and upper regions of social space, such that the present portrait of the margins of Austin would grow into a full triptych capturing the entire class structure and texture of the city, poor, middling, and rich. The second would turn longitudinal and interview the same characters along with another cohort of similarly located informants in five, ten, and twenty years to capture the work of time. The third would cut across media of analysis and reporting to mix text with audio, visual, graphical, and video materials and build a perpetually evolving hyperarchive of life in the Texan metropolis accessible online to readers of the book. A fourth and last extension would range across geographic space as well as across types of cities: just as Auyero and his students used Bourdieu's inquiry into social suffering in late twentieth-century France (Bourdieu et al. [1993] 1999) as a thematic and methodological springboard to delve into the underbelly of Austin, one hopes that *Invisible in Austin* will stimulate other sociologists to produce similar team studies of myriad other American cities, so that, by arraying them together, one would gradually stitch together a patchwork-like sociological portrait of the changing cityscape of the United States as seen from within and from below.

Notes

1. The term "precariat" originated with Italian labor activists and analysts of the 1980s (*precariato*) and was deployed a decade later by French social scientists concerned with the ramifying impacts of insecure labor forms: see particularly Castel 1995; Paugam 2000; and Perrin 2004.

2. This is part and parcel of the building of a "centaur state" practicing laissez-faire at the top and disciplinary supervision at the bottom, as shown in Wacquant 2009.

References

Bourdieu, Pierre. [1994] 1998. "The New Capital: Introduction to a Japanese Reading of 'The State Nobility.'" In *Practical Reason: On the Theory of Action*. Cambridge: Polity Press. First published in 1991, in *Poetics Today* 12 (Winter): 643–653.

———. [1997] 2000. *Pascalian Meditations*. Cambridge: Polity Press.

Bourdieu, Pierre, et al. [1993] 1999. *The Weight of the World: Social Suffering in Contemporary Society*. Cambridge: Polity Press.

Castel, Robert. 1995. *Les Métamorphoses de la question sociale. Une chronique du salariat*. Paris: Fayard.

Cerulo, Karen A. 2006. *Never Saw It Coming: Cultural Challenges to Envisioning the Worst*. Chicago: University of Chicago Press.

Dunstan, William E. 2010. *Ancient Rome*. Lanham, MD: Rowman and Littlefield.

Freeman, Richard B. 2008. *America Works: The Exceptional U.S. Labor Market*. New York: Russell Sage Foundation.

Hirschman, Albert O. 1970. *Exit, Voice, and Loyalty: Responses to Decline in Firms, Organizations, and States*. Cambridge, MA: Harvard University Press.

Hobsbawm, Eric. 1985. *Workers: Worlds of Labor*. New York: Pantheon.

Kalleberg, Arne L. 2011. *Good Jobs, Bad Jobs: The Rise of Polarized and Precarious Employment Systems in the United States, 1970s to 2000s*. New York: Russell Sage Foundation.

Lichtenstein, Nelson. 2002. *State of the Union: A Century of American Labor*. Princeton, NJ: Princeton University Press.

Noiriel, Gérard. 2002. *Les Ouvriers dans la société française*. Paris: Point/Seuil.

Paugam, Serge. 2000. *Le Salarié de la précarité*. Paris: Presses Universitaires de France.

Perrin, Evelyne. 2004. *Chômeurs et précaires. Au coeur de la question sociale*. Paris: La Dispute.

Shipler, David K. 2008. *The Working Poor: Invisible in America*. New York: Knopf.

Wacquant, Loïc. 2008. *Urban Outcasts: A Comparative Sociology of Advanced Marginality*. Cambridge: Polity Press.

———. 2009. *Punishing the Poor: The Neoliberal Government of Social Insecurity*. Durham, NC: Duke University Press.